Nabeel's Song

Nabeel's Song

Jo Tatchell

SCEPTRE

Copyright © 2006 by Jo Tatchell

First published in Great Britain in 2006 by Hodder & Stoughton
A division of Hodder Headline

The right of Jo Tatchell to be identified as the Author
of the Work has been asserted by her in accordance
with the Copyright, Designs and Patents Act 1988.

A Sceptre Book

1

A CIP catalogue record for this title is available from the British Library

Hardback ISBN: 0 340 89703 1
Trade Paperback ISBN: 0 340 89748 1

Typeset in Sabon by Hewer Text UK Ltd, Edinburgh
Printed and bound by Clays Ltd, St Ives plc

Hodder Headline's policy is to use papers that are natural, renewable
and recyclable products and made from wood grown in sustainable
forests. The logging and manufacturing processes are expected to
conform to the environmental regulations of the country of origin.

Hodder & Stoughton Ltd
A division of Hodder Headline
338 Euston Road
London NW1 3BH

To those born in a new Iraq, who will live in freedom.
To all the mothers who have suffered in the waiting.

Contents

BOOK II

Prologue

The wide streets of Basra are dusty and strewn with litter.
Rubbish blows across the cracked, uneven pavement, and the
noise of the city fills the air. Kerbstones, painted yellow and
white, are worn and broken from years of use. Although it is
the middle of the day the thoroughfares are busy. Traffic-
lights, suspended from sagging wires above, change fitfully
from red to green and back again. The army patrols and
battered Toyotas driving past ignore them, using their horns
to alert oncoming drivers. The city is poised and expectant.

Carrying his khaki knapsack, packed with bottles of spring
water, his tape-recorder, newspapers and a pocket guidebook,
Ahmed Goda, a journalist writing for the respected international Arabic newspaper *Asharq Alwsat*, treads carefully.
His eyes roam the dilapidated apartment blocks and commercial buildings of the country's second city. The sun is high and
the skies clear and blue, yet it feels to him like another world.
One of the first wave of foreign journalists to enter the city, he
is taking his first tentative steps in post-liberation Iraq.

Although some people seem cautious and subdued, most
shops have raised their iron security grilles and occasionally
he catches a face peering at him from within. In less extra-

ordinary times, he imagines that the tide of people and traffic on these city streets would be overwhelming, with vegetable traders, stationery sellers, hardware shops, furniture stores all vying for passing custom. As he progresses down the long market road children call, 'Hello, Mister – hey, Mister, how are you?' in broken English. He takes care to smile at them, and at the men who have started to appear in small groups of two or three. Some hang back but others gravitate towards him, calling greetings and questions. He has been expecting this. With their links to the Allied forces the foreign media are the only source of up-to-date information.

'Have they captured His Excellency the President the Leader God Placed Him?'

'Will Bush come?'

'Why are they letting the loyalists escape?'

'Do you not know they are leaving from the north of the city?'

'Hooray, we welcome you. Thank you, thank you.'

Knowing that most Iraqi people are not sympathetic to Arab journalists, who had, in the main, been supporters of Saddam Hussein, he pauses for a few minutes to answer each question individually. Of course, he has never been a supporter, and he knows many of the Iraqi writers and journalists in opposition in London, but the men with him will not know this. He smiles, and hearing the small Allied group guarding foreign media behind him, carries on into the city. Several men follow him and share news of the reprisals the Ba'ath loyalists are meting out in the name of their missing leader. 'They are animals and the world must know of it,' says one of the men, running beside Ahmed. 'My neighbour, my very good friend, his boy was killed for taking a cigarette from a soldier and waving at them when they drove past in their tanks. Tell your people that this is what they are doing to us. What little boy in the world would not want to watch a parade of tanks and soldiers?'

Another weeps as he tells of an elderly couple living on the west of the city who had been strapped to chairs, doused in petrol and set alight in the street because the woman had been seen bowing to an American soldier. Their charred bodies had been left outside their home as a warning to all collaborators.

Ahmed can see that, while there is evident relief at liberation, the diehard nationalists are not giving up easily. In the heart of this city, the talk is of Iraqi Ba'athists starting to kill others. It would appear that the spectre of Saddam reaches so far into the psyche of his beleaguered people that they cannot now rejoice that he is gone. Some fear not only the possibility of his return but occupation of another kind. And while many other Iraqis are celebrating the fall of Saddam, the future is still uncertain.

As he walks further into the city, the crowd trailing him grows, drawing in men from doorways and shop fronts. Still unused to the waves of foreigners in the city and doubtful, in part, of their motives, their mood turns. What had started out as excitement at seeing a foreigner walking through the streets taking photos and asking questions has turned to resentment and thinly disguised anger.

Ahmed nods affably to the crowd. Peering down a side-street he is keen to give the impression that he knows exactly where he is going. But the further he moves from the main road, the more threatening the mob becomes. He can sense malevolence in the crowd now. He hears snatches of their hushed words to each other and knows they are suspicious.

'You are Arab, yes?' A man stabs a finger at Ahmed's back.

'Answer me. Are you an Egyptian? You look like an Egyptian.'

This is a leading question. Many Arab countries, and many Arabs, have supported Saddam Hussein's regime over the decades, Egypt among them. Despite this, Ahmed knows he must tell them the truth.

'I am an Egyptian,' he replies, reaching for the bottle of water in his knapsack pocket. 'What of it?'

Before he can say more, the crowd is jeering at him. A tall, angry-looking man steps out of the mob. 'We don't trust the Arab journalists any more. They don't like the Iraqis.'

Keen to avoid any misunderstanding, Ahmed addresses their concern. 'I am with the Iraqis. I am a journalist and I have lived for many years in London. Believe me, I care for what you have been through.'

But the crowd twitches with doubt and anxiety. 'Look, I am writing a piece for an Arabic newspaper, *Asharq Alwsat*,' he tries to reason with them. 'I count many of your exiled countrymen as friends. I am here to tell things the way they really are here, not to gloat or spread propaganda.' He did not like to use his friends and connections as a bargaining chip but, under the circumstances, he has no choice.

'We know all about the Iraqi exiles,' the ringleader sneers. 'Friends of the regime. They took our money and treasures with them when they went and now they live like kings while we starve.'

'What do these people living in London and America know of things here?' shouts another. 'Have any of them ever tried to help us?'

The crowd raises a resounding 'No.'

Ahmed raises a hand to speak. 'Listen to me,' he shouts. 'I

4

may be an Egyptian but I know what has been going on here. I have a good friend, an Iraqi man, who has suffered as you have. The president made him an Enemy of the State. Yes, he escaped – but only just. His brothers, sisters and cousins were not so lucky. They were beaten, tortured and left for dead. I talked to him just before I came here and he told me he is happy I can make this trip to write honestly about the situation here.'

'Pah! A million cowards have fled this place.' The angry man spits back at him. 'They were the lucky ones.'

'No, no. This man was a poet. His name is Nabeel Yasin.' He grasps frantically at anything that might save him. 'Though he has suffered he would consider me a friend.'

Remembering times spent with Nabeel at the Kufa Gallery in London and at the newspaper, Ahmed shares other facts that might ring true. 'He wrote a poem called *Brother Yasin*. He was put on Saddam's blacklist . . . an Enemy of the State.' He closes his eyes and waits for the crowd to surge forward, but no one moves. He hears silence. Unsure of what is happening he opens his eyes.

The spokesman is quelling the commotion. His face registers recognition.

'*Brother Yasin*,' he says, raising his voice to the crowd. 'I know it. He talks of the man who wrote *Brother Yasin* and *Brother Yasin, Again*.' Suddenly the man pulls away from the others and begins to recite:

'*Here I stand in life's desert,*
Composing a song to pass the evening
Holding my questions in my hands.

I am the last wretched wiseman in a time that
    detests wisemen.

*I am the last one clutching the dying embers as the fire
burns out . . .
I am the last to burn . . .*

A second later, from the back of the crowd, Goda hears two
voices pick up where the first has left off. Others join in.
Clearly, many know the poem by heart. Ahmed stands
motionless, astounded, as they deliver the words line by line.
They have almost forgotten about him and any anger they
may have felt towards him has evaporated. Can this *really* be
happening? Surely these people can't know anything of a
blacklisted poet of the 1970s.

Back in London, Ahmed knows Nabeel well. During their
many conversations about art, politics and the trials of living
in exile, he had not been aware that Nabeel's celebrity
extended back to Iraq. Of course, the signs were there,
now Ahmed thought about it. He had heard that Nabeel's
poetry was on Saddam's infamous blacklist – a long, com-
prehensive catalogue of banned literature that included Virginia Woolf, Sartre and even Tintin. But Ahmed had not
realised his friend lived on in the public consciousness.
Neither, he thought, did Nabeel.

'Is it really possible that you know of this man?' Ahmed
asks those closest to him in the crowd.

'Of course,' says the tall man, mildly offended by the
question. 'He is famous here.'

They tell him the story of *Brother Yasin*. The poem had
been a sensation in its day, published, read and recited across
the country. It spoke for a generation. The follow-up, *Brother
Yasin Again*, written in exile, had also found its way into the
country, passed through the underground from person to
person, held up as an emblem of hope in a dark decade.

The story astounds Ahmed. His friend in London has no idea that his work has lived on in Iraq, that these epics have captured the mood of the times. He has been away for well over twenty years.

The tall man draws the crowd away, repeating his favourite lines until they all join in, stamping on the ground in unison. '*Brother Yasin, Brother Yasin Again, Brother Yasin, Brother Yasin Again.*'

They pull Goda into the throng, hailing him now as a hero. 'Where is the poet?' they clamour, taking it in turns to slap Ahmed's shoulders.

'Is he in good health?'

'Writing more poems?'

'Do you think he will write again for his people? Tell him he has many fans here still. Tell him he must come back to Iraq.'

Ahmed wants to laugh. He is a lucky man. Who would have thought Nabeel's name would mean so much? How strange and serendipitous life is. What a story he will have for Nabeel when he returns to London.

The tall man rolls up a shirtsleeve and holds out his arm. 'You must write your name here on my hand. I want the name of the man who is the friend of the poet Nabeel Yasin.'

Ahmed fumbles in his bag, finds a pen and begins to write.

BOOK I

The Swallow Tree
Summer 1954

Sabria sings as she works the dough. It is a slow lament of her own. These songs, with their rambling verses of half-formed thoughts and sad, swooping melodies, come to her every morning as she moves about the house. Her hair, thick, black and straight, swings from side to side in the early-morning sunlight as the melody dies to a hum, and is reborn a minute later, inspired by figures from the world of myth and legend, perhaps, her last pilgrimage to Karbala, her sister Makkya's troubles in love, the cool water she has drawn from the well in the courtyard or, as on this morning, her two older sisters, who died during the cholera outbreak in the year she was born.

Leaving the dough to rise, she goes to the well and draws two large tin buckets of water. As she walks back, she feels the baby twist inside her. She sings louder, directing her voice at her belly. This baby likes her singing, she is sure. Unlike Yasin, her husband. He listens as she waddles about the house, occasionally wincing and clicking his tongue until he can hold back no longer. 'Wife! In all the time we have been married I have not once heard you sing a happy song. Not once. Why must everything be so sad?'

She sets down the buckets and spins round to face him. 'Do I tell you what to sing?' she hisses. 'What you choose to sing when you are working is your own business. What I sing is *my* choice. If you do not care for my sadness, you should go out. Anyway, you know that all Iraqi songs are sad – it's traditional.'

Yasin raises his eyebrows and smiles at her. She scowls back. 'Go and leave me in peace,' she says, and nods towards the front door.

The domestic routine has played itself out regularly over the fifteen years they have been married. Whenever Yasin is at home and not out laying track in the deserts to the south and west of Baghdad, Sabria knows she must get him out of the house as early as she can. Otherwise he becomes restless and wanders aimlessly about the house, distracting her from her chores. Since he is not in the habit of eating breakfast, or no more than fruit and yesterday's bread, he's best out of the way.

'Buy some onions,' she calls to him, as he pulls on his outdoor shoes. 'If you go to the market late, they will be cheaper. I need two bobbins and some white cotton, too. Don't forget, or the boys will have no trousers fit for school. And before you ask, no, I cannot go myself, and Bibi is not here to go for me. Go to al-Shawwaka market, to the haberdasher's at the back.'

'Yes, yes, my wife.' Yasin sighs, wrapping a fresh white cloth over his patterned skullcap. He waves, and she watches him disappear across the sandy courtyard and out through the battered tin gate. She knows exactly where he will go, the route he will take, and for how long he will be out. A creature of habit, he will wander across the cultivated fields of Karradat Mariam to the little coffee shop at the river's edge. He will meet with the other men of the neighbourhood – the old, those on leave, professional and military men, and others driven from their homes by their irritated wives – and while away a few hours playing dominoes and sipping cardamom coffee, which he loves. He often stops to see it made, watching as the thick mixture rises slowly to the top of the tall aluminium jug and is poured, hot and syrupy, into long rows of glasses. Its smell is enough to distract him from whatever task he has undertaken.

He will settle himself at his favourite lucky domino table, one ear trained to the old Philips radio behind the counter, and wait for friends to arrive. Soon the room will echo with conversation and laughter, the gentle click-clack of *misbaha* beads and the news from Radio Baghdad. Yasin will be occupied blissfully for hours.

Now Sabria prepares the bread oven. She lays sticks and brushwood in the large bronze grate, then fans the flames with a frond until the embers set the new kindling alight. The fire will do now for her bread, then later for tea, coffee and a fish stew. It is a delicate balance: too much wood early in the day and the domed bread oven, which Yasin built against the back wall of the compound on the day they moved in, will smoke for hours. Too little and the fire will die. In the many years that she has performed this morning ritual, she has failed only a handful of times. Now such things are second nature.

Sighing, Sabria finds herself caught off-guard and momentarily unable to move. She is already exhausted and the sun is not even half-way up the sky. The baby inside her has robbed her of energy and she can only get about with considerable effort and slow deliberate movements. Standing beside the oven, she offers a small prayer that the baby will come soon. In the meantime she must try to rest. The housework can wait. With Jafar and Juma'a, her teenagers, at school and Yasin out, she might relax a little later.

Bibi, her ever-vigilant mother, had scolded her roundly just the day before: 'You do too much. They don't lift a finger to help because you won't let them. They should look after themselves for a week or two until the baby comes. Three demanding children and a house to keep – that's too much for anyone.'

Sabria knows Bibi is right but she cannot hope to change anything now. It is easier for her to continue doing all the work herself than to instruct her men how to cook, clean and wash. If she can get the sewing done, perhaps she will put her feet up for a few hours.

Sabria has come to treasure the brief moments of calm when the house is empty. She can think, imagine, plan and even sing without fear of upsetting anyone. When they come home and the tiny compound is filled again with chaotic comings and goings, her time will no longer be her own.

Besides, her mother and Sabria's sister, Makkya, will be here soon. They will help. They are spending the morning shopping at the market and promised to be back before noon. Sabria knows they will come much later. It is to be expected. Her mother has probably been accosted and is, at this moment, crouching on someone's floor with her stick and her bags of herbs dispensing advice. A seer, a wise woman and herbalist, Bibi makes herself available to anyone who asks. It is an obligation, a duty bestowed by the gift itself.

'What should I do, Bibi? My wife, she cannot sleep and she has terrible pains in her shoulders . . .'

'My husband is sick, it is his stomach. Can you give me something for him?'

Above the wide cliffs of her cheekbones Bibi's eyes look deep into those of her patient until the truth is revealed. As she listens and looks, never blinking, holding their gaze, she is reaching into the bag at her feet and pulling out a sprig or two with instructions to boil, drink or keep about the person. For as long as Sabria can remember her mother has carried herbs and special powders with her in the folds and cuffs of her robe and *fota*, the black cloth headscarf she wraps about her face. And while the gift itself has not been passed on, Sabria knows she has inherited some of her mother's insight.

After checking that the yeast is doing its work, she discards her house slippers, pads to the washstand and splashes her face with cooling flower water. Her youngest son Nabeel tugs at her skirt and, momentarily irritated, she shoos him away. 'Leave me alone, Nabeel. Go and play.' Half in a daze she makes her way to the shade of her room, unease blossoming inside her. 'I am tired,' she says to the child, 'and I have a lot of sewing to do. But if you are good, I will tell you a story when Bibi comes back.' She sits in the wicker chair in front of the old Singer sewing-machine, with a half-completed shirt and material for three pairs of trousers at her side, then stares out to the swallow – *sununu* – tree in the yard.

Little Nabeel knows that his mother is not quite herself. It has troubled him for days. He can feel that something big is about to happen but no one will say what it is. He scratches shapes and letters into the sand with the stick his mother uses to check for snakes hidden in the grass. He has always been good at entertaining himself.

Sabria watches him from the window as she cuts trousers from the grey cotton and pins them in place for sewing.

Nabeel is four and about to be joined by another brother or sister. How rapidly time has passed. He is no longer her miracle baby but a little boy, full of his own opinions and such a strong, wilful spirit. She smiles as she watches him run round the well, singing one of his own songs. 'Nabeel,' she calls.

'*Nabeel*,' she repeats the name to herself, almost as if she is hearing it for the first time. No one in the family has been called Nabeel before, and it isn't common in Iraq. Such looks she had had from everyone the day she announced it to the family. Even now it is strange to think that her son was named after her brother Rashid's favourite brand of cigarette. But it had been the only possible name for him.

◈

'Sister, if you have another boy you must call him Napoleon,' Rashid had said emphatically, waving a ticket for the Napoleon cigarette lottery at his sister, who lay resting on a mattress.

'Whyever would I do such a ridiculous thing, brother?' she had said, astonished.

Rashid spoke as if his reasoning was flawless and obvious to even the dim-witted: 'Because this ticket is for a prize draw set to take place on the day your baby is due. And, sister, I have a strong feeling that if the baby is born on that day and it is a boy, I will win.'

'Win what?'

'A lifetime supply of Napoleon cigarettes! I feel it is a most auspicious name, sister.'

'To be named after a cigarette is not, in any way, auspicious, Rashid,' she had said, dismissing the notion with a flick of her fingers. 'How could I ever face my child knowing I named him after a French leader or a cigarette?'

It wasn't until the baby was born, and Rashid called in to tell her he had won first prize, that she knew her brother would not let the matter be. 'What did I tell you, sister? One thousand cartons of high-quality cigarettes. Thank you very much, Mr Napoleon,' he had crowed triumphantly. 'It would be unwise to ignore such good fortune, don't you think?'

'It seems so,' Sabria admitted reluctantly. 'But I can't call him Napoleon, can I?' Rashid had raised his eyebrows and waved a lighted cigarette at her and the infant.

Encouraged by her brother's good fortune, Sabria had settled on the Arabic form of Napoleon's name, announcing to Yasin that they would call their third son Nabeel. She knew her husband would not protest: in the years they had been married she could not recall him objecting to anything of any importance.

Now that baby boy is an opinionated, garrulous four-year-old, with a seemingly inexhaustible desire to know about everything. He follows his mother everywhere, enthralled by her stories and explanations of the world. Unlike her other two sons, who are growing away from her, Nabeel loves nothing more than to curl up in the shadow of the hissing paraffin lamp, his head against her knee, listening to the legends of old Iraq that Sabria tells him. His favourites are tales of the present king, Faisal II, of his youth, his impetuousness, his travels to faraway countries, and of the enormous blue-domed palace he built on the outskirts of Karradat Mariam. In her imagination, this palace, a new home for the monarch, was a wondrous place, worthy of fairytales about the powerful emperors, cruel monsters and spoilt dynasties who dwelt within.

Soon the bread oven is hot enough to begin baking. The smoke has all but died away and only the white-hot embers remain. Leaving the sewing-machine, Sabria fetches a raffia basket from the kitchen and walks to the oven with the soft dough patties. As she turns to close the screen door a spasm grips her and she sinks to the ground, sending them rolling into the sand. She knows the feeling: the baby is getting ready to come. The pain passes slowly and she looks up. From the corner of her eye, she sees Nabeel throw the snake stick at the well and jump for the forbidden *sununu* nest. She has lost count of the times she has told him and his friends to leave the hatchlings and the swallows' eggs alone. But the more she warns him away, the more intrigued by it he becomes. All of the neighbourhood children have been after them that spring, and it has taken extraordinary vigilance on her part to stop them plundering the nest.

Sabria knows she must ensure the birds' safety. Swallows are an omen of good fortune. They fly in from the south, returning to the same nest each spring, and lay their eggs. Man must not interfere with them – the scriptures are emphatic. The *sununu* are one of Allah's holy creatures, to be protected. She rises to her feet and is about to scold her son when she checks herself. Pausing to watch his agile frame arch upwards into the branches toward the wall, she wonders if he will stop short of the nest or reach for the eggs. With his bare feet gripping the trunk and one arm coiled round a branch, she watches his small hand reach expertly into the nest and feel for an egg. From overhead the mother bird darts about distractedly, sending out urgent alarm calls.

'Nabeel! Nabeel!' Sabria shouts, clapping her hands angrily. The sound bounces off the brown mud walls of the compound. 'Get down! You are in so much trouble, my son, that I don't know where to begin with you.'

Startled, Nabeel loses his footing and falls to the ground in a cloud of dust. Breathless though she is with the onset of labour, Sabria goes to the tree, grabs him by the ear and drags him into the house. 'How many times have I told you? *Sununu* are sacred, and stealing eggs is bad luck – for all of us. Don't you understand? I want good luck for my new baby.' She twists his ear hard. 'I know what you would have done with those eggs. Probably smashed them against the wall or rolled them along the road with your friends until they broke. You are a cruel, wicked little boy. Don't ever think of trying that again. I am your mother – I always know what you're doing. I have eyes in the back of my head.'

Nabeel runs crying back into the yard and hides in the crack between the compound wall and the house. Sabria picks up the dough patties, dusts them off as best she can and puts them into the oven. Then she wedges herself behind her sewing-machine and begins to stitch again. The baby will come soon and there is no one but Nabeel to help her.

Bibi, Sabria's mother, takes control. On returning home, she finds her daughter doubled up on the ground as the first contraction strikes. Under her instruction Makkya directs the elder boys, when they return from school, ordering them to get more wood and keep the fire going at all costs. 'Keep the kettle filled and the water boiling at all times. This is a most important task. Do you understand?' The boys nod solemnly.

Bibi brings the heavy copper kettle and pushes it at Jafar. She clicks her fingers at the free-standing iron tub and draws the pair to her. 'I will not have time to keep an eye on you. We will need water for the bath as well as the kettle. Do not let me down.'

Yasin returns from the market to find the compound buzzing with activity and his wife well into her labour. With everything under control, he settles into a chair in the shade of the verandah with Nabeel, and Makkya's children, Salah and Taha, at his feet, waiting for his orders. He is not unduly troubled by the unfolding drama: he has lived through it enough times to know it is best to keep out of Bibi's way until instructed to do otherwise. 'You three are to play outside until this is all over,' Bibi calls to the boys. 'There is nothing you can do now except to be no bother to anyone. Yasin, see to it.'

Yasin winks and gathers the children to him, promising sweet treats if they keep out of the house.

Bibi gathers into one hand the carefully laid-out bundles of leaves and clove, jasmine and juniper oils from her wooden cabinet. With the other, she picks up a kettle of freshly boiled water and a stack of muslin cloths, then she and the barefoot Makkya disappear into Sabria's room, closing the door behind them. An instant later the shutters are drawn across the window.

Although he is only four, instinct tells Nabeel he needs to keep his promise to Baba, his father. With his mother undergoing some unpleasant ordeal in her quarters, and the air of concern in the compound, he can't settle to anything. He has never seen Bibi, a little old lady, move with such agility and purpose.

And although Baba is sitting quietly, as he always does, he shifts a little as if something sharp is on the seat beneath him.

From his mother's room Nabeel hears her short, breathless cadences, snatched words and cries. He sneaks closer to the house but Baba calls him back to the tree. 'Mama is having a baby, Nabeel,' he says, putting his arm round Nabeel's shoulder and pulling him close. 'Bibi and Aunty Makkya are helping the baby come into the world.'

'How long will they be in there?'

'I cannot say. But when the baby is born we will bless him, just as we did Jafar, Juma'a and you.' And with Baba's simple explanation every question, worry and fear withers away. Baba has promised two things: that Mama will be with him again soon, with a new baby brother or sister to show him, and that he can eat as much fruit and bread as he wants. 'Just as soon as your brothers have baked it you can eat it.' This seems like the perfect arrangement. There is nothing better in the whole world than bread straight from the oven.

With his elder brothers engaged in their tasks, and Yasin's eyes fixed anxiously on his wife's door, Nabeel is free to roam about the mud house and the sandy courtyard unobserved. Bored by his cousins' stone-throwing game, he starts to climb, not the swallow tree but up on to the roof. No one has ever said the roof is out of bounds, have they? And even though his mother is still behind that closed door and cannot see him, she will know if he tries to climb the swallow tree again. The one-storey roof is easy enough to reach: the wall at the side of the house is uneven, with lots of little ledges for climbing. From the table inside he can slide out through the open window on to the ledge. From there, he has only to grab the overhanging grass fronds and swing his legs up.

Now he can see right across the courtyard, to Baba, his brothers and cousins, tall and spindly against the bare ground. No one notices him. Either that or they don't care that he is up there on his own. He lies down on the fronds that cover the roof and listens to the strange sounds that punctuate the calm of the late afternoon: his mother's occasional cries, the sound of water being drawn from the well and poured from bucket to copper kettle to bath. He wonders what the new baby might mean for him and Mama. She has been the only constant person in his life and he knows that everything is about to change. Mama had told him about the baby, how much fun his new brother or sister will be and how he must not be afraid. 'You'll have someone all to yourself.'

What did that mean? Maybe like Jafar has Juma'a. To have someone like that would be exciting, but he couldn't help wondering if it also meant that he would no longer have Mama to himself.

Lying there with the mid-afternoon sun on his back, the grass bristling against his bare legs, he hears Jafar and Juma'a shouting below. He watches them fight over the discs of bread as they pull them from the oven and drop them into the large round table-basket woven from dried palm fronds. The smell, which he loves above all others, reaches him but he doesn't want to go down, not just yet. Instead, he gathers a handful of pebbles from his pocket and drops them one by one over the edge of the roof, watching as they make little pits in the dust. Then he rolls over and stares straight up into the cloudless blue sky.

He is roused from his daydreams by Bibi's voice and rolls back to see her standing before Baba with her arms outstretched. She is smiling, wringing his hands in hers and kissing his cheeks. And Bibi never smiles. Nabeel can see every one of her remaining teeth, small and quite white for someone so old. Baba is smiling too. Jafar calls to her and she nods. Juma'a holds up the kettle and tells her the water has boiled again. She pulls leaves from a hessian bag at her waist and pushes them into a small earthenware pot at her feet. Juma'a pours on water and Bibi swirls the brew. Although he doesn't fully understand what is happening, Nabeel knows that his mother's ordeal is over.

Bibi sets an ornamental glass on a brass tray and puts the earthenware pot next to it. As she walks back to the house, she starts singing and as the ancient song drifts up to him he feels lighter and more excited than he ever has before. He raises himself and lifts his arms skywards, expanding into the space about him. It feels as though everything is growing bigger, his eyes seeing further, with more clarity and detail than usual. He turns this way and that, scanning the horizon with his arms outstretched. All around him there are other houses like theirs – little circles with shaded verandahs round an open courtyard. In the distance he can see two barefoot women carrying huge pails along the road. Further away still he can see grass and scrub, and beyond that, in the far distance, the railway line where Baba goes to work, running off across fields and scrubland into the desert. Turning slowly, he sees orchards, meadows filled with fruit trees, everything from dates to apricots. On the other side is the river Tigris. He imagines it must be as big and furious as a sea. All around there are friends, and friends of friends, cousins and aunts, people who love him, doing so many things. It is a big world just going on and on. And he is part of it.

Birds scatter from one of the neighbourhood trees, sweep round them and settle again. He thinks of what Mama had said about the swallows, how they fly each winter to Africa where it is warm, joining with all the other swallows fleeing the harsh winters in Europe. They fly out to the horizon and keep going. Then, one day in spring, they return, not just to the same country but to the same house and the same nest. How is that possible?

He has only to turn round again and gaze at the blue skies to feel his heart soar. Spring is becoming summer, and all around him it is as if the world has cracked open to reveal its secrets. He stretches further up, and tips his head back, crying out into the fresh, clear air, '*Ateer, ateer, leyteny.*' I want, I want to fly.

The People's Revolution
Summer 1958

'Mama, look! The snake is coming. He is nearly in our house.'

Nabeel, now eight, and his little brother Jabbar are hopping up and down impatiently as they tell Sabria of the Lebetine viper's progress across the sandy courtyard. 'He has left Ali's house, Mama, and he is coming to ours, slithering along in the sand. He is a big, beautiful one. *Please* come and see, Mama.'

'He will be our snake,' Jabbar squeals, with the wilful certainty of a four-year-old.

'And the bowl? Is that still where I left it?' Sabria calls to them from the well, knowing that either of them, in his eagerness, may have forgotten to replenish the water, or even knocked it over.

'Yes, Mama,' the two boys chorus. 'It's still there.'

'And I filled it,' Jabbar says proudly. 'Nabeel put in the salt but I got the water and poured it.'

Sabria sets down her bucket and moves to the gate where the boys are crouched. It isn't that she doesn't trust them, simply that things have to be right. There are no second chances with snakes.

Cautiously she treads backwards through the courtyard, her shoes leaving only the faintest impression in the sand. The

25

bowl, a simple brown earthenware dish, brims with salty water. Broader at the base than at the lip, it will not tip over when the snake begins to drink, yet it is shallow enough for it to reach in easily.

'Don't go too close,' Sabria breathes, returning to the bronze grate where she is about to start cooking rice. 'And if I see either of you throwing stones I will punish you severely. You must *never* tease a snake.'

The two boys run from the shady part of the courtyard and out through the doorway, a huge wooden frame, nailed together from reclaimed railway sleepers that Yasin had liberated from the depot at the old Western Baghdad railway station. Across it are nailed strips of silvery aluminium – flat-beaten from empty cooking-oil cans, with patches of red and yellow paint still visible.

Half ignoring their mother, the boys crouch at the compound gate to watch the snake as it slithers along beneath the brown mud wall. Jabbar tugs at Nabeel's shorts. 'Shall we move the bowl? Maybe he cannot see it.'

'No,' whispers Nabeel, 'it's too dangerous. And *you* are only four, so you should do as I say because I am older.' He holds Jabbar tight by the arm, both boys frozen a few feet from the snake, which has stopped moving and is eyeing them with its head raised and motionless. Nabeel reaches slowly for his seven-eyes talisman. A tiny piece of rock with seven gnarled fingers and a spherical hole at the end of each, it has been glued into his hair with asphalt at his mother's instruction by an old mystic living on the outskirts of Karra-dat Mariam. Rolling it between his thumb and forefinger, he feels a reassuring sense of its protection come over him. To Jabbar, he whispers, 'We will win, you'll see. But to win we must be patient and wait for him to come in his own time.'

Cautiously at first, the snake arcs sideways towards the bowl, leaving a series of identical S-shaped tracks in the sand.

The boys know that much depends on the snake taking a drink from their bowl. Their mother, like everyone they know, has often told them that a visiting snake brings good fortune to a house and everyone in it. But first it must drink the offering.

'So if he drinks from the bowl, he won't bite us and we'll have good luck?' asks Jabbar, still confused.

'I've already told you,' Nabeel says impatiently. 'If he drinks the water he is our friend for always.'

'But what about people who don't live here? Will he bite them instead?'

'I don't know,' Nabeel hisses testily, flicking his brother's ear. 'All I know is that Mama says we must be good to him and not scare him away, because then it'll be good for us.' Crouched in the sand, the two boys consider their next move.

Deep respect for life is at the centre of Sabria's world. Once, Nabeel had woken in the night to find a deadly camel spider dangling above his face. He had screamed hysterically for his mother. She had cupped the intruder in her hands and carried it out to the yard. 'Why didn't you kill it?' he had asked her, as she tucked him back under his blanket.

'Why kill it if you don't have to? He doesn't want to bite you, after all. Spiders are sacred too. Remember, it was a spider that saved the prophet Muhammad by spinning a web across the cave so that the men chasing him wouldn't think to look in.'

Yasin had been known to brave a wry joke at her expense about her love of wildlife. 'Be careful where you sit,' he would say to guests, as he stared up at the ceiling. 'This place is crawling with wildlife and the roof may collapse at any time.' And it was true. The unbaked mud house was like a zoo, with spiders, desert rats, geckos, lizards, beetles and insects living in the roof and wall cavities. And, other than scorpions, the children are under strict instructions to respect them all. Of course, respect never stopped the boys chasing geckos up the walls or pulling their tails, which would drop off, or stamping on cockroaches as they scuttled across the kitchen floor.

Sabria interrupts the boys with a call for lunch. They eat quickly, wordlessly, scooping handfuls of the slow-cooked okra stew and cardamom rice into their mouths with pieces of flat bread, eager not to miss the snake's progress. With empty bowls pushed in unison to the middle of the table, they bolt back outside – to discover that the snake has gone. They walk out to where they had last seen it, and the dust round the saltwater bowl is undisturbed.

'Mama,' Jabbar's bottom lip quivers, 'Mama, the snake is gone. He does not want to be our friend.'

She smiles and strokes his thick hair. 'Oh, my son, you must not worry. He is just resting from the sun. He will come again. You'll see.'

With the younger boys engrossed in making friends with the local wildlife, the two elder brothers, Jafar and Juma'a, spend much of their spare time out of the house on more adventurous missions. Both are now studying, Jafar at Baghdad University and Juma'a in his first year at the Institute of Teachers. Jafar goes off each morning on the bicycle given to him by Sabria and Yasin. Even the bicycle was blessed. Nabeel had watched, enthused, as Sabria made her eldest son ride over two raw eggs as a sign that he would not be smashed to pieces in an accident.

Both young men are immersed in the emerging counter-culture of protest politics. They spend their evenings at rallies and meetings. Jafar has taken up with the Arab Nationalists while Juma'a is a Communist. And while their outlook differs, they, along with most other political groups in the country, are united in their dislike of the puppet monarchy set in place by the British after the overthrow of the Ottoman Empire. Sabria listens to their news with forbearance and the motherly desire to keep her children out of harm's way.

'It is our duty to be active. The king will never give people like us a voice, Mama.' Jafar had said once, when she had expressed concern that he might be getting too involved.

'And it suits the British. Do you not think they intended things to be just this way? Faisal II is an innocent pawn, being played for their own ends, but that uncle of his, Abd ul-ilah, controls everything and everyone. Now there is a chance for us to be part of something new. A republic."

'Perhaps you are right, my boy,' she said, 'but the question neither you nor your Communist brother can answer is which of your parties will take the lead in this glorious new Iraq you dream of. It sounds like no one has much of a plan.'

Now, for the first time in years, change is in the air. In smoke-filled cafés across Baghdad the blueprint of a new age is being drawn up by young thinkers and idealists. For the first time ordinary people are talking openly of their disaffection and their desires for the future. There are proud boasts of a modern Iraqi republic taking its rightful place at the centre of the Arab world. Egypt has taken the lead and deposed its ruling oligarchy, and the Iraqi underground is humming with rumours of its own revolution. Yet despite all this, Jafar and Juma'a – and almost all of Iraq – are stunned by the news to which they awake on 14 July 1958.

Sabria, rarely asleep beyond six, rises to her usual routine. Slipping out of bed, she taps her slippers against the wall to rid them of beetles and scorpions, then pads out into the yard. She draws the first, chilled, bucket of water of the day and pours it into an enamel bowl. Then she rinses her face. As the rest of the household, Yasin, Jafar, Juma'a, Nabeel, Jabbar, and their cousins Kamil and Amir sleep sprawled on mattresses spread through the few tiny rooms of the compound, she lights the fire, fills the kettle and wedges it into the grate. Even the baby, Aqbal, her fifth child and her first precious daughter, has yet to stir. Today they will all breakfast on a little leftover bread and cheese, the boys' favourite.

As she busies herself unwrapping cheese, she reaches for the valve radio on the sill, acquired by Yasin at great expense. Baghdad Radio – the country's only station – plays folk songs interspersed with news, Qu'ran readings, religious discourse and the occasional nugget of gossip from the world of film and entertainment. It is as good a way as any to keep in touch with the world outside her home, and, because she cannot read, provides fuel for her discussions with her family and the neighbours. With the green power light glowing, she knows the set will soon warm up.

From the first cracklings of the small oval speaker it is clear that something unusual is going on. The presenter's voice, normally so mellifluous and calm, is distorted, the words muffled and unclear. She tries retuning it, banging the huge battery and moving the aerial this way and that. The voice is now almost breathless with hysteria.

The army has stormed Baghdad. Marching from Jalawala,

a huge barracks on the Iranian border, troops have swamped the centre of the city, taking control of the radio station and government buildings. 'This,' the voice reaches a crescendo, 'is the voice of the people's revolution.'

'Jafar!' Sabria rushes in to her eldest son, asleep in the living room. 'Jafar! There is a revolution. The army has taken power. It's on the radio. They are going to storm the palace. You had better get up!' Within minutes the house is alive, the two eldest boys and Nabeel pulling on shirts, shorts and sandals, then running excitedly out of the compound and into the fields. Ignoring the calls of their mother to return for breakfast, they disappear towards the centre of Baghdad, to watch events unfold.

Angling the radio so that she can hear it across the courtyard, Sabria settles Jabbar to play with Aqbal. The radio announcer is encouraging people to take to the streets and show their support. Solidarity and unity are demanded of all citizens, and a new era is promised for Iraq. Yasin is working in the scrubland to the west of the city. She wonders if he has heard the news, and prays that he is on his way home. In the meantime there is the prospect of visitors, all, no doubt, eager to share what they know. She must be ready to receive them.

She draws two large buckets of water, then two more, from the well, takes them up the steps, past the swallow tree, and pours them into the huge earthenware water tank set against the back wall. This great structure, rough though it looks, has transformed her life. The clay cleans and cools the water, and holds such a great quantity that the family bathe more frequently than any other household in the neighbourhood. It is nothing short of a miracle. Wiping her brow as the heat of the day rises, she drags the bronze grate to the bread oven. Tea and bread will not be enough today: she will bake a salted fish too. By the time the sun goes down, everyone will be hungry and the house will probably be full.

Hearing the commotion, Makkya rushes out of her room and across the courtyard. The two sisters embrace.

'Are we ready for this revolution?' Sabria says, as she pours tea and pushes the last of the *ijja* Makkya's way.

Before her sister can reply, the radio crackles with another news alert. The royal family is being held captive at the palace. The radio spares no detail. Unprepared for the might and determination of the military, Faisal II and his family have surrendered, emerging from the palace with their arms above their heads. The women of the palace had been wailing, holding out copies of the Qur'an, in supplication, and many loyal servants have been taken captive too. All were hauled into a chamber inside the palace. Some had tried to escape and been shot. The announcer tells the people that it is the end for Faisal and his family. The two women listen in silence, dreading the horrors taking place less than a mile from where they sit. Makkya watches the two children play on the rug and Sabria stokes the kindling in the grate, saying a prayer. Spontaneously they break into a lament that fills the air, drowning the radio.

Sabria picks up a fragment of blue Kashani stone from a ledge, where it glints in the early-morning light. One of the boys had found it in a pile of rubble during the building of the new royal palace, which had taken years. Now, it seemed, the royal family would never live there. Of course, she understands that their downfall was inevitable. As Juma'a has often said, 'They serve themselves. It is only a matter of time.' Even so, it has come as a shock and Sabria can't help but feel sorrow at their end.

'Let us hope there is mercy and some are set free,' Makkya says, 'the servants too. What have they done to deserve death? Perhaps some have lost themselves in the confusion.'

'I'm afraid there may be no hope for any of them.' Sabria sighs, and both women nod solemnly to each other.

The first visitors to the house, Sabria's neighbours, bring no news. They come to sit and drink tea, preferring to wait with friends than to be alone. It is only when Khawwam, Yasin's only son from his first marriage, arrives, breathless and excited, just before noon, that they have confirmation of their suspicions.

'The king is dead,' he crows. 'They shot him. There are people everywhere, fighting, and the city is on fire.'

Sabria gasps. 'Are you sure?' She pictures Jafar caught up in the mêlée.

'Yes!' insists Khawwam, mistaking her sharp intake of breath for disbelief. 'I have it direct from the guards at the barracks.'

'But why?' the neighbours chime in. 'You would think they would spare them, give them safe passage into exile at least, as Nasser did with King Farouk.'

Khawwam nods. 'Maybe that is so. Nobody knows for sure. General Kassim is leading the revolution, but it wasn't him or his squad who captured the people at the palace. A second squad came without warning and executed them. No one knows who gave the order.'

'And the rest of the family? What news of them?' asks Sabria.

'All dead. Every one.' Khawwam looks uneasily at the ground.

News of the king's murder spreads quickly across the capital. Jafar, with the mobs thronging the wide streets from the edge of the Old Town, hears it from a runner who witnessed the events at the palace. At this news, the euphoric mass of young men surges forward, charged with the zeal of the righteous victor. Men brandishing guns, iron rods, wooden staves and knives bellow slogans at the sky, '*We are the Arab United.*' Jafar, delirious as he twirls through the crowds, knows his long-cherished people's republic is about to become reality. Yes, it will mean compromise, coalition, perhaps, but it is happening. He dares to hope that the Arab Nationalists will lead the way and Nasser will find himself elected leader of all Arab nations. But that is for another day. Embracing his fellows, he shouts and chants until he is hoarse.

The crowd fans out from the Old Town across the bridges and into Karkh. Its eye seizes on the huge Italianate statue of King Faisal I that stands at the centre of the roundabout close to the British Embassy. Twenty feet high, made of polished black granite, the king sits on a magnificent stallion, rifle raised to the heavens in triumph. Once a symbol of Iraq's imperial might, it now recalls the past injustice of a ruling élite whose self-interest condemned much of the population to poverty. Swarming over the base, men tie lengths of rope together, then lasso the horse's legs and neck, and the monarch's head. Then, as one man, they heave in their hundreds on the rope until their hands are raw and their bodies ache. With one mighty effort the foundation block cracks, the mob cheers and the statue begins a slow, graceful topple. With sweat pouring down the back of his neck and the tightness of sunburn on his face, Jafar pushes his way to the back of the crowd as Faisal's shoulder shatters on the ground. He wants to roar but the air is choked with dust billowing into the air. Squinting at the place where Faisal stood, there is nothing now between him and the brilliant sky.

For the little ones, Nabeel and his schoolfriends, Karim, Adnan, Adnan's brother, Taleb, and little Ali, the momentous events mean only one thing: adventure. They can hear the roar of the crowds coming from the direction of the river as they stand on the highway close to the house. As they run onwards, drawn to the sound, the street fills with cars. People throng the pavements as far as they can see in either direction.

Earlier that morning they had set off not knowing where they were heading. They had gone towards the river, taken the shortcut across the railway line and through the gates of the children's cemetery, where Cousin Bulbul is buried. Despite their haste Nabeel had paused at the grave to say a short prayer. It was something of a habit. He missed his chubby-faced cousin. Bulbul had been wry and funny: he'd liked to pretend he was a great Hollywood film star. Whenever you ran into him, the first thing he would do was pluck an imaginary comb from his shorts and slick back his hair, Elvis-style. Bulbul had been part of the gang, a good fighter, an accomplished mischief maker, a clever boy fond of kicking footballs until dusk, pocketing lizards and racing oil drums down the street as old men shook their fists. He had died without warning, like his mother before him, less than a day after taking to his bed with a fever. Nabeel watched as they washed and blessed the little corpse. He had asked Uncle Rashid, his mother's closest brother, if he could carry his friend to the cemetery. They had buried him that sunset, covering the body with earth, then returned, in the silent darkness, to the family home. Bulbul would have loved all this excitement.

Now Nabeel nods at the boys, jumps up and they run on towards the centre of the city. They stop beside a sappy oleander from where they can see the victorious army advancing down the boulevard, firing guns into the air. 'We are *this* close,' Ali whispers, holding his thumb and forefinger together and closing one eye. 'We will see this all for ourselves. No one will have to tell us about it because no one could be closer than we are now.' They wave at the hundreds marching, in their colonial greens, long shorts, khaki socks and shiny black boots, yelling the slogans of revolution at the top of their high-pitched voices, hoping to catch the eye of a passing soldier.

When an elderly man moves up behind them and clips Ali's ear, the spell is broken. 'Boys!' he bellows. 'This is a dangerous army of revolutionaries. Get off home before you find yourselves in terrible trouble.'

Spinning round, the boys stare into the lined face of an old man they recognise from their street. Behind him a second man, white-haired, his teeth stained yellow with tobacco, jabs a bony finger at them. 'Do as he says, or we will tell your mothers. They will beat you for your disobedience.'

'But, Uncle, we only want to see. Can't we just watch the soldiers and the tanks and then go home?' begs Ali.

'This is not a game, little boy. The king has been killed. Someone shot him dead.' The man looks straight at Ali, aiming his stick like a gun. 'They might kill you, too, for fun.'

'They've killed the king?' Ali's eyes are wide.

'Dead, dead, dead. His family too – sisters, uncles and all their servants – dead and left for the buzzards. We saw the body of Abd ul-ilah ourselves,' he continues, relishing every detail. 'They brought him out and tied a rope round his neck like an ox. Then they dragged him through the streets from the back of one of his own royal cars. Believe me, now that they've killed the prince regent, they'll kill anyone. If I were you I'd go home before they come for you.'

Nabeel tries to make sense of what the old men are saying. He knows they are telling the truth, but he can't bring himself to believe it. The palace is close to the house and his school. Can the royal family really have been so bad? Sometimes, waiting at the bus stop outside the palace to catch the bus to school, he has seen them come through the gates and they looked like anyone else. 'But why would they kill the king?' he asks. 'I saw him two weeks ago in his car and he smiled at me. He was nice.'

'You are young. You would not understand,' wheezes the tobacco-stained man. 'Sometimes people want change and the only way to make it happen is to force it.'

The two old men cackle at each other as the boys wriggle free and duck back into the crowd. Soon all four are racing silently through the sand towards Karradat Mariam. As they go, Nabeel pictures the king's face as it had been when he had seen him through the window of his car. He and Hamoudi had been on their way to the international railway station to do some trainspotting before school. The grand old building, built by the British, was a favourite haunt. They would sit amid its bustle and commotion at rush-hour watching the huge locomotives arrive and depart. The smell of steam and the great rumble of the engines were irresistible. From there trains departed for far-off cities, and countries he had only seen in an atlas, setting off through the desert sand, bound for the unknown.

The king had driven past in a silver and maroon Cadillac as Nabeel and Hamoudi waited to cross to the station. Juma'a had said the car had been a present to the king's father, Ghazi, from *Hitler*. The boys had waved and erupted into a spontaneous rendition of the national anthem. The king had looked out at them and smiled.

Nabeel runs through the open compound gates into the house and skids to a stop in front of his mother, bending to catch his breath. 'The king is killed,' he gasps.

Sabria holds him close and he catches sight of Ali's parents sitting in the shade, nursing small glasses of tea. They wave at him solemnly. 'We know, *habibi*. We heard it on the radio,' she says, clasping his face in her hands. 'Come and sit with us. Uncle Rashid is here, and Aunt Makkya.' She shepherds Nabeel to the table and pours him some water from the jug. 'So, tell us what you saw. Did you find your brothers?' He picks out an orange from the bowl beside the teapot and gulps down several segments, then launches into a garbled account of falling statues, soldiers, murdered kings, fires and giddy insurrection.

It is long after dark when Juma'a and Jafar return, and Sabria is glad to see them. The only casualty of the day is one of Jafar's shoes, lost in the excitement. A curfew has been imposed so they all settle on the terrace to talk. 'Who wants a baked aubergine?' Sabria asks, as she pulls several from the ash of the stove and passes them round in a thick earthenware pot. 'Even revolutionaries must eat.'

In the shadows cast by the paraffin lanterns, the elder children and neighbours talk over the extraordinary events that have overtaken their country. In the distance, gunfire and the occasional explosion ruptures the night, causing the smallest children, Jabbar and Aqbal, to twitch in their sleep. But it seems there is a chance that Kassim may bring with him a new era of equality and optimism.

The following morning, Sabria reaches for the radio and starts to clear up in the courtyard. The battery is weak but the voice that comes from the speaker is calm and clear. Strident martial music plays in the background, and blessings are offered to the people for their loyal support. Then she hears Kassim's voice, pledging to give Iraq back to her people. Sabria draws her *fota* into place and tucks a paper fragment of scripture, given to her by the local Imam, into the lining by her temple. No one else is up. Yasin had arrived home in the early hours and lies asleep in his white robe on their bed. It was a late night.

When she steps out into the courtyard to draw water, she sees it. There, in the sand, leading to the saltwater bowl, is the unmistakable S of a snake.

Yasin Hussain and Sons
Autumn 1962

A long extension cord runs from the house, out through the kitchen window and into the yard. It is made of several different lengths of wire twisted together with coloured electrical tape and winds across the lawn, under a bright woollen rug, up the side of an old wooden table and eventually disappears into the back of a new black-and-white Pye television set. A two-pronged extendable aerial hangs upside down from a branch, twisting fitfully in the morning breeze. Under the leafy canopy of the almond trees, the screen is filled with the cartoon antics of Walt Disney. The volume knob is set on full, distorting the sound beyond recognition, yet no one seems bothered. Yasin, seated on a woollen rug, wheezes with laughter. Apart from the films they show once a week this is his favourite programme.

All seven of his children are seated around him, Jafar and Juma'a, now in their twenties, twelve-year-old Nabeel, eight-year-old Jabbar, Aqbal, Tariq and even the bright-eyed toddler, Amel, all with their eyes glued to the screen.

Their deaf-mute cousin Kamil is with them too. When Sabria's brother Rashid lost his wife, he had been so addled by grief that he was unable to take care of his two sons, Amir and

Kamil. Sabria had agreed to have them until he could cope again. It had worked out well: even though the house was cramped the boys seemed to bring with them a welcome calm. Amir had eventually returned to his father, but they had all agreed that the timid Kamil was so content at al-Bayaa that he should stay. Now, he attends the Institute of Hope, Iraq's first school for the deaf, where he has bloomed. And he loves Nabeel too – even now, he chooses to sit as close to his cousin as he can, his head resting on the other's shoulder.

When they first came to live with the Yasins Nabeel had been the only one who understood Kamil. He had created a special sign language which, in time, all of them came to use. 'We understand each other because there are only five days between us,' was Nabeel's reasoning. 'We see things in similar ways. That is all.' Behind them, three local children are perched on the garden wall. Everyone squeals and jigs with laughter as the cartoon cat is repeatedly hit with bricks, a flying dustbin lid and a hammer. It is the highlight of everyone's week.

Yasin especially likes to be outside where the air is fresh. Beyond the shadows he can feel the autumn sun penetrate his lean leathery cheeks and warm him to the bone. The sun soothes the dull aches that still run through his body from the accident. As it had been at Karradat Mariam, so now, in their modern house in the newly built neighbourhood of al-Bayaa, the garden is his sanctuary. Its lush green foliage and grass make a stark contrast to the inhospitable desert scrub where he has spent so much of his working life. But, then, his whole life now is in sharp contrast to what has gone before.

Drifting in and out of the programme, Yasin plans his day. Once the credits on the Friday film matinée roll, he will cover the television with the tarpaulin and walk to the mosque, or perhaps through the market and on to see his brother in al-Rusafa, on the other side of the river. He would like to stay at home, but he knows Sabria will not tolerate it. Besides, it is good to go visiting on the day of rest. He and his brother can stop for tea and, though he does not smoke, he likes to sit with the other men as they puff on their *narghila* water-pipes. The pace is slow and the talk honest. Then, at the end of the day, he will return for dinner and the evening news. But for now there is nothing to do but sit and watch.

Since the arrival of the television, Friday morning has become a fixed date in the neighbourhood calendar. A double bill of cartoons and a big Hollywood movie – John Wayne, Tyrone Power or Tarzan. If they are lucky it might be the children's favourite, *King Kong*. They have seen it four times in as many months. They know every last plot twist by heart and cheer the ape as he wreaks revenge on his would-be captors. There is only one television station in Iraq and the schedule doesn't change much; the same shows are often repeated within weeks. But no one much cares, such is the novelty. Yasin's is the first family in their neighbourhood to own a set and he is as proud as he can be.

Perched on a metal camp chair beneath the far wall of the compound, Sabria nurses a cigarette. She relishes the peace television brings to the house. A bottle-green shawl is gathered round her neck and her thick hair is twisted into a chunky plait. She is deep in conversation with Makkya.

'Sister, don't even try to talk to me about your finances. You would lose money in a gold mine.' She shakes her head. 'There is no point in denying it. Investing prudently is not in your nature. "Ask thy purse what thou should buy". You must do business with your head, not with your heart, or you will be destined to remain poor.'

Makkya starts to sing under her breath.

'You are a Mullaya – a singer – not a businesswoman. But the boys can help you. There is no point in letting pride ruin you both.'

'You should not interfere.' Makkya throws up her hands indignantly. 'The man who has pledged to buy the house is a good man. Poor, yes, but he is honest. He has no wife and with four children to feed he is struggling. He is paying me all he can and I think it a fair price. Besides, the deal is done. I have made him a promise. As for the house we are buying, it is a good one at a fair price. Only you could find anything wrong with it.'

Sabria rolls her eyes and shakes her head. Since they had moved from Karradat Mariam, and Makkya had remarried and moved in with her new husband, she had become less prudent than ever. 'Sister, the house is overpriced. Marriage has turned your brain to dust. You must withdraw! Tell your buyer he must find a little more if he wants your house. I will send the boys out looking for somewhere more suitable.' Makkya clasps her hands together, closes her eyes and begins to hum under her breath.

Sabria presses her cigarette butt into the tin ashtray at her feet, gets up and goes inside, frustrated.

Yasin watches her, marvelling inwardly at his wife. If Makkya would only listen to her, things would get better. Of that he is certain. Sabria's prudence and instinct in all matters fiscal has saved his own family. While Makkya seems intent on trading down, their own prospects have improved beyond all recognition in the years since General Kassim came to power. Juma'a and Jafar might disagree but they are young and it is in their nature to be dissatisfied. But for him, the outward signs are there for all to see. Kassim had a vision for

43

Iraq and, slowly, it seems he is making good on his promise. They have possessions, their children are all well educated and the whole country has dragged itself into the twentieth century. Even the peasants and country folk are reaping the benefits of Kassim's new society. Throughout Iraq ordinary people are prospering and, through a combination of education and hard work, the Yasin family is making a determined bid to become middle class. The shift is almost imperceptible until you stand back and view it from a distance.

There is the new house in al-Bayaa, made not from mud but from bricks and mortar and with electricity, plumbing and fresh running water. Both Jafar and Juma'a have graduated from university into white-collar jobs. And there are many smaller signs of the family's progress up the social scale: the summer before last they bought a green Mitsubishi electric fan; the calendar that came with it, containing glossy colour pictures of kimono-clad Japanese models, still hangs proudly on the wall, a full year out of date now. The ammonia ice fridge has changed their lives, along with the water-purification tank. But without doubt, the television set takes pride of place. Just five years ago, Yasin could never have imagined such things existed. Yet here he is, a man of means with his own prospering business and his own television. For where Kassim's vision ended, his wife's tenacity and determination had begun.

Already in the middle years of his life when he married Sabria, Yasin, a widower, had expected to work on the railways until he dropped dead or was deemed too old to be of any use. There was neither a career path to follow nor any real expectation of advancement. In fact, he had hoped for nothing beyond delivering a regular wage to his family. He

44

had felt no bitterness or dissatisfaction with his lot. Quite the contrary. That was how life was, even after the accident.

In 1949, driving back from a three-month stint track-laying down near Najaf, he had lost concentration and spun off the road into a ditch. The car had crumpled and folded in on itself as it nosedived down the embankment and hit the ground. Yasin's legs and back had been smashed, the bones split and shattered. While he was still unconscious the doctors had told Sabria that his injuries were so severe he would be a house-bound cripple for the rest of his life. When he had come round a few days later he remembered nothing of the accident; nor had he any grasp on how serious his injuries were. The only real shock he expressed was when he discovered that he was wearing hospital pyjamas. Yasin had never worn pyjamas. 'You're like an old English gentleman,' Sabria had teased. 'I should make you a nightcap to go with them.'

Many weeks later when he was discharged, and the full impact of the accident had been revealed to him, he had become depressed. He imagined that the family fortunes would take a turn for the worse and felt he had let them down. As the money dwindled and the goodwill of neighbours, family and friends could no longer be relied upon, Yasin had panic attacks. It was Sabria, determined that the family should thrive, who had stepped in with a plan to save them. Her sewing business had always given them extra money. She was a respected dressmaker and often had to turn work down. Now she took on every order she could, working into the early hours for weeks at a time to complete a job. With the money she earned from her loyal clientele, she met the demands of their young family until, slowly and painfully at first, Yasin grew stronger. First, it was small victories, but with Sabria's encouragement he was walking again, shuffling about the house. The turning point came when he declared he would do the family shopping at the al-Shorja dry-goods market. In the months that followed, he honed his bartering skills with the traders and built up his wasted muscles, then finally declared himself well enough to work.

Yasin was still in pain but he bore it with fortitude. He worked through the next decade until, out of the blue, Hassan, an aged Kurd businessman and friend of Yasin's half-brother, offered him the lease on his stationery shop. 'Yasin, I am old and tired of this city,' he explained, one afternoon, over coffee in the back of his shop. 'I never thought I'd want to leave it but I do. I don't recognise it any more, with all these houses being built. How long before all the fields are gone, covered with factories and schools, eh? Don't get me wrong, schools are a great idea – but do we need so many? I don't know where I am half the time.' He shook his head. 'Once I knew everyone in this neighbourhood, every man, woman and child, by name. Now, there are so many strangers. I want to sell you the shop and retire to Kirkuk. I have three daughters there to look after me and I will live with one and enjoy myself with my grandchildren.' He brought out a sheaf of papers, ledgers and accounts from a wooden chest. The business had a healthy turnover and Yasin needed no convincing. He had long dreamed of owning a business and though he had never imagined himself as a stationery supplier, the opportunity was too good to pass up. So, at the age of sixty-four, Yasin became a shopkeeper.

With the formalities in order, Yasin had taken the whole family to see his new empire on the outskirts of al-Bayaa. The shop was in need of repair, but Yasin listened patiently to his family's ideas and had soon made the place his own. New paint, new shelves and new stock, with lined books, ledgers, receipt pads and HB pencils for everyone, from office clerks to schoolchildren. There were racy coloured papers, too, and sheets of tissue for party favours. There was even a rack of books, chosen by Nabeel, for those customers who could read. Above the door they fixed a hand-painted sign, elegant white lettering on a cobalt blue background: 'Yasin Hussain & Sons: Granada Stationery.'

The final credits roll on *Tarzan – Lord of the Jungle*. Yasin raises himself from his chair and switches off the set. He will leave his wife and her sister to sort out their differences and come back when the dust has settled.

Taking a cloth for his head from the chair by the terrace door, he calls to his wife, 'I am going over to Rusafa. Then I will be at the shop doing the stock-take. Send Nabeel and Jabbar across – they can help.'

Hearing the gate shut, Sabria calls Aqbal in to help her with dinner. 'Jafar, Juma'a, before you go out, bring the babies in.' Her low voice carries out to the garden.

Jafar prods Tariq until he goes to fetch his sister. Juma'a hauls Amel into his arms and takes her in, depositing her on the tiled floor.

'Will you go to work?' Sabria asks him.

He shakes his head. 'But if you want me to help you here, Mama, I will.'

'No, but be back for dinner. We are having *masgouf*, fire smoked and grilled carp.'

Juma'a thinks of this and the pickles and salad in the fridge. After spending the afternoon with friends, discussing the latest strategies designed to promote the Communist philosophy among Iraq's middle classes, he will be hungry.

Outside, Jafar is talking with Nabeel about Hemingway again. Despite the decade between them they are close, and Jafar often allows Nabeel to come with him to political meetings. In 1959, when Nabeel was just nine, he and Juma'a had taken the younger boy on the International Workers' Day Festival demonstrations. In retrospect, this had perhaps been reckless: the crowds were rough and the march had turned violent. By nightfall the Nationalists were fighting with the Communists and they had been forced to take Nabeel on to the roof of a bus out of harm's reach. Rocks and stones, sticks and even knives were out that night. To Nabeel, it was the most thrilling thing he had ever witnessed.

'Jafar, come on. I'm leaving,' Juma'a calls. 'Our bus will be here any minute.'

Jafar leaves Nabeel and walks towards the gate. 'See you later, brother.' He salutes and closes the gate behind him.

Sabria watches twelve-year-old Nabeel looking longingly after his brothers and knows that one day soon he, too, will find his way into politics. Whether that will be a good thing remains to be seen. The elder two are setting quite an example, arguing at every opportunity with each other and anyone foolish enough to engage with them. Even Uncle Rashid, a man without a political bone in his body, has been drawn into the fray. Sabria is concerned about the people they talk of, the Ba'ath party. An offshoot of the Ba'athist organisation formed in Syria in the late 1940s, the name is on everyone's lips. Juma'a seems convinced that they already pose a threat to peace and liberty. 'They have no heart and they will stop at nothing. I can only hope they don't win any popular support.'

It seems true that they are ruthless and determined. In 1959 one of their number, Saddam Hussein, a one-time assassin in the employ of the CIA, had hunted down prominent Communists and even tried to assassinate General Kassim in a bid for power. The attempt failed and Hussein succeeded only in shooting himself in the leg. He had been forced to flee the country and settle in Egypt. But even without him Juma'a says that others are waiting for an opportunity to seize control.

With the older boys gone, Sabria encourages Nabeel, Jabbar and Cousin Kamil out of the house. 'Go and play football.' She shoos them towards the door, pushing a ball at Jabbar. The brothers pull on lace-up sneakers and run out of the gate. Kamil lags after them, his sandals dragging in the sand.

To Sabria the peace now is blissful. The three youngest children are still with her, but they are quieter than the boys and happy playing together. She thinks her friends will come soon, bearing little bowls of food or other offerings as they do most afternoons.

The first through the gate are the two teachers from the local school. Sabria hears them call her name and hurries out to greet them. She admires them enormously. She cannot read but she enjoys the company of independent educated women. 'Dear friends, come in, your timing is perfect. The house is quiet at last. I have only my sister with me, and the little ones. Shall we take our tea outside?'

She ushers the women on to the terrace and returns to the kitchen to make tea, pausing only to drop a pinch of saffron into the rice and take the simmering stew off the heat. Makkya has forgotten their earlier exchange and squeezes her sister's arm. 'Go and sit with your friends. I will bring the tea.'

Outside, Amel is asleep on a rug under the orange tree, and Aqbal and Tariq are playing hopscotch in the corner of the compound. Sabria tucks her long legs beneath her on her wooden chair and listens as the conversation takes shape. This is the way she learns of ideas and opinions. Shia'a, Sunni, Christian and Mandaean Sabian, rich, poor, educated and illiterate are equal in her house. All have something to teach her.

The younger of the two teachers, Zaynab, brings out fabric from a canvas bag. 'Sabria, you made me a skirt only two months ago but now I want another the same.'

Sabria reaches for the bag. 'Did you go to the same place?'

'Yes.'

'Next time we must go together.' She turns the fabric in her hands and rubs it between thumb and forefinger. 'But you chose well. This is quality cloth. And what a lovely colour. I can make you another the same or we could try a new style I found in the newspaper.' She gets up and scurries into the house, returning with a neatly torn page. Her tiny fingers hold up a picture of a model wearing a skirt and matching jacket.

'*Shukran*, Sabria!' Zaynab is ecstatic. 'This is so smart, and thank you for thinking of me, but do you not think it is too much?'

'Tsk. It will be perfect for you. You're a teacher and you should show you are a woman of confidence and learning.'

Then the gossip begins in earnest, who is doing what, where and with whom. Sabria shares all that she knows about politics from her sons and in return her friends confide in her.

When Jabbar and Nabeel return Sabria sends them out again to the cavernous tobacco shop in al-Shawwaka market for ready-rolled cigarettes. 'Get sixty,' she whispers, out of earshot of the teachers, pressing coins into Nabeel's hand.

It's a treat for them to go to the tobacconist's. The boys love to watch the sweet, moist Virginia tobacco being shaken out and rolled into cigarettes – *and* they get to spend the change on something sweet. Once rolled, the cigarettes are wrapped tightly in pink tissue paper and presented like a bouquet. On their return home the boys compete to see who can fit the most cigarettes into his mouth before lighting and passing them out to the women through clouds of smoke and laughter.

Makkya goes inside to make the first of many fresh pots of tea. It will be a long afternoon of laughter and talking. The lengthening shadows cast by the orange tree shield them from the sun until it disappears behind the wall, and the first signs of dusk play across the sky.

'Today we must all eat together,' Sabria says. 'Go and call your children and husbands. The gate here is open until the last one goes to sleep.'

The Palace of the End
February 1963

On 8 February 1963 the Ba'athists stage a successful military coup, proclaiming victory to the people of Iraq on the television and radio. Sabria, Jafar and the younger children are at home when the news breaks. Nabeel and his father return, breathless from hurrying through the chaotic streets. They had been minding the shop when they heard a wave of grief-stricken cries coming from the street outside. In the morning heat they watched as hundreds of women in black *abayas* ran from the market, wailing, 'They have killed Kassim! Our blessed Kassim is dead.'

The family gathers round the television set to watch men dressed in the uniform of the Ba'athist National Guard proclaiming that Kassim is no more. 'There is a new government and a new regime. This is the dawning of a great age of peace and prosperity. Your new government will make Iraq a great country once again. All those who would seek to compromise this great and noble cause will be rooted out and punished as traitors to our great nation. There will be no mercy.'

Everyone is silent for they understand what that means for the family. The day before, a gang of Ba'athist guardsmen had attacked Juma'a with a hammer, chasing him through the streets. He had only just escaped, running all the way across the river to a friend's house in Rusafa to hide. Later he had spent five hours in hospital. Jafar looks down gravely at his mother, curled up on the sofa. 'Mama, Juma'a will have to stay away until things settle down. They will be looking for him. There will be a purge and it will come soon.'

Sabria sighs. 'These men are like no one we have seen before. They will not stop unless someone stops them first.'

And she is right. Before the evening is out the National Guard arrive to arrest the twenty-one-year-old Juma'a. Inside the darkened living room, half asleep, Yasin hears them outside the gate. He barely has time to stand up before the soldiers are ripping sheets of aluminium off the gate and breaking into the yard, brandishing automatic weapons. Yasin stands calmly in front of them, placing his hands symbolically across the door to the house.

'We are here for Juma'a Yasin and we know he is here so do not bother to lie, old man,' the young sergeant snaps, pushing Yasin aside with his rifle butt.

'Don't speak to me like that,' Yasin says quietly, his eyes narrowing. 'This is a private house and I am a respected citizen in this neighbourhood.'

'You cannot enter our house without invitation,' Sabria shouts.

They push her out of the way and begin to ransack the rooms.

'We have all the authority we need,' says the leader. 'We can enter any home where we believe dissenters are hiding.'

A younger man chimes in excitedly, eager to say his piece: 'There are Communists here so this house is on the list.'

Yasin stares at him. 'Why do you have to go about it like

this?' he says, as the contents of cupboards and drawers are turned out on to the floor. 'He is not here. He has gone to visit friends in the south. We do not know where he is.'

Angered and unable to find Juma'a, they snatch Yasin instead. Sabria and the rest of the family close in around the squad of seven men and somehow pull him free before he is dragged out through the battered gate. 'We will be back for your Communist son,' barks the sergeant. 'When you see him, tell him we called. And let this be a warning to you all.'

The following evening, the previous day's execution of General Kassim is broadcast on national television. Without warning the screen cuts from the nightly news broadcast to a soundless image of the general, in full military uniform on the stage in Baghdad Radio's concert hall. Yasin, Sabria, Jafar, Nabeel and the little ones all stare blankly at the screen, wondering what is about to happen. Is the General still alive after all? Is he going to speak? But before anyone can cover the children's eyes, Ba'athist officers enter the scene, raise their guns and shoot the General in the head.

Nabeel watches in confusion and disbelief. Whatever their reasons for wanting power, Abdul Salam Arif and Hassan Al Bakr, the new president and his prime minister, have done a terrible wrong.

It takes the National Guard almost two weeks to track Juma'a down. He avoids coming home but they find him at the school where he works and arrest him in the middle of a lesson he is teaching. 'Keep reading. I will be back in a moment,' he tells his pupils, as the guardsmen push him from the room. They throw him into an unmarked van at the school gates. As he looks round the group of men, he recognises one. It is Hassan, the son of a family in the neighbourhood.

When Sabria and Yasin discover from a teacher friend of

Juma'a's what has happened to their son, panic descends on the house. Nabeel and Jabbar look to their mother for reassurance, but she turns to Yasin. 'Husband, this cannot be good.' She quivers. 'They will hurt him, I know it. He will provoke them and they will make him pay. He is too proud to keep his mouth shut.' Then she stops and her eyes widen as fear takes hold of her. 'They will put him in the Palace of the End. Sister Noua told me they are rounding up the Communists and taking them to the basement of King Faisal's palace . . . Oh, Yasin.' She can't bring herself to say any more in front of the children and drops down to cuddle her two daughters, Aqbal and little Amel.

'Will they hurt Juma'a, Mama?' Aqbal asks.

'I think they might,' Sabria replies, unable to stifle the truth.

Yasin's indignation gets the better of him. 'Why take him? He is a decent man, a teacher. Surely they cannot arrest every single Communist in the country? I tell you, it is those stupid pamphlets and books he has hidden everywhere. They have got him into trouble. He must have offended someone high up, for this to happen.'

Sabria does not answer. She cares nothing for the reasons why her son has been arrested, only how she might get him back. Wrapping a dark *fota* round her head and pulling on her brown outdoor sandals, she heads for the kitchen. Then she takes Juma'a's papers from the drawer, money from the stone jug at the back of the cupboard, drops them into her square fabric shoulder-bag and leaves the house without a word to anyone.

She makes straight for the police station, less than twenty minutes' walk from the house. If he has been taken anywhere it must be here. The central jails, in Karkh and al-Rusafa, have ugly reputations and she feels sure they cannot have left him there – at least, not yet. Even Juma'a's big mouth couldn't have got him into that much trouble. Those places are for murderers and thieves, rapists and cheats.

All she has to do is find a familiar face, someone who knows her or one of her family. Who would deny a worried mother a little information? She curses herself for not thinking to bring any food with her. Food is the best currency – dates or almonds, or perhaps a little of her *kofta* would make a tasty bribe for the guards on the night shift. Who knows? She might even have her son home by midnight. That and other less optimistic scenarios play out in her mind as she races through the back-streets, towards the lighted windows of the police station. She hears the crowd before she sees it. Hundreds of people are demanding to know where their children, husbands and fathers have been taken.

Tall and imposing, Sabria carves her way through to the front desk. Shoulders back, she stares straight at the bewildered junior officer taking names and shakes her son's papers at the grille. 'Juma'a Yasin. Juma'a Yasin.' She shouts it again and again, until the guard drags her forward.

'Juma'a Yasin?' The young officer ticks off a name in a ledger of detainees. 'Yes, he is here.'

'And what is he supposed to have done? He is a teacher, not a criminal.'

'He is a Communist. Everyone arrested today is a Communist, an enemy of Iraq.'

She cannot deny it. She has always been proud of her eldest sons and their beliefs. She might not agree with them but she admires their integrity. Once, of course, Communism had been illegal, but during Kassim's rule it had become a vital if uneasy prop to his regime. Now it seemed the Ba'ath were about to punish them for their years of tacit support. And Juma'a? He had held the odd meeting and perhaps spoken at a few rallies, but he was no threat to anyone. Surely sharing a few books with his friends wasn't a criminal offence?

'What will you do with him?' She keeps any outward trace of anger at bay as she speaks. 'There are thousands of Communists in Baghdad. Do you intend to imprison them all?'

'Yes. All traitors will be arrested and punished. Your son will be held here until we receive our orders. Now go home. You are beginning to annoy me.'

'Don't think I am going anywhere, young man. I will wait here until he is freed.'

The police station empties slowly as parents, wives and other relatives leave to worry at home. Sabria stays on a bench at the station throughout the night, praying quietly. Occasionally she shoots a glance at the guards as they pass, or shouts her son's innocence at the reception hatch. At last she, too, admits defeat and returns home, crestfallen. When Juma'a is released two weeks later, it is not because of her efforts but because there is no longer enough room to hold him. The guards had opened the cell doors and told the prisoners that they would be back to collect them when they had dealt with the backlog.

Juma'a plays down his arrest, telling his parents that it was little more than scare tactics. 'They are just flexing their muscles, showing who is in charge, nothing more.' But they arrest him again three days later and this time they beat him with clubs and burn him with cigarettes in their quest for names, dates and places. When he falls unconscious during the third day of interrogation they throw him out on to the street.

The only good thing to come out of these brushes with the nascent Ba'athist machine is the discovery of its disorganisation. While Juma'a is in prison for the second time, three officers from the larger al-Rusafa division of the militia visit his home in al-Bayaa to pick him up. As Sabria listens to them explain that his school is in their jurisdiction, she realises they are unaware that the al-Bayaa force is already holding him. When the house is raided by yet another group of officers, this time from the Ba'ath Central Office, she calculates that they might play this hopelessly inefficient system to their advantage. 'Think about it, Yasin,' she says, sharing her theory with him that night. 'If none of the different security forces know when Juma'a is *in* prison, how will they know when he is *out*? So, from now on if they come asking for any of our boys we should tell them they are already in prison.'

Juma'a, though bruised after the beatings, is sanguine about the future. 'Don't worry, there's no organised command, Mama. The Ba'athists are just bullies. They will get bored and the purges will stop. There are not enough prisons for us all, anyway. They would have to arrest half the country to be rid of us.'

By April, however, the new administration is busy building more jails. First, they appropriate the country's premier air base, the al-Rashid military camp in south Baghdad, renaming it Central Prison No. 1. Then they take over schools, police stations and, finally, Baghdad's national football stadium. Built during the late 1950s as the country's first world-class sports facility, it had been the centrepiece of the new city under Kassim. The Yasin children had all squeezed under the fences to watch the inaugural match between the Iraqi national team and a squad from Algiers. It had been a glorious afternoon as they sat among the crowd.

And it is here, at the end of April, that Juma'a finds himself. Only this time there is no international fixture. Instead he is imprisoned beneath a stretch of stadium seats, in a newly built concrete pen, awaiting a punishment his captors have assured him will be unimaginable in its agony.

Sabria knows something is wrong when Juma'a fails to return for dinner. 'He said he would be here,' she tells Yasin, as she combs Amel's hair. 'Rashid is coming to visit Kamil, and Juma'a promised me he would be back.' Yasin, though not usually given to passing comment, asks her to be calm and to wait until the meal is over before she becomes too concerned. 'Let us eat with Rashid. If Juma'a is not back by morning and no one has come with news, we will go looking. Take heart, if you can. He has been arrested before and he has always been released. He is a good man. They all learn that in the end.'

'I wish I shared your hope,' she whispers.

Despite Yasin's comforting hand on hers throughout dinner and Nabeel's attempts to distract his mother by telling her old Iraqi folk tales, Sabria cannot sleep. Instead she lies across her bed, imploring the Imam Ali for mercy and deliverance of her son. She pictures his white-bearded face, as it is represented in the decorative portrait on the wall. Little Amel and four-year-old Tariq wake and climb into bed next to her. And in the darkness, with the children by her side, she stares at the moon shadows on the ceiling above her.

As the first rays of the sun light the sky Sabria rises to prepare dough for the day's bread. The process is automatic, and gives her something to do as she frets. As soon as Nabeel and Jabbar wake, she sends them to the police station to ask for news. When they return an hour later with nothing, she abandons her chores, gathers food and money and prepares to leave. 'Boys, take your sister to school with you today.' She clicks her fingers and pushes Aqbal towards them. 'Bibi, you will mind Tariq and Amel for me.' Bibi has no chance to reply before her daughter sweeps past her and out of the compound, then strides towards the bus stop at the end of the street.

Sabria can't help but wonder at the nature of things. Life had just become easier for everyone and now another regime has forced itself upon them, bringing fear and misery. As for Kassim, he hadn't deserved to die. His critics said he had neglected the issue of Arab Unity, but he had achieved much at home. Even Kamil had benefited: at the Institute of Hope he had learned to read and write and was developing into a skilled carpenter. What will happen to him now? The Ba'athists are not the kind of party to run schools for the deaf. They are all so young, and such uncontrollable hotheads. Only last week Nabeel had been standing at the bus stop and had watched, horrified, as a National Guard officer fired three bullets straight into a policeman's head. The murderer had pocketed his pistol and run off into the wasteland beyond the rows of shops. And now Saddam Hussein has slipped back into the country, to aid his uncle, al-Bakr, in ridding the country of undesirables.

Sabria spends the morning criss-crossing the city in a fruitless search for Juma'a. Circling back towards the house, she decides to try the old school. A neighbour has told her that the basements are being used to house prisoners. A guard bars her way but tells her that most of the Communists are being held together at the national stadium.

From outside, the grand sports ground looks as it always has. Inside, she knows it is bedlam. Lined up along the wall outside, a row of armoured cars waits, like metal teeth, in the sand. Clusters of jumpy young men, no more than boys, swarm at the gate. Pausing to shake her sandals free of sand, she hears one shout to her, 'Where do you think you're going?'

'I am trying to find my son,' she says, inclining her head down so that she does not appear imperious. The guard, young and striking in his khakis, swaggers over. 'Listen,' he whispers, pulling her out of earshot, 'I can't tell you whether he is here or not. There are so many that I don't think anyone knows for sure.' Seeing his colleagues watching him, he jerks his Kalashnikov at Sabria and pulls at the fluff that passes for a beard round his jaw. 'I can't do any more for you,' he says, putting on a scowl. 'Just make sure you're not around when the fat man comes.'

Shielding her eyes from the sun with her hand, Sabria meets his eye. 'I know you have a list of prisoners,' she says, and before he can speak, she describes her son. 'He is a teacher,' she looks at the boy's smooth, gentle face, 'a little older than you. Perhaps he taught you, or your brothers and sisters.'

The tactic of talking people round comes instinctively to her. She is soon in full control, and when a second guard wanders over she is half-way to getting the information she needs. 'The lady is looking for her son. He sounds decent enough. Can we get the ledger out? It wouldn't hurt just this once, would it?'

The second National Guardsman looks at Sabria, then nods. 'As you like.' Inwardly Sabria's heart is soaring. She has only to keep going a little longer and she will have what she needs.

She follows them through the gates and looks around. Beyond the endless rows of seats there is just the ground, dry and deserted. She wonders where the prisoners are kept but dares not ask. Suddenly the stench of ammonia, faeces, urine and sweat hits her, and she realises what they have done with the prisoners. They have built rough concrete rooms under the seating and packed the men into them. There will be thousands of them in semi-darkness. She rushes in front of the guards. 'Is my son here? You have to tell me!' She grabs the shoulders of the younger man and shakes him.

He is about to speak but stops at the sight of a jeep roaring across the ground. He pushes her back through the gate. 'Shut your mouth! Leave now before you land me in prison too.'

Sabria refuses to move, facing him.

'Please go,' he begs. 'In the name of Allah, go. Trust what I say. The man coming now will kill you just for sport. It is Kutaiba. He crushes people by sitting on their bare chests until they suffocate.'

The boys, Nabeel and Jabbar, are waiting at the table when Sabria gets home. She says nothing but brings out a stack of bowls from the cupboard and passes them round the table. They watch as she spoons out lentils and okra in tomato sauce. 'You, at least, will be pleased there is no meat today, Gandhi,' she says, breaking the silence, teasing Nabeel, who has become vegetarian, with a new pet name. 'The man in India is to be much admired. His diet at least kept him peaceful.'

'Mama, what has happened to Juma'a?' asks Jabbar.

'He is at the stadium. He is being held there by a man called Kutaiba.'

The boys look up at her.

'He is so fat that there are no clothes to fit him and he smells like a drain. He is the vilest man I have ever seen.' She cannot continue but, rather than break down in front of the boys, she goes into the yard under the pretence of checking the gate.

'I will find him,' Nabeel says conspiratorially, to his brother.

'I could come too.'

'No, Jabbar. You will not come. It will be dangerous.'

Jabbar cups a hand over his mouth, excited. 'OK, Gandhi,' he says, and then, after a pause, 'but do you think that man is as fat as Mama says?'

'He can't be. No one is that fat.' Nabeel pushes his chair away from the table and runs outside.

The next morning he leaves the house before breakfast and runs along the sandy paths behind the rows of houses until he finds the main road. By bus it is not far to the stadium. As the buildings of the city centre sail past, he grips his schoolbag. The situation is deadly serious, yet the idea of seeing the mighty Kutaiba is exhilarating.

Nabeel steps from the bus on the opposite side of the road and cautiously approaches the huge stadium gates. Crouching behind a line of cars, he looks at the soldiers gathered outside. Parked next to the gates is a jeep, and two men are inside it, one whippet thin at the wheel, the other so large that the doors have been removed to accommodate him. It is Kutaiba. With his breath coming fast and shallow, Nabeel approaches the jeep and pulls his thin, adolescent frame up to its full height. 'Mr Kutaiba, you have my brother inside your prison and . . .' he reaches out to Kutaiba with his hands '. . . he should not be there. Juma'a is a teacher, and his school needs him back.'

Kutaiba raises a leg and kicks Nabeel in the stomach, so hard that he hits the ground. As he tries to get up he falls back, winded, gasping for breath.

Kutaiba laughs, hauls himself out of the jeep and retrieves his machine-gun. The guards stand to attention, a ripple of nervousness passing among them. 'What is your name?' he says, his monstrous thighs straddling Nabeel.

'Nabeel Yasin.'

Kutaiba looks down at the boy and prods his ribs with a boot, then turns and walks towards the open gate. 'Yasin, Yasin, Yasin.' He spits out the name with a ball of phlegm. 'I should go and find that brother of yours and tell him you came visiting . . . and then I will squeeze the very breath from him.' He throws back his head and roars at Nabeel, 'Now get away from here before I do the same to you.'

Juma'a spends his days trapped in an agonising routine. Periods of intense pain are followed only by the expectation of more pain to come. He is held in a four-metre-square concrete space with no window and twenty other men. There is nothing to drink, and only a small tin bucket for a toilet. Water, foul-smelling and still, is ladled out twice a day, passed from one man to another in a tin cup. Food, when it comes, amounts to little more than scraps of bread and day-old rice or millet slops. Sleep, and the comfort of a simple mattress, is a memory he dare not even recall. The only chance he and his fellow inmates have to rest is through their own self-imposed routine; three men lie down to sleep while the others stand against the walls, timing them against the patrols of the guards. It continues day and night, interrupted only by the arrival of the guards at the cell door. If one of their number returns from the interrogation room in particularly bad shape they break their rhythm and allow him to sleep longer.

Sometimes they return naked and bloody. Sometimes they don't return at all.

Like most of his cellmates, Juma'a is not aware that he has committed any specific crime. Two men believe they are there for releasing white doves in a gesture of peace back in 1959. Another two have been incarcerated since February but have not been charged. They had been working together as engineers for the Ministry of Oil when they were arrested and marched from their offices by the Ba'ath militia. Their colleagues had looked on without daring to protest. The only conclusion anyone can draw is that the Ba'athists are using the purges to settle old scores.

Juma'a knew that the butcher from the market in al-Bayaa, had been imprisoned over a dispute with one of his customers, now a leading Ba'athist. 'It is lawless out there,' one of the engineers had whispered to Juma'a, when he had first come in. 'I heard that one of those militia dogs raped a girl because she would not have him as a husband. He went to her house with a Kalashnikov and his brand-new uniform on. He told her she was being punished for the sin of refusal.'

Juma'a knows that this is probably not rumour but the truth. Leila, a girl in their street, has suffered the same fate. Everyone, it seems, has such stories to tell.

The younger of the two engineers, his mind in tatters, worries about his wife constantly. Each morning he imagines he can hear her voice outside the gate, calling for him. 'She has come for me,' he says confidently, between bouts of tears at having left her to fend for herself. 'I had no chance to explain,' he whimpers. 'She is no good on her own.' Plagued by equal measures of shame and fear, he had clutched at his colleague and made him promise to look after her if he got out first. 'I have let her down, I can only pray for her now. But you will help her, won't you?'

His colleague, hollow-eyed with exhaustion, promises, with Juma'a as his witness, to take care of his friend's wife. 'Such a promise is all very well, but you must not give up hope,' he had said, as his grateful friend wept on his shoulder. 'We will all be free soon and this misery will end.'

Outside spring turns to summer and the heat inside the cell becomes intolerable. All the men have now dispensed with their clothing and stand or crouch naked in an effort to keep cool. Even at fifty degrees centigrade the guards refuse them water for days at a time. Their tin bucket is removed only when the uneven concrete floor begins to run with the overflow. Unable to avoid the filth, Juma'a and the other men develop sores across their emaciated bodies. Infections travel through the jail in waves, laying waste as they go. In the cooler days of spring, they had demanded justice. By high summer all thoughts of protest are forgotten. Within days new prisoners are broken by the conditions. And so it goes on, life slowly ebbing away as the temperatures soar.

One afternoon, when the heat of the day is at its peak, a new arrival, the thirty-sixth man, is rammed into the cell. He has been beaten, and the wounds on his head and arms run with blood. At the sight of him the married engineer collapses. Exhausted, starved and dehydrated, he dies at Juma'a's feet. The Ba'athist doctor, who signs the death certificate, writes that he has suffered a heart-attack. The news reaches the men in hushed whispers, passed from cell to cell through the windows. 'They always write it up as heart failure, no matter what,' says a man who has seen many such deaths now. 'If they call it a heart-attack they absolve themselves of responsibility. What do you expect? However this turns out, they will not be held to account.'

While the engineer is the first to die in their cell since Juma'a's arrival, news of other deaths across the camp come daily. Some die of disease and dehydration, others are murdered or die during interrogation. Salam Adil and Hasan Wayna, the secretary and deputy head of the Communist Party, are executed while in custody. At night, squatting and unable to sleep, Juma'a hears the sound of body-bags being dragged across the sand to be driven away and dumped in unmarked graves out in the scrubland.

Despite everything, he manages to stay sane. He marks each day in his mind by breaking down the weeks, days, hours and minutes into tiny chunks of time. It is a trick that more experienced inmates have passed on. 'You must not think of the world outside. *This* is your world until you are free. If you lose your mind, they will drag you out and shoot you.' Every day is an exercise in self-deception. There is no prospect of a trial, of being found innocent or, it seems, of release. As far as he can tell, no one leaves the stadium alive. While he is here, his only goal is to see out another day.

Sometimes, as others around him stare aimlessly or mutter to themselves in prayer, he closes his eyes and allows himself to think about his library. This is his luxury, his escape. He thinks of little Gandhi, who hid his books on the evening of his first arrest. Nabeel had known that they would be as good as a written confession to the militia so he'd dug a pit and buried them in the garden. On his first release Juma'a had scolded his brother for not wrapping them up.

He closes his eyes, turning them in his mind, recalling their weight and texture. Marx and Engels, *The Manifesto of the Communist Party*, with its rough red cover. Charles Fourier and François Noel Babeuf's contributions to socialist thought, *Le Nouveau Monde*, then Comrade Mao Zedong on Marxist philosophy. He has them all in front of him, even Tolstoy, Dostoyevsky, Turgenev and Gorky. He stops at pages he knows well, quoting passages that he learned by heart as a teenager. In his head, the collection is intact.

From time to time the routine is broken. The cell door opens and Juma'a is dragged to one of the steel-clad torture chambers. Led through the corridors of the stadium, he often hears the cries of others reverberating round the walkways above. It has no impact on him now.

So far he has stood up well to torture. Resisting pain has become a bizarre challenge for which he has worked out his own simple strategy. The less he resists, the more bearable it is. In fact, by letting go, the pain itself is relieved. He has begun to learn their ways, and to anticipate their next moves. Among themselves, and from time to time with prisoners, the guards refer to the range of their cruel practices as the 'menu'. Newcomers are subjected to the *mezzes*, minor hardships, such as being beaten up, lashed or perhaps burned with a cigarette.

The *entrées* are more imaginative. Wali, a cellmate and former clerk, had been locked in a cupboard with a bag of starving feral cats. The creatures had been left until they were deranged with hunger and had started to cannibalise each other. When released on their bound human prey, they had begun a frenzied attack, witnessed by many of the guards as if it were sport. Wali was guilty only of holding a small gathering of socialists in the front garden of his mother's house. Frequently the guards used vipers instead of cats. They cause death by toxic haemorrhage.

It is the *desserts*, in which physical and psychological

torture are combined, that are the worst. They bring in a prisoner's wife, daughters and sisters and rape them in adjacent rooms so that they can be heard. They torture children, too, to induce parental confession.

Juma'a knows they want him to confess to being a Communist, passing on a pamphlet to a comrade or going to a rally. But so far they have no evidence, and so their questions never change.

We know you are a Communist. Where do you meet? Who do you see? What are their plans? Give me the names of those who are leading you. Tell me where they live. Tell me, and you will live.

When their words stop, the beating begins. He thanks God he has neither wife nor children to worry about or mourn him. If he had no family at all, he would surrender completely. But he misses his parents and siblings and, in quiet moments of darkness, he has found himself wishing, not for his own deliverance but for the safety of those at home.

It is late summer and they come for him at the first light of day. They pull his naked frame away from the wall, then drag him along the corridors, kicking him for being slow. He wants to walk but his legs are of little use now. He cannot see: he has been made to wear a black blindfold. At the familiar dull echo of the metal door leading to the torture rooms, he reminds himself that his goal is simply to stay alive. They drag him to the ground, rope his rotting feet together and hang his emaciated frame, head to the floor, from the blades of the large ceiling fan. Blood floods his brain and dark, throbbing shapes form behind his eyes as he tries to draw on the essence of life itself. He tries, for a long while, and then, as the fan is switched on and blood chokes the arteries of his brain, he blacks out.

When he comes to, slumped on a floor sticky with his own excretions, he can hear voices in the next room. In the airless heat, the hood still pulled tight, he feels himself breathe and his ribcage touching the floor. The breaths are thin and shallow. His lungs and ribs hurt and every movement brings a surge of pain from different points on his body but he is still alive. He is dimly aware of a key turning in the heavy steel lock. Maybe they have come to pick up wherever they left off. Perhaps they will use the electrodes on him again. He neither knows nor cares. He has lived through something, and if he is lucky he may do so again tomorrow. And so it may go on until, one day, he will appear at his mother's gate.

Two Shrines
Late Summer, 1964

Juma'a is released in the autumn of 1963, following a swift counter-coup by Abdul Salam Arif. When she first sees her son Sabria weeps uncontrollably. He is hollow, frail and deaf in one ear. She has only half of him back, she says. But although they have broken him physically, Juma'a has emerged from prison more determined than ever. 'I will not hide at home. I will appeal to the education minister and get my old job back,' he says, to the astonishment of his family as they gather round the dining table. 'If I shrink into the shadows they will have won. I should keep my life as it was, and show them that dignity cannot be destroyed.'

Sabria is overjoyed when Juma'a gets word that he can start teaching again, but knows it will anger his enemies. How long it will be before the Ba'athists regroup and Arif is himself ousted no one can tell. Instinctively, though, Sabria knows they will not be at bay for long. 'Mark my words, Juma'a. Al-Bakr is waiting in the wings for his moment to come again. They are hungry dogs, looking for a way back in. This time we must be prepared for the worst.'

For once no one disagrees. Not even Juma'a. He has word that the Ba'athists are already making inroads into the major institutions. From the police and the army to the judiciary, from government officers to lecturers, they are gaining popular support with working-class men everywhere. Saddam Hussein, the Ba'ath Party's head of security, has put the fear of God into even the most dutiful Party members. 'Let us be thankful we are still united,' Sabria tells her children, when she hears of his reputation as a torturer. 'They will break the country into tiny pieces if they have their way.'

Bibi's death, in the summer of 1964, plunges Sabria into grief and darkens her mood further. Not even Makkya and Sabria's other sister, Noua, can comfort her. Bibi's passing, she tells them, is an omen: 'We are about to enter a period of uncertainty and turmoil.' Her usual defiance, the optimism with which all of the Yasins have grown up, has deserted her. 'We have already suffered but there is worse to come, my children,' she tells them over the dinner table, on the day after her mother's burial. 'Enjoy what goodness you can and I will pray for us all.' Sabria is devout and though the others, including Yasin, are not, it is always somehow understood that she does enough praying for all of them.

Prayer has been rewarded throughout Sabria's life. Unhappy at being unable to conceive a third child, she called on the Imam Hussain, and it was to the Imam Ali she turned when Juma'a was imprisoned. On these and other occasions she thought nothing of bringing together her friends from the neighbourhood to hold a vigil. The women would meditate, working towards a fevered display of breast-beating and chanting. Then, suddenly, they would stop and relax, smoking and talking as if nothing had passed between them. Neither does she think twice about taking the long, uncomfortable ride to Najaf or Karbala to make a blessing at the shrines there. Even when she has no particular plea to make, she has faith in the efforts of the true believer. As with the fragments of prayers sewn into the lining of her cuffs to ward off evil spirits, the benefits are cumulative.

Late in the autumn of 1964, a month after Bibi's death, Sabria decides to make a pilgrimage to the shrine of Sayyed Muhammad. Fifty miles north of Baghdad, it is near Dujail, marooned in the desert that rolls up to Samarra.

She tells Yasin of her plans as she digs out her *mesbehe* and her seven-eyes talisman from a drawer and goes to fetch Nabeel, who will accompany her. She finds him hidden in the back room with his nose in a book. These days, books and newspapers accompany him everywhere he goes. 'Gandhi, you must get some sleep. Tomorrow we are going to the shrine of Sayyed Muhammad.' She clicks her fingers, and tells him it is time to close his book.

'Mama, please. Can't you see? I'm reading for school. I have a test on Monday. What about Juma'a, or Aunty Makkya?'

She lowers herself to face him. 'Do you think I was born yesterday? I may not be able to read but I know this is no schoolbook, child. This is one of your new books from Maktabet al-Muthanna bookshop. There is no test, I think. I will wake you at dawn.'

'Mama, this is Sartre. It's philosophy. I'm telling the truth.'

'I know all about Sartre. Don't tell me they're teaching him at your school! Have you forgotten what happened to your brother? This is one of the books you buried in the garden. You need protecting. That is why we will go to the shrine together.'

Nabeel closes the book and stuffs it inside his shirt. 'Well, let me bring it with me then,' he grumbles. 'I can read it on the bus.'

'Good. Now, sleep, and we will have an early breakfast.'

73

Nabeel knows his mother's wishes are not to be ignored. With Bibi gone, the house is sad. Perhaps this pilgrimage might help her regain her happiness. 'Will we take our lunch with us?' he asks.

'Of course! You do not go to the Sayyed Muhammad shrine without lunch.' She is smiling. 'I have a basket in the kitchen filled with bread and rice, spices, pickles and okra.'

Nabeel smiles back at her. The picnic lunch, cooked communally and shared with other pilgrims, is his favourite part of the trip. 'Perhaps,' he says, thinking of the mouth-watering figs sold in long strings at Samarra, 'we might get a little something sweet from the hawkers on the way up too. It will be a great day and I promise I'll read the Du'a for you.'

Sabria looks at him. 'Why are you so keen all of a sudden? Maybe you have a school test, after all? You are never this eager when we go to Karbala.'

'Mama, that's different. You know I don't like to make the sacrifice any more.'

Sabria's good mood is extinguished in an instant. 'You're an ungrateful boy. You, my miracle baby, owe your life to the Imam Hussain. You should be making the pilgrimage to Karbala every year and sacrificing yourself to him, with all the thanks your heart can muster.'

After delivering her first two sons, easily in quick succession in the early 1940s, Sabria had naturally expected a third. But as time passed there was no sign of one. The Second World War ended, the year of the drought came and went, and Jafar and Juma'a continued to grow. She watched them walk, talk and

Nabeel and Jabbar, 1965

play together in the dusty backyard. She watched them start school. Jafar lost one tooth, then another, and her hopes for another baby turned to despair.

Yasin remained gentle and forgiving, but the idea of being pronounced barren was a humiliation that Sabria could not endure. Bibi had passed her a variety of herbs and potions designed to stimulate her organs while the local mullah had provided spiritual assistance. Passages from the scriptures were copied in green and orange ink on to tiny pieces of papyrus, then blessed and sewn into the lining of her *fota*. Perhaps they would bring a change of fortune.

After six years of failure, she decided to reach out one last time to Imam Hussain. She believed she lived an exemplary life, praying daily, giving alms and making regular pilgrimage to the site of his martyrdom in Karbala, and felt certain that if she pledged even greater devotion he would reward her with a third child. One afternoon, standing before the portrait that hung in the family room, she had called to the Imam Hussain to give her a child. This time she promised the child's blood if it were born.

Less than ten months later, after she had given birth to a healthy baby boy, she set about keeping her promise. With baby Nabeel on one shoulder and a bag of clothes, she joined the thousands travelling to the Festival of Ashoura.

They travelled the ninety kilometres to Karbala on a long wooden train crowded with pilgrims, stopping at every station and in the scrubland between to pick up more. Sabria imagined Yasin toiling hard on these tracks and felt proud of the part he had played in ushering so many believers towards salvation. 'For trade and prosperity.' It made her laugh. The British had certainly not intended *this* when they planned their great railway.

The pilgrims sang inside the carriages and on the roofs, and shared their food. A group of three women beside Sabria cooed over the infant Nabeel. Before they had even reached al-Musayyib, each had confided in Sabria that they were journeying to the shrine to pray for the blessing of children: they were cousins, all childless, and desperate for a future. As she nursed her own precious son, Sabria decided to help. Since she had been so fortunate, why not these women too? She told them her story and promised them some of Nabeel's blood as an offering. 'Let us meet tomorrow,' she said, and suggested a place she knew in the town.

By the time the train arrived, the sun had already sunk to the west. The huge golden shrine, with its four flowering minarets, stood high against the flat horizon. Sabria's stomach tightened in anticipation. Karbala was the bridge to Paradise. Carried by the tide of pilgrims pouring from the station, she found her way down the narrowing streets towards the sacred heart of the city, past long tables piled with *harissa*, stewed lamb, oil and bread for the hungry pilgrims who had travelled from the other side of Iraq and beyond.

One woman, seeing Sabria with her baby, invited her into her cool, quiet house and brought her a generous bowl of stew and salad. She offered her a place to rest, and Sabria accepted gratefully. As she lay down to sleep she considered the sacrifice she and her son were about to make. One day, she thought, Nabeel would understand and value it as she did.

Before dawn the next day she dressed Nabeel in a simple black robe overlaid with the white cloth that would bear the blood of sacrifice, then joined the column of pilgrims heading by firelight for the shrine. The streets were teeming with bystanders, singing and dancing. From the balconies above men and women sprinkled flower-water on to the lines of worshippers as they passed. Nabeel woke as cooling, fragrant drops fell on to his face.

As they neared the shrine, the sun pushed above the horizon and soon the air was hot and sweet with the smell of blood. The noise had risen too: women turned circles outside the mosque, wailing and beating their chests. Men in black robes lashed themselves with chains.

Sabria gasped as they were pushed through the arch into the shade of the *haram* within. Passing between the latticed walls, she struggled to take it all in: the gold, the lanterns, the walls of inscribed crystal tiles soaring high above her. She could hear the chink of coins being pushed through the latticework around Hussain's grave.

One of the shrine attendants, a tall man in black, had beckoned her towards him. Stepping forward, she had held out the baby and waited for him to raise the ritual sword, *q'ama*, in his arms. Heavy, with an embellished handle and a long, straight blade, it required some effort to keep it steady. Holding the sleepy infant firmly to stop him wriggling, Sabria began a slow hum of ancient prayer. With his band of seventy-two followers, Hussain had come to claim the caliphate that was rightfully his. But the brigade had been overwhelmed at Karbala and all had been slain. But in contrast to this tragedy, Sabria was blessed: now her son was about to receive the cut of life, not death.

The attendant drew the knife three times from the centre of the baby's skull to the midpoint of his forehead. Beads of blood formed instantly along the cut and fell in rivulets on to his white wrap. They bloomed, like roses, across the cloth. When the cloth was crimson, Sabria mopped her son's brow with a clean corner of her tunic. She nodded at the sword, pulled the baby over her shoulder and carried him out into the noisy courtyard, where his angry cries were lost in the clamour.

With the sacrifice made, Sabria had gone to meet the three cousins from the train. She walked slowly through the milling throng, trying to remember the street and the coffee house where she had suggested they meet, knowing that, in the spirit of the festival, they would be welcomed and plied with refreshments. Among the hordes of bloodstained pilgrims, Nabeel was the youngest. She stopped for a moment to wipe his wound with a cloth soaked in vinegar. 'We have kept our bargain, *habibi*,' she whispered proudly. 'You are a real pilgrim now.'

The women were waiting, with clear-eyed hope. 'You show us true kindness, Sabria. We are at your mercy.' They crowded round the baby, admiring the cut. 'What faith you must have!'

'*Shukran*,' Sabria replied, then invited each woman to dab her finger in the baby's blood.

In the afternoon Sabria and Nabeel had rejoined the jostle of devoted pilgrims as they re-enacted the Battle of Karbala and the martyrdom of Hussain. Then, as it had been in history they burned the makeshift camp. Rows of tiny suns, bright, flaming pyres, drew exhausted pilgrims to the outskirts of the town for the final hours of mourning. Sabria watched as a pilgrim caught fire: a spark touched the tail of his robe and huge flames leaped up his back. Others beat him with their scarves, working frantically to put out the blaze as the crowd looked on, waiting for the bonfires to burn down and the final prayers to begin.

Later, as the festival drew to a close, and the last sounds of grief were carried into the air with the smoke from the fires, Sabria scooped up a fragment of charred wood and a thimbleful of the powdery grey ash. 'We will take this for Baba,' she had whispered to her baby, 'and for your brothers. It will keep us all safe until next year, when we will return.' Then she had bundled him up and begun the walk back to the station to catch the morning train to Baghdad.

Memories of Nabeel's first sacrifice replay in Sabria's mind as they begin their journey to the shrine of Sayyed Muhammad. She wishes that the teenage son beside her would make the annual sacrifice willingly. She has tried to persuade him many times, but he no longer listens to her. She sighs, disappointed at letting down the Imam Hussain. People, chickens, crates of vegetables and huge vats of cooking oil are crammed into a dilapidated eighteen-seater Mercedes public taxi. It carries them noisily along uneven roads out of the suburbs and on through the outlying villages.

Nabeel looks at the scant buildings and wonders what it is like to live here, isolated and cut off from the city. Out here, communities grow old together, supported by tiny market stalls and basic schools. No libraries, no book markets or universities. What on earth do they do with themselves? Children trail along the roadside waving as they pass, then hanging back and throwing stones that strike the side of the vehicle with faint clangs. They are making the best of it, he thinks, reaching for his Sartre.

After a couple of hours, the charabanc pulls off the road and on to a track that leads through the scrub. Ahead is the blue-domed shrine of Sayyed Muhammad. It stands alone and proud. Nabeel is thrilled at the sight of it, here in this desert. He loves the purity of its presence, its loneliness, its folly.

Standing on the scrub with the warm wind at his face, he senses the significance of the place and his own small voice in the order of things. Other buses arrive, and worshippers wander off, women, children and old couples, all with bags and pans. There is nothing here – no stalls, no hawkers of trinkets or food – so pilgrims come equipped with everything they need to feed themselves.

Nabeel is hot and clammy in his shirt. He can feel the Sartre book chafing his thigh as he struggles across the sand with the rucksack. He pulls the book out of his trouser pocket and tucks it into the waistband at the back.

'We will go in first. Then we can eat,' she says.

The shrine is covered with decorative tiles, its low dome nudging the paler sky. Thousands of little wooden cradles are scattered around, offerings from parents on behalf of their babies. Left there to the mercy of the desert wind and sand, they spread out like an ancient forest.

'Do you want me to read the Du'a prayers to you?' he says, putting his arm round his mother's shoulders.

'Of course. That is why I brought you,' she says, and guides him through the huge doors. Ever since he learned to read he has recited with pride the Du'a inscribed in large calligraphic murals on the walls of the shrine.

Positioning himself close to the mural, he feels no flicker of self-consciousness. He clears his throat and starts. Now that his voice has broken he relishes the sound of each word as it rolls off his tongue. The lines and verses are rich with meaning. As he finishes each line he pauses, and his mother repeats the words back to him.

By the time he has finished the first section, a small crowd has gathered round them. He sings a second, a third, a fourth, and the crowd grows until he is swamped by pilgrims, all calling back as he intones each line. He wonders if the scribes had ever imagined how far people would travel to read their words. At home when he fills his notebooks with verse and stories, he is thrilled at the prospect that somewhere, in some other time, maybe long into the future, his words may find an audience.

'Let us move on.' Sabria interrupts his thoughts and shuffles back into line with the group, all of whom are eager for the next instalment. 'Let us hear another.'

The crowd clap and chant in unison, 'Ya, ya, ya, ya.'

He begins a low chanting of the first line, but stops abruptly. An old man, white-haired, bent almost double with age, has begun his own song. His shoulders are hunched as he peers up at the wall but his voice is deep and mellifluous. He delivers each line slowly, with a deep resonance, like an actor. His voice has authority and is loud enough for all to hear. The crowd turn their heads as one.

'Come, come, ignore him, *habibi*. Sing for your mama, please!'

'No, Mama, not while that man is singing too.'

The crowd are still.

'He's not saying the words properly. Hey, Mister, you've got the words wrong.'

The man continues to sing, following the words on the panel.

'Mister!' Nabeel's voice is rising now. 'You have it wrong.'

The crowd gasp and the man stops mid-verse, turning to face them with a look of confusion.

Sabria pulls her son to her and hisses in his ear, 'Stop that this instant! Perhaps he is old and cannot see the words properly. Have you thought of that? Let him be. He is a pilgrim, just like we are.'

Sabria drags him away from the group. 'While I implore the prophet to spare our family, you are busy making trouble.'

'But, Mama, he has it all wrong. Someone wrote the words in a certain way and we should all honour that.'

Sabria gathers her *abaya* as if to leave and watches as her son stands still, his feet dug defiantly into the floor. Nabeel has always been so strong-willed. Now his passion for words is asserting itself. She remembers when, as a young boy, he stole the carbon rods from an old radio battery and used them, like giant black crayons, to write verses in thick, childish script over the brown walls in Karradat Mariam until he was scolded by a neighbour. Today she sees him as a performer.

Looking back at the diminutive old man, she hopes he understands. As for Nabeel, she must warn him to be careful.

'Whatever you may think of the world, little Nabeel, you cannot spend your life at odds with it. Think about those things you want to change, then speak. And before you do, ask yourself if the result will be worth it.' She puts an arm round his neck and draws him away. 'Let us go and have lunch.'

He scowls at the old man and follows his mother. She always gets her own way, he thinks. It runs in the family. Bibi was the same. 'Do this, fetch that, get rid of the other.' Bibi always managed to persuade people to do things for her. She had Jafar traipsing from desert to mountain to fetch herbs — southernwood, camomile, khilla. Hearing of his plans to visit Basra, she would pull him to one side. 'Go to al-Khamisiya. I like the *sheih* bushes there. Fetch some leaves.'

No, it is impossible to argue with his mother, as it had been with Bibi, and, besides, Nabeel knows that an argument now will jeopardise the prayers she holds so dear. But with all that has happened, he wonders why she still believes in the power of prayer. Nabeel enjoys the spectacle of the rituals, but to him, neither his mother's entreaties nor his grandmother's seeds will make any difference to the way the world turns. These days, he is more inclined to believe Juma'a, who has turned his back on prayer, maintaining that the good life will arise from a new society and a new kind of politics.

Seated together on rugs, they unpack their baskets and lay out the contents, meat, rice, raisins and nuts, in small bowls. The group shares everything, from the communal fire to the water they have in their flasks. They will throw spices into the flames and agree that the food is delicious.

As he talks to his mother he can tell that her spirits have

lifted. Sacrifice and atonement are as balm to her. He is glad that the trip has helped, but from now on he is to be his own man. He will decide where he goes and what he believes. His mother's ways are no longer his.

He finds a stub of pencil in his pocket and digs out his book. He writes, in small, neatly sculpted script, 'The Beginning' on the inside back cover under the picture of Sartre. He will speak his mind and tell of life as he sees it. Like the ancient messengers whose prayers he has been singing, or Sartre whose words burn in the pages of the book he holds, he has decided to make his world count for something.

The Dream of Brother Yasin
Summer 1971

It is close to midnight when Nabeel parts with his university friends close to the old *souq* in al-Rusafa, on the eastern side of the Tigris. The group had met to read through scenes from *King Lear* in preparation for a poetry night but, as usual, they had lost track of time and purpose. It usually ended that way at the Christian Club: high spirits, bottomless pots of bitter cardamom coffee and the air thick with the blue smoke of American cigarettes.

Now the twenty-one-year-old is alone, in his Westminster flared trousers and French blue shirt, a pencil-sharp figure strutting along the pavement. The air is still heavy with the heat of the day but the night sky is clear and he can see the stars. Without his sparring partners on hand to distract him his thoughts return to Lear. 'When the mind is free, the body is delicate, when the mind is free, the body is delicate,' the words circle round his mind, like a mantra, as he heads down through al-Haydar Khana towards the banks of the Tigris. Turning to look at the moon, he knows that when he reaches Shuhada Square he will be lucky to catch the last bus home. If he misses it, he will pick up a taxi – the few still looking for trade will be collecting revellers from outside the city's many associations and clubs. If not, he will walk the four kilo-metres home. He has done it many times before, usually because he has spent all his money. He reaches into the pocket of his shirt and pulls out a crumpled packet of Baghdad brand cigarettes, lights the last one and throws the empty packet into the gutter. At least, he thinks, a walk would clear his head.

The streets in this commercial part of the city are dark and deserted, all of the tiny shops shut behind their heavy steel grilles. Above them, beyond the washing-lines strung between the old Ottoman windows and balconies, are rows of squat apartments and roof terraces. None of the windows is lit. It is eerily quiet. No cricket, market-stall chatter or even a car on the out-of-town highways rises above the sound of his footsteps as they echo between the stone walls. There is only the occasional hiss of a stray cat from a doorway or a sheet of newspaper being blown along the ground by the light summer breeze.

He tips his head back and stares up at the *shanasheels*: houses with first floors that overhang so far out they almost meet across the narrow, winding streets. By day one can barely breathe in the crush here, people jostling and barging, the street traders shouting, vying with each other. What luxury it is to walk uninterrupted towards the al-Qushla, the imposing stone government buildings. He follows the weak light from the streetlamps on to the Martyrs' Bridge and crosses the river. The water below swirls black and silent, and he knows it carves a generous loop from the elaborate Abbasid Palace to the shimmering minarets of the Mustan-sariya and al-Wazir mosques, and on out of the city toward the Taq Kisra. He stops and looks down at the reflection of the Al Qushla clocktower dancing on the water. What as-tounding curves: they have the grace of a dancer.

Nabeel has always loved the Tigris for its constancy: it cuts the same path now as it did for his father and his father's father, and back and back without end. He thinks of all it has witnessed in the passing of countless civilisations: Sumerians, Babylonians, Assyrians, the Abbasids and Mongols, the Ottomans and the British. People have come and gone, peacemakers, despots, tyrants and martyrs, and still it goes on, a reminder that his and all these past worlds are fleeting and of no real consequence. He walks again, pacing along the pavement, feeling the dips where the tarmac has blistered in the heat. And as for this second Ba'athist regime, with whom the fight has now begun in earnest, it, too, will pass one day into history.

The knowledge that he is becoming one of the city's most celebrated new poets has filled him with pride and ambition. In these uncertain times, the poet's aim is to reach people with truth. Where once he had been frustrated that his words were overlooked, now people want to hear what he thinks. As soon as the Ba'athists had marshalled themselves and pushed out President Arif in 1968 things began to change for everyone. With al-Bakr now president, the Ba'athists had learned from the mistakes of 1963 and three years into their second rule the purge against self-expression shows no sign of abating. They have come for Juma'a again, several times in fact, keeping him alive because they think he can lead them to more powerful men, but their actions seem only to make him more determined to resist. Like Juma'a, Nabeel knows how important it is to remain unafraid. The Ba'athists make a pretence of fairness and collaboration but all around him people are succumbing to fear and silencing themselves.

Before he finished his studies at the University of Baghdad, he started writing for one of the city's most respected publications, *Alif-Baa Magazine*. The editor gives him some freedom to write about what he sees. His reputation, and the notoriety he is acquiring in the literary cafés and beyond the university campus, don't worry his boss. Far from it. He is encouraged to speak out. No doubt they will come for him sooner or later: he will be hauled off and told to toe the line. Mama has always said the Iraqis love tragedy. As they crave poets, so they crave martyrs. From the Imam Hussain onwards, the culture has embraced it. Nabeel knows his family is not the only target: many across the country have suffered in the crackdown on writers, poets and artists.

Now, at Saddam Hussein's request, the Mukhabarat have even set up a guard station at the *Alif-Baa* offices, and everyone's papers are checked morning and evening. He tries not to take it seriously. It is the inconvenience that gets to him. Though his last poem *Picnic* has already been published to good notices, he doubts that the collection he is working on now, *The Poets Satirise the Kings*, will be passed by the censorship board. Some on the board are men he knows, writers themselves, who are not without sympathy, but they will be unable to help him. The poem is vicious satire and Saddam Hussein wields the power on the cultural board. He might only be *vice*-president but he acts as if he is the premier. One day he will push out Ahmed Hassan al-Bakr. Then there will be no latitude. But Nabeel has made his choices, knowing what he faces.

And this is as it should be. As his mother told him only the week before, 'It is your duty to write. You have been blessed in ways that others have not. And, though you should be careful how you do it, you must use your talent.' Poetry was more than duty. Apart from his adored Nada, poetry is his life, his way of fashioning meaning from the world around him. What else could he do but carry on? He was not equipped to do anything else with his life.

Poetry had brought Nada and Nabeel together. He had just finished a reading at the university poetry festival and had been listening to the students as they gathered round him, asking for advice and explanation.

'Are the pressures of modern life too great to yield classic poetry in the great tradition?'

'Are you creating a new form or do you seek inspiration from the masters?'

'Should we build on the motifs of the great poets, like Omar Khayyam, al-Mutenabi or al-Sayeb?'

He had been weary and wanted to get away. The conversation was tedious, the students asking questions only so that they could talk about themselves. He had considered walking away, knowing it would add to his mystery and unpredictability, but then, out of the corner of his eye, he had caught sight of a girl. Her thick, shoulder-length hair bobbed as she turned away from the group and headed to the courtyard outside. He had seen her only for a split second but her image was etched into his mind's eye: dark eyes in a perfectly oval face. And he was certain she had been looking straight at him. He smiled and, without a word to anyone, walked off the steps towards the courtyard.

On that occasion he had missed her, but a week or so later he saw her again, stepping out of a car at the main gates of the university, clasping her books to her breast. He watched her come up the steps, and lower her eyes as she darted past him. Nabeel was sure she knew who he was. Most people did – his reputation at the university was growing. But he could not be sure. If she knew nothing of poetry . . .

At that point, of course, he had not known that she, too,

was studying literature, and a high-born privileged Hashe-mite, descended directly from the family of the Prophet Muhammad. He had no idea that she had seen him walking through the literature faculty muttering poetry to himself and had been hoping to meet him, too.

It was a slow courtship. They had started to catch each other's eye, smile and wave as they passed in the lecture halls. Then they had found themselves in a group of students who had gathered in the courtyard to talk about the literature lectures they were attending. With the offer of a novel, Hemingway's *The Old Man and the Sea*, their romance began. At first they were awkward and shy with each other. 'Do you think he is the greatest living writer?' he had asked her.

She had shrugged. 'How can anyone be the greatest?'

She was certainly not in awe of him. No, she *liked* him. He was sure of it. Eventually, talking outside the faculty gave way to glasses of tea at the students' club, and Nabeel was soon in love. Now she is his inspiration. He has been writing fur-iously, submitting articles, opinion pieces and poems to Baghdad's best magazines and newspapers, *Alif-Baa* and *al-Jumahrriya*, as well as the children's magazines *Majallty* and *al-Mizmar*. He writes verse for Nada too, offerings of love, and thanks.

They have become the golden couple of the campus; he a rising star, she his elegant and clever muse. She goes with him to readings around Baghdad, poised, with her hair in tendrils, on the sidelines. But it is the time they spend alone that he treasures, when his achievements are forgotten and she is simply the beautiful girl who has become his friend. They meet at the library, with plans to study together, and find themselves talking in a quiet corner instead. She lights a cigarette and talks of the essay she is writing, then finds herself telling him of home, her three sisters and life with her family.

Earlier that year Nabeel had decided to take her home to dinner with his parents. It was an unorthodox move, since they were neither engaged nor in the process of arranging a marriage. In fact neither set of parents had any idea that their offspring had found each other. But such was the strength of his feelings that he needed them to meet her. 'They will love you as much as I do. It will be better to have it out in the open,' he promised, trusting his intuition.

Sabria's face lit up when she saw Nada. The girls, Aqbal and Amel, now in their teens, were pleased to have another woman in the house, and Nabeel's brothers, though divided in their politics, found themselves falling for her too. Even Yasin, not prone to sentiment, had gazed, soft-eyed, as she talked of her family. She had been a sensitive guest, well brought up with an easy charm. Sabria had sighed with pride and as they both left she pronounced, 'They will be married. Mark my words.'

Nabeel, too, has dared to think that one day soon Nada will be his wife. Sometimes, between jazz nights at the Lawyers' Club and dancing at the Journalists' Club, he imagines the future they might share.

There remains one thorny issue between him and his dreams of life with Nada: her parents. Soon he must meet them and declare his interest in their daughter. He has heard much about her father, Hamed, who was once the General Director of Finance but was forced out by the Ba'athist administration of 1963. He sounds like a man of conviction and principles. Her mother is always impeccably dressed, anxious for her daughters to marry well and for their lives of

Nabeel and Nada, 1971

privilege to continue uninterrupted. Despite his confidence and reputation Nabeel wonders if they will take to him as his own parents and siblings have to Nada. Many problems stand in his way, not least tradition, religion and class. But he has never been one to let convention put him off. His own family had not abided by the strictures of tradition and class and in one generation, they have leaped up the social ladder of success. Jafar is now an economist, Juma'a a teacher, Jabbar an able student, and the younger three, still at school, are well educated, with prospects and talent.

Now he is walking through Martyrs' Square. There are a few dim streetlights and the cement pavements guide him through the shadows. For Nabeel, in the heart of the night, it is a short-cut. He emerges to cross the wide boulevard that runs out towards al-Bayaa, and sees the last number forty-five bus waiting at the station.

He climbs to the top deck. As children, he and Jabbar would lounge on the leather-seated rows of the first-class section until the conductor came to inspect their tickets when they would jump back, claiming they had been in second class all along. Tariq probably still does it with his friends. Tonight the seats are all empty, and he sits down, pulling a scrap of paper from his back pocket. He sees the scattered lights of the city spreading out behind him, the great highways that carry the traffic to and from Jordan and Syria, the wide streets with their tramlines, flanked by ancient Ottoman town houses and, to the west, modern homes, hotels and department stores. There is so much new construction but it is the old monuments, the Abbasid Palace, the Khadimiya mosque, that are the most glorious. The bus sways down the road towards Al Bayaa, passing the Music and Ballet School, the Iraqi Painters' Club and the minarets of the al-Bayaa mosque.

As they travel westward, the larger buildings stand out in silhouette against the dark scrub in the moonlight. When they had first moved from Karradat Mariam to al-Bayaa in 1958, this land had been untamed. His family had been among the first to move into the area and its brand-new houses. Back then they had wondered if their street would remain alone, marooned on the outskirts of the city, but within a few years, houses were springing up close by, on the ground where Nabeel and his siblings had played football.

Eventually, they will probably have to move again. When Jafar and Juma'a settle down, they will surely bring their wives to live at the house. Then there will be arguments and it will be decided that they must have a compound with more rooms to accommodate each family. It is hard to imagine any of his siblings married. Juma'a is so serious, still consumed with politics and principles. And who can blame him?

Jafar is a much more likely prospect for marriage: he has abandoned his Arab Nationalist stance for a leftist one, is nearly twenty-nine and, to Nabeel, the kindest man alive. He would make someone a good husband. He has always admired his elder brothers, and now Jabbar and Tariq admire Nabeel. It is the way, he supposes. Together, they try to look after their independent-minded sisters, Aqbal and Amel.

Stepping out of the bus at al-Bayaa, he feels the cooling *shamal* from the northern highlands. As the bus disappears round the bend he ruffles his thick black hair and lets the air get to his neck. He is blessed. He begins the slow descent into his own familiar neighbourhood singing words that come from deep in his heart:

Brother Yasin,
On the way to the family,
Surrounded with a chain of blood,
I catch in my hand
The beautiful islands . . .

The road he is on leads out of the city to Babylon, Karbala and beyond. He passes the street sign that reads 'Babylon'. The white arrow on the light green background points straight ahead. It thrills him to see it: Babylon is the last haven. Beyond it, the land is uninhabitable, arid scrubland, wide stony plains, sand and wadis, powder dry for most of the year. Only a few pastoral nomads, who drift across the borders from Saudi Arabia, Syria and Jordan with the dust storms, can live there. Babylon and the mighty Euphrates, with its fertile banks, are the first and last bastions of civilisation.

A white taxi slows beside him in the hope of a fare. He waves it on. His eyes travel over the streets of Al Bayaa with its panorama of flat rooftops and television aerials. How big it has grown. The haphazardly built houses with pathways trodden between them in the grass have made way for an organised network of streets. Nabeel has always loved the mix of people here, shopkeepers, textile traders and craftsmen living beside academics, teachers and journalists. Even poets. Though life is becoming less predictable, the area feels as safe and familiar to him as his own face.

He turns into his street and sees the silhouette of the family home, the lantern above the gate guiding him, like a beacon. The door swings open silently and, slipping off his shoes, he creeps across the cool tiles of the hallway. In the kitchen he sees that his mother has left food for him – the journey has made him hungry. There is kofta, rice and minted diced cucumber. He eats quickly, in the dark, not wanting to wake anyone. The tiled kitchen, with its hot oil oven and wooden fridge, is still his favourite room. When they had first moved here after the revolution it had seemed the height of modernity. Mama had cried with happiness when she first saw it. He remembers how he had pulled at her overalls as she brought in warm bread from the clay oven outside. He and his father had built that oven! The house had seemed so big then. Now it is a wonder that it contains them all. Still, they manage, jostling for space. He cannot recall a time when it was any different. There has never been any peace: half of the family snores, Amel spends her time under the kitchen table with a book, never around when there are chores to be done, and the quick-witted Tariq is always playing one practical joke after another. . . . As Mama always says, the knife of the family does not cut.

Tonight the house is full to bursting. The mattresses and quilts from the store cupboard are, no doubt, all on the roof; the girls usually sleep next to their mother, but tonight Cousins Taha and Salah, Uncle Rashid and Kamil are here too. He steps over sleeping bodies and smiles. No one has been beaten or arrested and no one is sick. Carrying a jug of water and a glass, he tiptoes past two more sleeping forms on their rolled-out mats, searching for somewhere to lie down.

'Mama,' he whispers, catching the outline of his mother in her room. She is up, pretending to be engaged in some essential household task.

'Nabeel, you're back. I prayed for your safe return tonight.'

'Mama, you really shouldn't wait up for me like this.'

'Tsk. I was doing some sewing for Tariq. That boy gets through trousers like most people get through a bowl of almonds.' She closes the wooden sewing basket with its woven lid. 'Where have you been? No trouble tonight, I hope.'

'No, Mama, I have been with friends, reading Shakespeare.'

'And you return at this hour? Nabeel, tell me. I will ask again. Has there been any trouble tonight?' She leans forward and pulls his face into the light. 'The wounds we make with words are greater than those made with swords. Remember that.'

'It was just reading, Mama, I swear.'

Satisfied that he is telling the truth, she takes his wrist and squeezes it. 'Go and sleep, my son. You can tell me about Mr Shakespeare in the morning.' She turns to extinguish the kerosene lamp.

Tomorrow they will sit together in the shade and drink sweet black tea. They will exchange the news of the previous day. And then he will begin to write the poem about his family that has been calling on his mind during the long journey home.

The Writers' Union
Autumn 1972

As he walks to the front door, Nabeel calls, 'Mama, I'm at the Writers' Union tonight. Please don't wait up.' She doesn't answer. He draws back the cast-iron bolt, opens the door into the courtyard and waits, the ritual of departure playing out as it has ever since he was old enough to leave the house alone. He speaks slowly, exaggerating each word: 'Mama, I know you can hear me.' He hears her house shoes whispering across the tiled kitchen floor. Hush, hush, hush, and suddenly she is there, peering at him. Nabeel stands before the only mirror in the house, beside the front door, smoothing and straightening his shirt, tugging at the lapels of his expensive new beige sports jacket. He cocks his head to one side and pulls the packet of Baghdad cigarettes from his top pocket. Smiling awkwardly at himself, he feels the first flutter of nerves.

'Gandhi,' snaps Sabria, 'eat before you go. Surely you need something to line your stomach? I have –' He cuts her short with a dismissive wave. She will leave him some rice, bread, other simple things for when he returns, she thinks. He always eats at night these days. Sabria rolls her eyes and goes back to the kitchen. The door snaps shut and his footsteps are soon lost amid the sounds of early morning. The faint waft of the cigarette he lit on the step reaches her like an echo.

Nabeel had said it was just a reading, nothing special. 'A few close friends gathering in someone's living room.' But she knew this was a lie. A neighbour had heard on the radio that he had been invited to read at the Iraqi Writers' Union. Perhaps he will perform *Cry on the Obelisk of Sadness*. She cannot read his poems but she often gets one of the others to recite them when Nabeel is out, and they all think this one is his best. 'Yasin,' she calls from the kitchen, a wave of pride breaking over her, 'this is such an evening. We have a famous poet for a son. All the struggles and sacrifice, and now this! Yasin! Do you ever listen to anything I say? Yasin?'

Yasin reclines on a rough mattress, his head and neck propped up on brightly patterned cushions. His gnarled hands are folded across his belly, which rises and falls beneath his linen shirt to the rhythms of sleep. Standing over him, Sabria tuts. 'Yasin, do not pretend you cannot hear. You should be happy and proud. Seven children, all clever, well educated and *now*, through little Nabeel, with a name that will be recognised and honoured.'

Yasin opens one eye, swivels it towards his wife and is once more in awe of her. 'Yes, you are right,' he says, knowing it is best to agree with her on matters relating to the children. ' "An honest voice in a country awash with sycophants and propagandists", that's what they say about him.' Nabeel's vision of the future is bleak, too bleak for Yasin, but perhaps it is in the nature of youth to be disaffected and angry. He tries to recall if he was ever thus. He wasn't. But whatever he thinks of Nabeel's poetry, there is no denying that it has struck a deep chord in educated and ordinary people alike. And that is good. He closes his eyes.

Nabeel arrives at the steps of the elegant sandstone building just after six, and pauses to look up at the words carved over the main doorway: The Iraqi Writers' Union. This is the temple of his endeavour. He sees the last of the sun, now a dusty amber ball, dip below the horizon and knows it must be time. He drops his cigarette, smoothes his coat and pushes open the heavy doors.

There is an excited hubbub in the foyer and all eyes turn to him. He sees a poster pinned to the far wall. 'Nabeel Yasin. Hear the poet recite his work.' *He* will be standing on that stage tonight. He hopes things go well, for while he knows he doesn't need the support of these people now, he wants their approval. There are so many great poets he must live up to, from Ma'ruf al-Rusafi, to his favourite al-Jawarhiri and other contemporaries like the poetess Nazik al-Malaiyka, al-Bayati and al-Sayyab. Older men in tailored suits begin to float from the shadows towards him. He spots Hameed, a teacher friend, and waves in relief. 'Hameed! I'm glad to see you here tonight.'

They are soon joined by others, poets, playwrights, a novelist and several newspaper journalists. As introductions are made, Nabeel feels goodwill swell around him and carry him forward into the courtyard garden at the rear. 'Here.' Abbas, another friend, gestures at a lectern. 'This is your perch for the night.' Nabeel is thankful they will be outside: he is too hot to read at the back of some great airless hall choked with cigarette smoke and expectation.

He goes to check the makeshift stage. Strings of coloured

lights swing in the gentle breeze round the podium. Behind him, the garden fills. It is going to be a large audience, made up of writers and critics, all of whom know the tricks, the devices and the form, and who will scrutinise him closely.

The secretary walks up to the stage, and Nabeel, standing to the side, takes a last drag at his cigarette and stubs it out on the ground.

'We have before us tonight one of Baghdad's most talented young poets. In five years he has become widely read. His work is uncompromising and at times difficult but it seeks the truth. We are honoured to have him at the Iraqi Writers' Union. Ladies and gentlemen, I present the man they call the poet of our time, Nabeel Yasin . . .'

As he waits for the applause to die away, Nabeel's heart is pounding.

'Tonight he will read from *The Poets Satirise the Kings*, which he has been working on for over a year. This is the first time it has been read on Iraqi soil – or anywhere else, for that matter.'

The ripple of laughter leaves Nabeel feeling more nervous than ever.

This new work has been much anticipated and rumour in the literary world is wide-ranging: it is good, it is bad, it is a sellout, a long, poorly composed diatribe – or a composition touched by genius. Yet he has shown it to no one but Nada. The only thing anyone else can know for certain is its title and that it is to be published in *Status*, the blacklisted Lebanese literary magazine. Many people inside Iraq have requested illegal copies be sent to them in the post. He will not be surprised if there is an extra print run.

Finally the moment has arrived. He will speak and be damned. Standing behind the lectern, he begins:

He led me then, into a forest of tears
A forest fencing in another forest
And we separated from each other
Under a gate of candles

Al Nifferi guided me on a cold flame
Hell passed under me
And Al Nifferi commanded it should be a
peaceful, good home . . .

. . . my country was fighting me beneath a gate of dried
 blood
Fighting me!
Have you heard of a country fighting its own sons.

The audience sits forward, straining to hear every word. As he continues, verse after verse, Nabeel can feel their rising excitement. The soft cadences linger in the air like the scent of blossom. They are spellbound.

No one sees the two dark-suited men appear at the back of the garden. Nor does anyone notice when, after a few minutes of note-taking, one slips into the administration office and picks up the phone.

These days, everyone is watching their back. The number of Ba'ath recruits and informants grows daily. There are rumoured to be several within the Writers' Union, though nothing has ever been proven. Mundhira, a relatively new member who works on one of the Ba'athist newspapers, has fallen under suspicion. Having inveigled his way on to the committee with undue haste, he has been caught by some colleagues in the administration office talking on the phone about other members. Confronted, he had shrugged and claimed he was sorting out the archives. While they know this to be a blatant lie no one has dared do anything about it. So a curious status quo has arisen. Tonight, however, Nabeel is not going to be cowed by the militia and their spies. He expects them to be here. He will read his work as he wrote it, in its entirety. This might be his only chance to do so. He only wishes he could make its political content more evident to all. But where is the poetry in that? 'There is plenty that needs to be criticised,' he had reminded Hameed and Abbas, when the three had last met. 'And besides,' he had added, 'if print censorship is to limit people's access to literature and poetry we become more duty-bound than ever to give readings.'

As the last lines of the poem fall away into the silence, Nabeel takes a long breath and bows his head. Above the applause he hears a passing fire siren. He has not prepared an encore but he could read a little from the new translation of *King Lear*. He was given the crisp paperback on his way in. But then he thinks better of the idea. This evening is his chance to make a personal statement, without recourse to the vision of others.

And he has more to say. Only last week Juma'a's Communist cronies had branded him weak for hiding behind verse, rather than taking direct action. They have even nicknamed him the Bourgeois Poet. Well, not tonight. Without stopping to consider the implications, Nabeel launches into an attack on those who would seek to suppress writers and artists, to stifle free speech and banish art from the minds and hearts of the people. 'This country has been conquered a thousand times, and its people with it. But through all this political exchange it has remained at the heart of culture, of learning, of great philosophy and thought. And so it must be today. No matter who occupies the seat of power, nor what minor philosophies they peddle, there is a greater human desire to explore the truth. Like the brave men and women of history and myth, we should not falter. It is these epic journeys, seen in *The Poets Satirise the Kings*, and in my other work, *The Head* and *The Meadow*, that could be our inspiration. Our battle is universal, and it can be won.' His own poetry, into which he weaves myth and history to criticise the Ba'athist regime, has now become an unambiguous vessel for his views. There can be little doubt now of his stance.

Afterwards the floor is thrown open to the audience who, it seems, all have an opinion on his work. Many members have brought friends from outside the union to the reading, and Nabeel meets a stream of enthusiastic well-wishers. If only Nada had come. Still, he will see her on Thursday when they go to the Roxy to watch a film. He might have finished the little poem he is working on for her by then, too.

It is a near-perfect evening. The gardens at the union are rich with the scent of date palms and oleanders, the lights soft. It is like being in an intimate little theatre. The union building had once been a hedonistic retreat – the Club of the Tenth, named in honour of the tenth prime minister of Iraq. It was established during the era of monarchy, and boasted a well-stocked bar, an extravagantly decorated poker hall, and offered late-night music and dancing. Close networks of friends and inner-circle contacts met there to share information, do deals and consort with unsuitably glamorous women.

No doubt the Ba'athists, who had closed the union once already, in 1963, would be delighted to do so again.

By midnight Nabeel, feeling pleasantly weary, decides to take a taxi home with Hameed and Abbas. The friends kiss the remaining members of their party goodnight and gather on the union steps to go out into the night. Outside, they hover on the empty pavement in the hope of catching a passing cab and are rewarded by the arrival of a large white Volvo, which emerges from the shadows and glides slowly to a halt next to them.

'Mr Nabeel,' comes a voice from a slit at the top of the window, 'you are waiting for a taxi, no?' Caught off-guard, Nabeel admits they are. 'Come then,' the voice continues. 'We will take you.'

Nabeel steps forward and peers in at the window. The glass, like the street, is black and impenetrable. 'Who are you?'

'We are admirers. We know you and respect your work. You are a *great* poet – a very great man.' A pair of heavy-lidded eyes appear at the window. The words are flattering, but the tone is sinister.

'I will stay with my friends, thank you. We still have things to discuss.' It had been a wonderful evening, and he wanted to keep it that way.

The car drives off and the three young men walk on in silence. Several minutes later the Volvo reappears, this time from the other direction. It accelerates on to the pavement and forces them to the wall. The man inside leans out of the window. 'Come,' he calls. 'It is difficult to get a taxi at this time of night. We will take you home for free.'

The three move away from the car and try to appear relaxed as they walk away, a little faster now, towards the al-bab al-Sharqi quarter. With a virtual curfew through the city, the streets, once teeming with evening traffic, street vendors and entertainers, are deserted. But there is bound to be a taxi in al-bab al-Sharqi. Only the sound of their footsteps, and the hum of the Volvo following them, breaks the stillness. Dark old houses loom up on either side of them from the pitted ground. The men walk faster and faster, until

Nabeel spies a short-cut that will take them away from the secret-police headquarters. He leads them into an alley, too narrow for a car to follow, and they break into a run half-way down the cobbled street, past a row of tiny, uneven shops, set on outwitting the driver of the car. They dive into another unlit, empty road and stop to grin at each other. They've given trouble the slip.

Their pulses have barely settled when the glaring beams of another car sweep round the corner. It is a white Peugeot 404, the preferred car of the secret police. It skids to a stop and several officers, silhouetted in the headlights, jump out and surround them. This time there are no invitations. This was an ambush, not the idle opportunism Nabeel had imagined. Perhaps a tip-off from someone at the union – maybe even from one of the men next to him.

Stealing a glance to the left, Nabeel sees a door close quietly across the street. His heart sinks. They are standing opposite one of the secret militia houses. The enemy is hidden behind the white exterior. How ironic that in their attempts to lose the Volvo they have run into a vipers' nest. To run would be folly now. He would be dragged into the house, beaten, shot or raped, to join the swelling ranks of the many who have disappeared under Saddam Hussein's four-year purge.

'Are you Sha'ar?' barks an officer.

'Are we *Sha'ar*?' Nabeel repeats.

'Yes, Sha'ar.' The men begin to laugh. 'You know, minstrels, pansy boys, fools wearing women's clothes.'

'No, I am *Sha'ir*,' Nabeel says defiantly, pulling away from Hameed's calming hand on his shoulder. 'A *poet*.'

'A man of words, eh? You don't look like much of a man to me.' Two officers prod Nabeel with steel batons.

He springs forward and punches the side of the captain's face. 'You uneducated barbarians!'

The men see to it that Nabeel does not throw any more punches: they knock him to the ground and kick his head and torso until he no longer moves. Nabeel is dimly aware of their steel-toecapped footsteps as they haul away his friends and the car roars off into the night. Then there is only silence.

Some time after five, when light first curls round the edges of the sky, voices above him bring him round. 'He is still alive, yes, still alive.' He sees that he is surrounded by the beggars of Baghdad. He is at the back of al-bab al-Sharqi Square, where the city's poor offer themselves for casual labour at the beginning of each day. A group of men, dusty from a night sleeping rough, hover over him in soiled, faded robes. Beyond their feet, just out of reach, he can see his copy of *King Lear*. As the men watch him he remembers the incident that brought him here. His face and hair are caked with sticky patches of blood, one eye is swollen shut, and his back and ribcage are badly bruised. From the searing pain in his chest, he is sure that at least one rib is cracked. He tries to stand, and begs for their help. 'I need a taxi. You must get me a taxi,' he wheezes.

The men are keen to help the bloodstained man in his best clothes. 'Were you robbed?' one asks, crouching to check his pockets for identification. 'Or was it the secret police?'

Nabeel winces, then collapses back to the ground. 'Yes.'

At this they scatter to wake shopkeepers and fetch water. 'Do you want tea? Bread? Let us get you some black tea.'

'No, please, just a taxi.' Two hoist him to his feet, and a third brings a chair from a nearby stall. He puts his hands on

Nabeel's head, then examines the thick streaks of blood on his own palms.

'It will dry. You are respectable enough to get home,' an old man reassures him, as they help him into a taxi. He thanks them and fights back tears of gratitude and pain.

When he arrives home Sabria is waiting. He hides his face from her, finds a mattress and curls up under a sheet. It is late in the morning when he wakes. He opens his eyes to his mother's horrified gaze. She crouches to look at her son's broken face. 'Why did you not tell me?' she cries. 'What have they done to you?' Tears fill her dark eyes. Nabeel mumbles the first excuse he can think of. He must protect her.

'Ah, Mama, it's nothing. I cut myself shaving.'

She knows he must be concussed, or worse, to use such a feeble excuse. 'This is no shaving accident. You may not have seen a mirror but I can see *you*. There's blood on the back of your neck. Are you shaving there too now?'

She goes to the wooden medicine box Bibi bequeathed to her, and returns with wads of fine cotton and a pungent ointment that she pours out of a glass vial. 'Press this to the wound,' she orders. 'Was this the Mukhabarat?'

He nods.

Propping him on the sofa, she brings him a herbal tea. It reminds him of his childhood and he begins to feel better. If he is careful, his injuries will heal.

The Small Matter of Friendship
Late 1972

Ali has been in the Secret Police for a year when the order to arrest Nabeel finally comes. He has been expecting it, of course. It was only a matter of time before he was asked to bring in one of the brothers: they live in his jurisdiction. He had hoped Nabeel would have the sense to move away or at least quieten down. But it seems that his old friend is determined to make a career out of upsetting powerful people.

Ali and Nabeel had been childhood friends, but while Nabeel had gone to university Ali had joined the Secret Police. After failing his baccalaureate at high school he had decided to make his own way in the world. But he had been unable to settle to anything until the recruitment officer had found him wandering aimlessly through the streets of al-Bayaa.

Like everyone else Ali had seen the posters. It was hard to miss them, with their garish colours and bombastic quotes from Michel Afleq, the Syrian founder of the Ba'ath Party.

United Arab Nation . . . immortal mission
Your history is glorious.
The past is full of heroes.

It's time we replaced these heroes with new heroes for today.

Join us and become a hero too.

Not for a moment had Ali considered enrolling. If anything, he had always held the security services in contempt. But as the recruiting officer began to explain the benefits of joining the Secret Police, a future crystallised in Ali's mind. The job offered a simple ideology – Arab Unity – a reasonable salary and the prospect of promotion; he could earn enough to buy a house in just four years. Then there were the fringe benefits of prestige, excitement and power. He passed the physical and was signed up.

In many ways Ali and Nabeel's lives had mirrored each other. The two families had moved to al-Bayaa within weeks of each other, and Sabria and Ali's mother, both tending small children, had struck up a close relationship. Most days they would agree to meet en route to the markets of al-Bayaa or simply chat together over tea, the children wandering in and out as they pleased. But despite the warmth of their friendship and their similarities, their attitude to learning set them apart. Sabria encouraged all of her children to be independent thinkers. As she was fond of telling her teacher friends, 'I want each of them to attend university. What they do after that is their own business. Education is the way out of a life of ignorance and menial work.' She knew, from looking at the miscreants around the neighbourhood, that education was the dividing line between those who did well and those who turned bad.

The children had never questioned her vision. Even Tariq, who had always been somewhat mischievous, loved school. They all seemed blessed with strong principles and a natural work ethic. Sabria encouraged open discussion in her household, from religion to politics and literature, and through her sons she too had acquired knowledge of the great works of Rumi, *The Rubáiyát* of Omar Khayyám, T.S. Eliot, Charles Dickens and Marcel Proust. 'Keep reading and take as much from it as you can. That is what will set you apart,' she told Nabeel and the girls. Yasin had helped too in his way: in passing on his mistrust of authoritarians and zealots, he had made his children aware of themselves – and of those who seek power for its own ends.

Ali had drifted through his teenage years, with no interest in learning so as he and Nabeel grew into adulthood they were living in different worlds. On the street, if they bumped into each other, they soon ran out of things to say. And although he remembered their adventures with affection, Nabeel could not help but wonder at the path Ali had chosen.

Now, at the end of 1972, their lives collide again. Ali leaves his colleagues at the station with a mumbled excuse. He may not approve of the Yasins' politics but he feels duty bound to alert them to the raid, even at risk to himself. If he didn't, his mother would never forgive him. He pushes off on his bicycle and weaves his way home, arriving just as the sun reaches its midday peak. His mother jumps to her feet as he kicks open the fly-screen. 'Ali? You're home early. What's happened?'

'They're coming for Nabeel tonight, Mama. I have to warn him.'

His mother is not shocked. The Yasin boys are forever under arrest, although she had not imagined her own son would arrest him. 'At what time?' She does not hide her contempt.

'Ten o'clock. There are a few on the list today.'

'And you?' She looks straight at him.

'I will be with them. I have no choice.' He looks at the ground. 'It is difficult for me, Mama. I must protect myself. This is my job. If they found out, I would end up in the cells with him.'

'Ali,' she falters, 'this will change everything between our two families. You must warn him now.'

'But I have to get back to the station, Mama, they'll be wondering . . .'

'Go now. There is no time for cowardly shilly-shallying.'

'OK, but remember, it is not me who has done this,' he hisses. 'Nabeel has enemies. He is reckless, and does not have the wisdom to censor his pen.'

'Maybe that is so, but this is about our honour. It is a shameful day indeed for our family.'

Sabria welcomes Ali. 'Ali, what a surprise! How nice to see you. Come, come,' she beckons, 'I am making tea for Yasin. The children are not here. But, please, go through. Say hello to Uncle Yasin. He will be pleased to see you. It has been a long time.' She looks back toward kitchen.

Ali feels uncomfortable at the sight of Yasin. Talking to Aunty Sabria was like talking to his mother, but today saying what he must is a daunting prospect. He looks over at Yasin, resting on the large aubergine-coloured rug and begins to rearrange the facts until they fit his conscience a little better. He might be a member of the National Guard but he is also giving this family a chance – and risking his own career to do so. If it were not for him Nabeel would have no warning at all. Perhaps, he thinks, as Yasin invites him to sit, they should be grateful to him.

He would have preferred to stand, but he settles himself uneasily against a hard-stuffed cushion, shifting this way and that in an effort to get comfortable. He smiles weakly as Sabria pours the tea, offering him the sugar with her other hand.

'Thank you, Aunty Sabria.'

Sabria peers at him from over the rim of her glass, aware that he is uneasy. 'Ali, is there something you need to tell us?' She drums her fingers on the tray. 'Is it your family? Your mother? Is she not well? I only saw her yesterday. I hope there is nothing untoward, *Inshallah*.' She looks down at his crisp cuffs. He is smarter now than she has ever known him.

Ali shakes his tightly cropped head. 'Oh, no,' he says. 'Mama is quite well. The rest of them too. She sends you her greetings. *Inshallah*, she will come over soon.'

'Good,' Sabria replies, 'And your father?'

'Fine, also,' he says. 'Thank you.'

All three sip their tea awkwardly. They have never struggled for conversation before.

'There is one thing,' Ali says finally, setting his cup on the table. 'It's about Nabeel . . .'

Sabria keeps to herself the shock of discovering that Ali is a member of the Ba'ath Party and the Secret Police. His mother has never mentioned it. She calls testily for her youngest daughter: 'Amel! Come down here.'

Within a minute the thud of footsteps announces the arrival of the studious twelve-year-old. She has been reading in a dark corner somewhere, Sabria knows, behind one of the clothes chests or the pile of mattresses kept for guests in the store-room on the roof. She is quiet but she has an exceptional mind. Sabria generally tries not to disturb her but now she has no choice. 'Amel, *habibti*, the police are coming for Nabeel. You must go out to the bus stop and warn him.'

'Today? How do you know?' asks Amel. 'Every day you think they will come for him.'

'Amel, do as I ask. Ali told us,' Sabria says, pointing to Ali, now standing at the door. 'Thank you.' She places her broad hand on his shoulder. 'And send my regards to your mother,' she calls, as he walks through the gate. Poor, simple boy. It is a shame. Yet he is just the kind they seek out, guileless teenage rebels looking for adventure and power.

And his mother! She must be so ashamed that one of her sons is a secret policeman.

'Amel,' Sabria turns to her daughter. 'Ali says they are coming at ten. Go now and wait until you see him get off the bus. Tell him to keep away. It is the local Secret Police so he'll be safe anywhere outside al-Bayaa.'

Amel rolls her eyes. One or other of her brothers is always in trouble. Of course she sympathises with them, but she is more concerned for her mother. The strain is beginning to show. With the boys often away, at meetings, protesting or in jail, the house is fraught with anxiety. Mama is tired from waiting up late for them and Amel's brothers are too busy with their revolutions to notice.

'How long will he have to stay away?'

'Just a week, perhaps a little more. Until things settle down and they forget about him.'

Amel knows that this means 'until something or someone else annoys them'.

'As if poetry were a crime anyway,' Yasin murmurs. 'He

should go and visit Rashid and Kamel. No one will think to find him in sleepy old Babylon.'

'Nonsense, Yasin. Rashid is a hundred miles away. Do you think Nabeel needs to go so far? Of course not.' Sabria reaches out to pinch Amel's cheek. 'Be careful with yourself, *habibti*. And take some fruit. It's warm today.'

'He will be all right, won't he?' Amel says.

'Of course, *habibti*, as long as you find him.'

'And what about Ali?'

'Well,' Sabria says, 'Ali will be back later, in his new shirt, pretending to look for Nabeel like the others.'

'Do not be too harsh, Sabria.' Yasin brings his palms together. 'Ali has been a good friend to us.' And his words bring peace to the room, as they often do.

It is sad how things have changed under the Ba'athists. There was a time, not so long ago, when it was unthinkable to doubt a neighbour. Now, since reclaiming power with few more than sixty people, the Ba'athists have successfully infiltrated the police force, the army and the civil service. Now they are gaining favour with the masses. It is easy enough for them to win support. With the promise of a brighter, richer future, the poor, disadvantaged and plain greedy willingly sign up, happy, it seems, to ignore the violence or even to participate in it. How ironic that the party's name should mean rebirth. Even the Communists are now trying to stay on the right side of al-Bakr and Saddam Hussein.

One thing is certain. The days of Secret Ibrahim are over.

'Yasin, do you not wish we still had Secret Ibrahim?' Yasin nods with a smile. White-haired and unthreatening, Ibrahim had been the neighbourhood's sole informant for years before the arrival of the Ba'ath. He could be seen cycling the bumpy tracks in his white shirt, always at the same stately pace. He never seemed to be going to or coming from anywhere in particular. He was just there. And all he ever did, as far as anyone could make out, was to cycle round, warning residents of planned arrests and house visits. Of course they knew he was in the pay of the Secret Police, an informant, a spy living among them, but he performed a vital function.

He was an intermediary, a double-agent, and the community had been left to get on with their lives. The children had thought him exciting. *Do you live in a special house? What secrets can you tell us? Is it true that you have a gun? How many men have you killed?* He had patiently answered their endless questions: 'Yes, I am a secret agent. And, yes, I have a gun, many guns, actually, but I have never killed anyone.' He had even made use of the little ones, appointing some as messengers. At the ring of his cycle bell, they would know he had a message or a warning. 'Listen, Nabeel. Tell your brother Juma'a to make himself scarce tonight,' he would whisper. Or 'make sure Jafar's friends do not go to tomorrow's meeting. That is all I will say.'

Once Sabria had asked him why he always warned them.

'I have no choice,' he'd said, with a wink. 'How could I stand here and meet your eye tomorrow if I had played a part in the arrest of anyone in your family today? A house divided cannot stand. We are neighbours, sharing the land, no?'

This had been the Iraqi way for as long as Sabria could recall. And though Ali, like Ibrahim, has a good, loyal heart he is unusual. The Ba'ath Party will be leaning on him, filling his head with obligation, threatening him with isolation and destitution if he should consider turning against it.

Amel bounds out of the house still wearing her grey school skirt and white cotton shirt. She carries a geography book in one hand and a bag containing two oranges in the other. She runs all the way and is at the number forty bus stop within a few minutes. According to the clock on the wall in the haberdasher's opposite, it is four o'clock. Far too early for Nabeel to be on his way home. He rarely leaves work before dusk, and nowadays even that is rare. Sometimes he doesn't get home until ten or so. Working on the principle that there is a first time for everything, she settles herself in the shade, her back against the wall and opens her book.

She watches people come and go, dutifully scanning each busload for Nabeel. What a life they all lead, her brothers. Although they're grown up they act like children, always out looking for trouble. They are principled enough, but not circumspect, too busy trying to change the world to notice how dangerous they have made their own. Not one of them stands still for long enough to change anything. Instead their days are filled with arguments, marches, protests, and grand pledges to their peers. Does everyone dream like this? she wonders, as another bus arrives and discharges men in crisp white robes and cotton trousers, mothers herding school-children and an elderly couple who grip each other's shoulders for support. Things will be different when she grows up. Her teachers have told her she can do anything she wants so she has decided to become a doctor. It is something practical, pragmatic, a real skill.

Her shadow lengthens beneath the dying sun, and the streetlights flicker on. She has long since given up on her book. She drops it into the bag and steps forward into the light. She is tired and hungry. 'Come on, Nabeel,' she thinks, as several people she knows disembark from another bus: two of her mother's cronies and one of Jabbar's Communist friends. She waves politely but does not want to be distracted. She cannot risk missing him. The sight of Juma'a arriving home from prison when she was a tiny child, a thin, strange, crop-headed creature, had remained with her down the years. Her mother's upset had left her, even now, with a mild sense of panic and fear. Everyone had rushed to him and he had said nothing. She does not know if Nabeel is as robust as Juma'a . . .

Around eight Nabeel struts off the bus in the Westminster flares, made for him by his friend, Tawfiq the tailor. Since Nabeel's friend Salman, the painter, introduced them at the beginning of 1969 they have been almost inseparable. Tawfiq is an energetic yet thoughtful man, and has become almost one of the family. He is also a great fan of Nabeel's work, which he had first come across in prison. While Juma'a was released after the first Communist purge in 1963, the tailor was kept without charge or explanation for five years at Noqret al Salman in the south-western desert of Iraq.

During his time in the notorious desert jail he'd learned to read. 'I couldn't help it,' he often joked, 'the prisons in Iraq are full of writers.' Beginning with smuggled copies of Chekhov, Tolstoy, Gogol, Pablo Neruda and Marx, he had progressed to the classics of English literature in translation and modern Arab poets, including Nabeel's earliest published works. On his release he had met Salman in his small shop in Qanber Ali, the old quarter, and discovered the connection. 'You must introduce me to your friend, Nabeel, I am his biggest fan,' he had said urgently. 'I should dearly love to meet him. I read *The Head* in prison and I carry it with me still. Now I am reading everything of his. Please tell me you will introduce me. I have a shop now – you know I am a designer and tailor. Please come and visit. I should like to make you both something, perhaps a new suit.' Salman had visited him the next day with Nabeel.

Amel spots the magazine before she sees Nabeel's face. He is carrying a copy of the *Mawaqif*, another banned magazine. She feels butterflies in her stomach. He is so careless. She slips discreetly through the crowds towards him.

She calls softly to him from across the scrub: 'Nabeel, over here.'

He peers out at his little sister, a halo of light round her black head under the streetlight. 'Amel! What are you doing here?'

'Mama told me not to come home until I found you. The al-Bayaa Secret Police are coming for you tonight. There is a squad, with Ali in it.'

Nabeel kisses her forehead. 'Thank you, little Amel. You've saved me. Quite a heroine, no?' He pulls out a cigarette. 'But now you should go home. It's late and you should not be out alone.'

His voice is kind and assured, just as a brother's should be, but under the streetlight she can see his eyes are steely and she knows he is thinking of Ali. She wonders if it saddens him that his friendship with Ali is no more, but she says nothing. He does not talk to her about such things.

'I will,' she says, grinding the tip of her shoe into the pavement.

'Good.'

'Shall I give Mama a message?'

'No,' he lowers his voice, 'she knows I will be fine. I will go to Aunty Noua.'

He knows he must get a message to Nada, too, telling her

119

what has happened. If she cannot find him she will imagine the worst.

'I will be back soon,' he adds.

'When?'

Turning away, he almost laughs: to that question, there is no answer.

A *Little Wedding*
July 1974

By their own choice the rites of Nabeel and Nada's marriage are simple. In contrast to most Iraqi weddings, grand formal affairs attended by hundreds, theirs is intimate and informal. Only fifty guests receive invitations to the reception at the home of Nada's parents, Hamed and Behija, in al-A'adhamiya, at the end of January 1974.

Arriving just before dusk, Sabria, Yasin, Aqbal, Tariq and Amel disperse, as the tradition of the Mahar demands, into separate rooms, one for the men, another for the women. Sabria and her teenagers, Aqbal and Amel, are barely able to maintain their composure in all the excitement. Although Nabeel is the third son he is the first of the Yasin boys to marry. The prospect of a wedding, even a pared-down one, has them revelling in glamour and ceremony. The girls have spent hours choosing clothes and discussing their makeup and are now transformed into beautiful young women. Their long satin dresses are complemented with scarves, bangles, necklaces and decorated shoes. Sabria dresses simply, as always, in her favourite cotton *thawb*.

Nada sits in the centre of the sitting room, perched demurely on a chair. She is wearing a white, silver and black satin robe. Sabria, Aqbal and Amel go to her.

'You look beautiful,' Sabria says, taking in the clear eyes and serene face. 'And this dress? It cannot be Selwa's?'

'No, Aunt. It's from Tawfiq. Selwa's dress fits well enough but Tawfiq designed this specially.'

'He has been busy, what with Nabeel's suit too. How lucky we are to know Baghdad's best tailor.' Sabria, looking as though she might burst into tears, stands to one side to admire Nada. The dress has been made with great care: the front panels and cuffs are adorned with fine beadwork. With a few family heirlooms – a necklace, bracelets and earrings – Nada makes an incomparable bride.

'Aunt, I want the waiting to be over. I'm worried about Nabeel. You know how he is sometimes, forgetful and anxious. Do you know if he managed to collect his suit?'

Nabeel's suit has been a mystery to everyone. No one except him has seen it and Tawfiq had not finished it when Nada last heard. Originally Nabeel had gone to see his friend with his own idea of what he should wear for the big occasion, a camel-coloured, double-breasted alpaca with wide lapels and a pat-terned lining. Tawfiq had refused to consider it. 'Nabeel, you are a friend so do not be offended, but that is not right for a wedding. You are the poet. Let me be the tailor.' With that, he had pulled down a bale of pale blue gabardine with a sheen and thrown it open in the shop. 'It came in this morning. Look, very special,' he had said gleefully. 'It's from Greece.'

'Nada, the suit will be fine.' Sabria reaches for Umaima and Selwa, who have been fussing behind their sister, arranging the tendrils of her hair and adjusting the other chairs in the room. Nada jumps up to embrace Aqbal and Amel and soon they are talking and giggling together.

As the room fills, the guests are offered glasses of juice from silver trays. Sabria looks for Behija and sees her instructing a young cousin on how to carry one of the trays. Ordinarily she might have felt like an outsider, but they are making her so welcome. It had been a relief to discover that the other family is without airs. Behija comes across and embraces her. 'Are we not two proud mothers today? I think the union will be a good one.' Then, leaning into Sabria, she whispers, '*Inshallah*, they will bless us with grandchildren before too long.'

Sabria makes a blessing with her hands. Behija may already be praying for grandchildren but Sabria is still giving thanks that the wedding is taking place. It had almost never happened. First, a cousin had discovered that Nada had been lying to her parents – telling them she was staying late at the library to study when in fact she was with Nabeel – and had threatened to tell her father. Then Nabeel had announced to Sabria and Yasin that he intended to marry Nada but he would ask her father *himself* for his daughter's hand. Sabria had rebuked him. While she understood his need to strike out against the old way of doing things she knew that Hamed would almost certainly be offended. The rites of marriage had remained the same for generations. The elder men of the groom's family would sit with those of the bride's family. They would make conversation and drink before finally making their request on the absent groom's behalf. Hamed would expect this. 'Hamed and Behija have four daughters, and they are very wealthy. Hamed will not consider a proposal made in any other way. These traditions exist not for you but for them.' Even the usually unpartisan Yasin had voiced his disapproval. He had been looking forward to the day when he would go to meet the estimable Hamed to discuss the union of their families.

But Nabeel had gone alone to request Hamed's permission to marry his daughter. Hamed, as Sabria and Yasin had predicted, had turned white with shock at the impertinence but he loved his daughter and respected her choice of husband. 'Send your father and uncles. I will speak about the matter when they come.'

'Uncle Hamed, I will give you my word that my family will return to ask you again in the proper way. I have to know that you will grant us your permission.'

Outside the door he and Hamed could hear Nada and her sister Noha whispering and scurrying about. Whether it was they who softened Hamed or his potential father-in-law's desire to free himself from the tricky situation, Nabeel wasn't sure. At any rate, he relented and agreed to bless the engagement, the *Khotoba*, as long as Yasin came to him immediately.

'From now on you do things by the book,' Sabria told him. 'You are fortunate that Baba was able to make a good case for you. Hamed recognises a good man when he sees one. It is only because they know Nada loves you that they are willing to overlook the insult. Do not expect them to tolerate any more of your nonsense. Since you seem not to care what kind of wedding you have, you should agree to one that will bring happiness to those who do care.' Nabeel had thrown up his hands and marched out, knowing that, as ever, she was right.

The Mufti of Baghdad who comes to perform the service wears a thick, embroidered cotton robe and cap. His arrival at the house signals that the ceremony is about to begin, and after a brief round of introductions a hush descends on both rooms. The women settle into their seats behind the bride, and even the children are quiet. Nada's neice, Umaima's little girl, who has spent the previous half-hour tearing around, now stands still as her mother strokes the shiny black hair that curls above her collar.

Leaving the door between the men's and women's quarters ajar, the Mufti begins the short ceremonial in front of Nabeel. His voice is strong and firm, carrying through the high ceilings of the hall to the women's room.

'Are you Nabeel Yasin?'

'Yes.' Nabeel's voice is clear and confident.

Nada, sitting in her yellow-upholstered chair, is stiff in anticipation.

'Do you take Nada Al Hashimy to be your wife?'

'Yes.'

At this simple word Nada's eyes, which have been shut, fly open. As Nabeel and his two witnesses step forward to sign the marriage ledger, the Mufti walks into the adjoining room and stands before her.

'You are Nada Al Hashimy?'

'Yes.'

'Do you take Nabeel Yasin to be your husband?'

In her enthusiasm, Nada forgets the long-held tradition that demands a bride remain silent the first time this question is asked. 'Yes,' she blurts. Behija clamps a hand across her daughter's mouth and her sisters dissolve into fits of giggles. 'Nada, do not answer him yet! What are you thinking?' she hisses.

Sabria smiles at Nada, so eager. However much in love a bride may be, she *never* answers yes at the first call. She must remain composed and keep her groom guessing. Sabria had heard of weddings where a sister or an aunt had leaned into the bride with a timely reason why she should not marry the man chosen for her – if she had never seen him, she relied on the intervention of others. *He is fat and ugly. I have seen him with my own eyes. You cannot marry him. He has no money.* Of course, it is different for Nada and Nabeel. They know one another and understand the commitment they are making.

To the Mufti's third asking, the bride responds with a confident 'Yes.'

With the ceremony complete, the women rise to greet the groom as he is led to the threshold of their chamber. 'Nabeel!' they chant, gathering behind Nada to pour their blessings on him. 'We bless you. May you live in peace with your wife and bear many children.'

And Nabeel makes his own salutations in return.

After the ceremony the traditional feast, Quzi, begins. Dishes are brought out and placed in long rows on trestle tables along the back wall of the dining room. Each vast oval dish is filled with rice, sultanas, almonds and pine nuts, topped with pieces of slow-cooked lamb. Later, there are sweets, and mounds of fresh fruits, apricots, peaches, pomegranates and soft dates piled in decorative glass bowls. The men and then the women fill their plates and, sitting where they can, begin to eat. The bride and groom sit together.

Later as formality gives way to celebration and the wedding cake is brought out, Makkya and Sabria snatch a sisterly conversation.

'Don't be sad.'

'Ah, Makkya. Can you believe it? Number three marries first.' Sabria is close to tears as she puffs at her cigarette.

'And you could not hope for a better daughter-in-law. You have done all a mother can. Any fool can see they're a good match.'

'This is true. She is like a daughter to me and she has the measure of Nabeel, that is certain.'

'It is you that presents the only problem here,' Makkya laughs, 'you are going to be a most formidable *hamah*!'

As Nabeel and Nada cut the cake, Sabria gazes down at the henna tattoos on the backs of her hands. In the lamplight they are like blurred squares of black ink. They have been there for a long time now, done by a woman from the village when she was a small child, not even five, as a sign of her devotion. And though her knowledge of the world has changed, her faith remains the same.

She is glad that Nabeel and Nada have been able to choose each other. She had been fourteen when she was sent to marry Yasin, a man she had never set eyes on. In the absence of her father, a rice merchant who had died when she was two, her mother had been keen to see each of her daughters married as soon as possible. Yasin had asked her brother Karim. Having worked with him on the railways for several years, Karim knew that Yasin was trustworthy and needed a wife: he was a widower with one son, Khawwam. An arrangement between the two sides had been easily struck.

Sabria had not been afraid, but she had thought about what she would do if she did not care for the man they had chosen.

She pestered her mother and sisters for snippets of information, making it her business to learn more about Yasin. 'He is good. He is a kind man, with a job. He will care for you well,' her sister had told her. 'Your brother Karim says his heart is big.' But while Sabria could not deny that what they said of him was good, much was left unsaid. Into this chasm she dared not venture. Instead she had lain awake through her last nights at home thanking the almighty for providing her with a future. In marriage, she would be given the chance of motherhood. And, whatever else life held in store for her, a finer role than this was unimaginable.

On the day, her sisters had combed and braided her hair, washed and dressed her and brought her out for the women of the neighbourhood to cluck over. In bright robes they had chanted farewell laments and danced to songs that promised fertility and good fortune. As dusk turned to darkness they led her out of the house in her finery and walked her down the dry track to her new home.

The instant she saw Yasin she had understood what her family had been keeping from her. He was old, with a face lined by experience and a head of white hair. While they had blessed her with songs of hope no one had thought to mention this fact. She had been left her to discover it for herself.

But she had grown quickly to love Yasin. He had turned out to be a good husband and had always taken care of her, working hard and without complaint. And now there are her seven children to show for their life together.

She wonders if Nada and Nabeel will give her the grandchildren she craves. Perhaps, like many modern women, Nada will leave it for a while. Certainly the two of them prefer to do things in their own way when it comes to their living arrangements. Rather than moving in with her and Yasin, they will go to the mansion that Nada's father had built a few years earlier in fashionable al-Mansour. Nada had taken her to see it while workmen were redecorating. Sabria had been awestruck by its size. 'All this for two people!' With its whitewashed façade and large French windows, it is as big as the Yasins' new home in the al-Sayydia district. Sabria had been upset that Nabeel was going, but he will not move out until the Zafaf, the high-spirited celebration of thanks that marks the end of the wedding

Wedding (Selwa, Nada, Umaima)

rituals, so she has him for a few more months. After that, if she is lucky, the babies will come.

Taking two glasses of tea from Nada's sister Umaima, Sabria goes to sit with her daughter-in-law. 'You will come to see me often, I hope,' she says.

'Aunty, we shall be at your table every other evening.'

'Good. You must let my other sons and my daughters take you out dancing or to the cinema, perhaps to the ballet.'

'Yes, and Nabeel must get to know Mama and Baba properly. It is not always easy at the beginning for a husband.'

'It will soon be second nature. You will have a house together and perhaps be thinking of starting a family of your own.'

Nada clasps Sabria's wrist. She has been expecting such interest from both mothers and is eager to divert it. 'Tell me, Aunty, am I supposed to cook for him every day? I cannot even boil an egg. I think his stomach will suffer going from you to me!'

'Ah, on that matter, I have already spoken with your mother. Whenever you need it, she will bring hot food to you. And I will have a stack of flatbread wrapped in a cloth for you to take home each time you visit. So, if you don't want to starve you had better visit us often. Now drink up! I should study the leaves.'

A Meeting with Saddam, His Excellency
the Deputy
March 1976

Standing in the nursery surrounded by a neat pile of white
baby linen, Nada is glad that only a few days remain before
the baby is due. Several little white robes, some loose vests,
the muslin cloths that everyone has told her will be indis-
pensable, wool and cotton blankets are folded in readiness.
This baby will be a stranger to them both, she thinks, yet they
are responsible for its well-being. She has tried to prepare but
it seems to be more a question of instinct than of application.
The baby is coming, regardless of anything else, and though
they had not planned it, it had always been going to happen.
She can't help but wonder at how destiny has caught up with
her.

At the beginning of their marriage they had agreed not to be
caught up in family life too soon. 'Art and children do not
mix. We are happy as we are, with our careers and each
other,' Nabeel had said, whenever their mothers had raised
the subject. Nada agreed. She had seen how her father, having
raised four girls to adulthood, had ended up as little more
than their taxi-driver, ferrying them to and from university,

friends' houses and then to work. Besides, Nabeel had not been ready for such responsibility. Aside from his love for her, poetry and politics were all that his heart had space for. Lost in his imagination, he was happiest with abstract ideas and his poetry. It seems only right that, following the success of *Brother Yasin*, his epic on faith and family, he should have the chance to reach the pinnacle of the literary world.

She had her own career plans, too. After leaving the al-Maktaba al-Watania library she had got a job at the Ministry of Culture and promotion was imminent. Even now she plans to return to work: her mother has agreed to help with the baby. She has always loved her job, rising early to begin indexing the documents that pour in. Her love of order seems ironic when she considers her choice of husband: Nabeel is a man whose possessions and mind unravel around him.

How quickly things change, she thinks, as the baby moves inside her.

She sets down the last pile of baby clothes and goes downstairs, then out into the garden that surrounds the house with greenery. There, she settles into one of the large wooden chairs, carved by Nabeel's cousin Kamil. He had given it to them with the bedroom furniture as a wedding present and she thinks it extraordinarily beautiful. Of all the gifts they received, his exquisite carpentry, with its carved flowers, trees, animals and ornate swirls, is her favourite.

She wonders if Nabeel has managed to finish his two articles for *Alif-Baa*. Perhaps he will be home early so that they can eat together. She hopes, despite the looming deadlines, that he will finish on time for once. She is feeling lazy and wants him to look after her. And she misses him. There are visitors every day, her sisters, cousins and mother-in-law, bringing fruit and advice, but it is her husband she craves.

The cool March breeze feels good on her face. She is lucky to have been pregnant through the winter and early spring. Any later and the heat would have made this arduous experience intolerable. Had Behija planned this too, she wonders. She is no longer as angry as she was when she discovered what her mother had done, but it still bewilders her. This pregnancy was all her mother's doing.

They might never have known of Behija's scheme but for Selwa's loose tongue. Always bad at keeping secrets, she had made some remark about 'the pills', which she had then tried to cover up. When pressed, she had told Nada what she knew. 'Mama was worried.'

'About what?' Nada asked.

'She didn't know why there was no baby after so long. I had to tell her because she was worried that the marriage was not . . . a good one.'

'Selwa, I don't understand,' Nabeel had interrupted.

'Don't be angry. Nada is pregnant now and everyone is happy. Where is the problem?'

'Tell me.'

'Look, she asked me why there were no children and—'

'And?' Nada and Nabeel chorus.

'I told her your marriage is real and good, but that you use birth control. I couldn't leave her worrying.'

'How could you say such a thing?' Nada had been incensed.

Nabeel had left the room. He knew that this had been the invitation Behija needed to meddle in their lives.

And indeed she had made the arrival of a grandchild her primary objective. She had enlisted the help of the family's gynaecologist, who had known Nada since she was a child.

'Every woman needs a child. We must get rid of everything Nada is using.'

The doctor called Nada in for routine tests, and told her she must dispense with whatever pills she was taking. 'It is dangerous for you. And do not worry, you will not be able to conceive even if you try.' Perplexed, Nada had obeyed while Behija had ransacked the bedroom at Al Mansour and taken away the remaining tablets.

Now, sitting peacefully beneath the orange tree, she accepts the episode as fate at work. She knows that, for her mother's generation, a child was Allah's most precious gift. Neither her proofreading and editing nor any of her other aspirations – poetry, travel, even love – counted in her mother's eyes as a grandchild would. Like Sabria, Behija adheres to the idea that nothing comes above the furthering of family.

And so many people are eager to help with the child when he or she comes. The knowledge that a loving family will envelop her baby, showering it with affection, pleases her. Suddenly she hears someone knocking urgently at the gate.

For Nabeel the day at *Alif-Baa* promises to be busy. The editorial team are finishing off the latest issue and his office is stacked with papers, he has two pieces to finish and other articles to edit. They are a small team at this political arts magazine, and they make it a rule to edit each other's work. Still, today he is longing to put down his pen and go home. Anywhere would be better than this airless box on a day like today. He is contemplating disappearing for some coffee when

Ibtisam, the journalist with whom he shares his office, rushes in, breathless and anxious.

'Barzan Tikriti is about to summon you,' she stammers. 'You are being asked to go and see His Excellency the Deputy, Saddam Hussein. I have been told to tell you to sit by the phone and wait for the call.'

'Saddam Hussein's brother has called me?' Nabeel swings round in his chair. 'Who told you?'

She opens her mouth to answer, but is interrupted by the editor and his secretary who have followed her in. 'We have a big problem.' Khalid, the editor, looks gravely at Nabeel.

Nabeel nods. 'I know. I've heard. You expect me to sit here and wait for them to call?'

'Yes, I'm afraid I do. It comes from His Excellency the Deputy himself. When his department calls, you will do precisely as they tell you. Do you understand?'

Nabeel understands only too well.

'And when you get there, say nothing. Even when you get to his headquarters and people are talking all around you,' warns Khalid's secretary, a recent Ba'athist convert. 'His Excellency the Deputy will read your eyes. He will know what is in your heart and mind.' He examines his fingernails. 'Be careful, Nabeel.'

Nabeel laughs openly. 'So he's added X-ray vision and mind-reading to his many other talents?'

'You would do well not to laugh about it. His Excellency the Deputy *can* read your mind – he reads everybody's thoughts. That is his gift.'

This way of referring to Saddam Hussein still puzzles Nabeel. Why are they no longer allowed to refer to the man by his name?

When the order had first come to the office Nabeel had

mocked it. Ibtisam had been harsh with him. 'Don't be a fool,' she had hissed. 'There are people watching us and notes are being taken. They will have you arrested.'

He knew this to be true. He and a colleague, Kadim, had once broken into the large grey filing cabinets of the personnel offices at the magazine. Kadim had picked the locks and Nabeel had removed three thick files on himself. Inside, documents from several colleagues reported on his movements. Page after page of intelligence, detailing anti-Ba'athist gibes he had made, clothes he had worn, people he had spoken to on the phone, restaurants he had eaten at. It seemed that no detail was too small to be included.

Now it seems he is to be taken in anyway. 'Why now, Khalid? There is always trouble over my articles.'

'Your echo is too loud, Nabeel, and your shadow too long. His Excellency the Deputy doesn't like you. You are popular, but you are anti-Ba'athist. It is clear in everything you write. You tell the world you do not like their attitude or their smugness, and people listen. Surely that is enough of a reason.' Khalid rarely spares him the truth. He is an honest, clever man whose opinions are to be trusted.

'You know I cannot promise to be silent if he abuses me. I will not.'

Khalid ushers the others out and closes the door behind them. He goes to Nabeel's desk and looks him straight in the eye. 'We had better hope that it is a warning, designed to scare us, and no more. You know their reputation. His Excellency the Deputy does not forget his enemies. And because I have tried to protect you, they will come for me too so, please, think before you act. Be smart. Be calm. You are a clever man. Do not be pig-headed. Save yourself and me any more trouble. Tell them what they want to hear.

You can be sure that His Excellency the Deputy will try to provoke you. He knows you are difficult and hot-headed, and that you will not accept compromise, so he will push you to join the Party. If you refuse him, well, you must be prepared for whatever happens.'

Nabeel nods. There have been many problems over the past five years. They have arrested and beaten him several more times since his début at the Writers' Union, but it is their attempts to deny his voice by banning him from Iraqi television and radio that have been the biggest blow. He lost his job five times in the previous year, relying on close friends to save him from penury.

The previous New Year's Eve, when he and Nada had been at a party with friends, Khalid had drawn him aside. 'You may be happy now, but there are problems ahead for us all,' he had warned. When Nabeel pressed him he had refused to elaborate. 'Another time. Let's enjoy the party while we can.' Nabeel had thought it must be the series of articles he'd written to mark International Women's Year. They had attracted much criticism in Iraq, which still amazed him; they were far less incendiary than most of his other writings. He had interviewed women of all ages and backgrounds about their hopes and dreams, their careers, their divorces, their ideas about fulfilment and the law. Some in the Party considered them anti-Islamic. Wali Baghdad, Saddam Hussein's uncle and the city's mayor, had used the furore to further his campaign against Nabeel. Together with Barzan Tikriti, he had proclaimed the articles profane, an insult to Islam, and took great delight in exhibiting letters of outrage and disgust from the country's most conservative towns, Tikrit, Fallujah and other towns, in the leading newspaper *Athawra* before sending them to

Saddam. Now, sitting opposite Khalid, Nabeel understands that it is neither these words nor any of his writing that is at fault. It is *he himself* who is the problem.

He can no longer place his colleagues in the firing line. Khalid, though a Ba'athist, has been loyal, allowing him to write without censorship, defending him in numerous editorial policy meetings against the petty bureaucracy of the Ba'athist Office of Culture and Media. Now, as he watches the cigarette smoke rise into the air and form a canopy above them, he knows his friend's loyalty must be repaid. Thus, at noon, when the beige telephone on his desk rings he picks it up and, in a few words, agrees to their demands.

'They are sending a car for us. Khalid and I are to be driven to the office of His Excellency the Deputy,' he tells Ibtisam, after he has replaced the receiver. 'He will see us at one.'

◆

The entourage of Mercedes 280's that collects the two men have blacked-out windows and contain ten plainclothes Mukhabarat officers. As Nabeel and Khalid sit in the back, they watch the city going about its business. The two officers remain silent.

'How ridiculous,' Nabeel whispers to Khalid, as they weave through the traffic towards the National Assembly, al-Majlis al-Watany, in Karkh, 'that they should want me to change my mind and become one of them. After everything I've said! Surely it would look stupid.'

'Please stay calm, Nabeel. This is not a game to be played with His Excellency the Deputy. He has the power to make things painful for both of us. Please remember that.'

They soon arrive at the reception building of the national assembly, Saddam Hussein's personal complex of offices on the banks of the Tigris. For many hundreds of years the area had been used for recreation but now anyone caught straying inside its boundaries is shot on sight. Inside the huge black and gold wrought-iron gates, the car stops. They are pulled out on to the concrete and strip-searched behind portable canvas screens. Pens, paper, money, cufflinks, all personal effects are taken from them. Then they are handed over to two military guards and marched in silence towards the main building.

'Such a shame,' Nabeel whispers. 'This is the best stretch of river. I used to play here when I was a boy.' Khalid does not reply but Nabeel remembers watching his friends swim across to the al-Rusafa side as he sat on the Karkh bank. Unable to swim, he had waved to them. During the building's construction, he had pestered the builders for offcuts of the smooth cream stone brought in daily from Palestine by the dusty lorryload. 'Uncle, Uncle,' he and his friends would shout, 'give us some and we will leave you in peace.' At home, he, his brothers and cousins had chipped holes in the slabs with chisels and fixed them to lengths of iron piping, turning them into dumbbells.

Now their playground is a military zone with sentry posts and razor wire. The people who once fished here and the boys who had watched for the sparrows on the date trees are long gone.

The guards lead them on through a set of vast armour-plated doors and, once inside the central block, down an endlessly curving corridor with door after anonymous door leading off it. Finally they arrive in a long, narrow room and are told to wait. Waiting is a normal part of the Ba'ath tactics of intimidation. The longer a man has to wait, without pen, paper, a book, even the opportunity for free conversation, the more time he has to think, wonder, worry and, eventually, fall to pieces. There is nothing to do but ask the same questions over and over again. How long will I be here? What do they want? What will they do to me?

For two hours the men sit in silence barely daring to look at each other. Then a lock turns and the door is pushed open. Nabeel's heart sinks. The man standing in front of them is Tariq Aziz, minister of media and culture, one of the Ba'athist luminaries, and also one of its most reviled. 'His Excellency the Deputy will not be seeing you, after all. He has been called to meet with the Vietnamese Deputy Prime Minister. However, he and I have discussed your case and I have a message for each of you from him. Your fate, if you will.'

This cannot be good. If anyone could hate Nabeel more than His Excellency the Deputy it was Aziz. They had come to blows in 1968, when Nabeel was a young reporter at *Athawra*. Aziz, cultural minister for the newly victorious Ba'athists, had begun his purge of ideologically unsuitable writers the day the Party took control. Although Nabeel had tried to hold on, reminding himself that he should 'be tougher than they are, and remember the Ba'athist aim is to delete all other philosophies', he had buckled. Aziz had been deliberately provocative: 'This is *our* newspaper, now. And our homeland, too. You and your comrades have failed.'

'You are wrong. No one can own a country or its people.'

'So idealistic, Nabeel! This is a new age. And the people need our vision and our rules if they are to prosper. Not your weak philosophies. Strength is the only thing people truly respect or need to live happily.'

At this Nabeel had lunged for Aziz over the desk. 'You lie. You want dictatorship. Power for its own sake.'

Aziz tapped the dial of the telephone on his desk. 'A professional man should not be so angry. What you fail to grasp is that people are joining us of their own free will. They accept what we are offering. As for you, I would be careful what you say to me from now on. I can bring the secret police in to remove you at any time.' Nabeel had ripped the telephone out of its socket and thrown it across the room.

In the intervening years Aziz has risen to become one of Saddam Hussein's highest-ranking aides and the architect of many of the Ba'ath Party's policies of fear and intimidation. It seems he has kept half an eye open for his old enemies too, making his presence felt in petty, intrusive ways. It was he who instructed the civil intelligence service to follow Nabeel. It was he who had signed the order denying Nada the right to enter the Ministry of Culture by the main door so she has had to use an entrance in a shabby back-street where petty criminals and black-marketeers ply their trades. The deliberate humiliation of a pregnant woman is entirely intentional: it is intrinsic to Aziz's latest brainchild, the Conversion Programme as Nabeel calls it. A vicious strategy, it focuses on coercing ordinary people into supporting the Party, by dishonouring them in front of their peers at work, perhaps by exposing some small secret, or refusing their children a food or medicine allowance. In this way anxious families are sucked into the fold, and more extreme measures, such as kidnap, blackmail and torture, are avoided.

And here they are, facing each other again. Nabeel nods at

Aziz. '*Marhaba*,' he says, deliberately informal. There is no point in being afraid. Jail is a threat, but he does not believe they will kill him. He is too well known. Ignoring Nabeel, Aziz turns to Khalid. 'You are fired,' he says coldly. 'Effective immediately.'

'But Khalid has done nothing wrong,' exclaims Nabeel. 'He is a member of the Party! A supporter.'

'You are sacked too, Nabeel,' Aziz continues implacably, turning to him as the guards remove Khalid from the room. 'But we realise that that is not enough to silence a mouth as big as yours. You and your family, will you never give up? So, there is more for you. From this moment you are an Enemy of the State. You are banned from working and publishing in Iraq. You have been placed on the government's blacklist, and we have withdrawn all material you have published from our public institutions and libraries. You are forbidden to travel and your passport will be revoked.'

The guards come towards Nabeel and, as one holds him, the other pulls out his identity papers and spreads them across a small console table. They open a large rubber-stamp block and hammer the words 'Enemy of the State' on to each page and enter the details in a log.

'Every police branch, every government office, every place of work, every border and port in the country will be informed.' Aziz's stare carries a hint of amusement, knowing that this is the one punishment that will cripple Nabeel. 'Now, since there is nowhere left for you to peddle your opinions, I suggest you go home, back to the scum that is your family. And do not think of protesting. We will be watching you and your Communist brothers even more closely than we have been until now. If you speak out again, you will find your-selves in the stadium, and you know how well we treat our guests there. I hope in the many years of idleness that lie ahead you will reconsider your choices and reflect on the things you have written. It will be hard for you without work. Especially with your wife about to have a baby.'

As he turns to go, he raises an eyebrow. 'There really is nothing left for you now.'

Three days later Nada goes into labour. She and Nabeel are at home, coming to terms with the news, when the contractions start. After calling for Nada's parents, who have promised to drive them to hospital, Nabeel double-checks the hospital bag and diligently counts the minutes between the tides of pain. By the time they arrive at the al-Hayderi maternity hospital, Nada is clutching him, her mother, even the car seat, unable to endure the agony any longer. 'It is the best hospital. They will make everything good for you.' Behija tries to comfort her daughter with soft words of experience. Nabeel is silent.

As he sits outside the ward on a long wooden bench with other expectant fathers, Nabeel's thoughts ricochet between his worry for Nada and his fears for how they will cope without money. He needs to be a good father, husband, provider, but how? As an Enemy of the State, he is no better than a beggar. Materially they are not in trouble yet; there is a house, furniture, a car, even Nada's job waiting for her after her maternity leave, but it will not be enough. Without his income they will slide into poverty. The car will be sold first, then the house and after that what will they do? They cannot live off others. For several years now he has provided Yasin with a living allowance for his parents.

But Nada's father has already embraced the imminent matter of the hospital bill and told him not to worry. 'It will be taken care of,' he said. 'We are your family.' He is grateful but he cannot let this happen again. As for his own family he knows that everyone will donate part of their own much-needed salary, or offer a portion of their savings, without question, to help them.

At just after midnight, a nurse walks out into the corridor and gives him the news. 'Your wife has had a baby boy,' she says, gesturing to the delivery room. 'You can go in, if you would like.'

His worry is forgotten, and he is seized by the moment. Skidding towards the glass wall of the delivery room, he stops at the sight of the tiny baby sleeping on the other side of the glass. His firstborn son, with long tufts of black hair, shrouded in a white blanket, and his wife, her arms around him, are lying together peacefully in bed.

By the following afternoon, news of the birth has spread through the family near and far. His own mother and father, brothers and sisters, Jafar, Juma'a, Jabbar, Aqbal, Tariq and Amel, Nada's sisters Selwa, Umaima and Noha, with their husbands and children, descend on the hospital with neighbours and friends from both sides of the family, some of whom Nabeel is not sure he has ever seen before. There is not one empty seat, and the corridor is filled with excited voices talking about the new arrival. Flowers lie against the back wall and as soon as mother and child are back at the family home with Behija these will be joined by gifts – toys, blankets, delicate gift boxes containing trinkets and gold charms of the Qu'ran, small blessings that mark the baby's entry to the world and protect him. The older women group round the baby, taking it in turns to hold him and make their own prayers and predictions. *Allah, may he bless this child. Allah, may he bless the mother of this child.* Nabeel feels giddy and unprepared. He doesn't want to leave Nada's side but knows he must work his way diligently round the room, like the good father. By the time Uncle Rashid comes to slap him on the back and push some money into his hands he has given up the pretence that he is anything other than overwhelmed. 'Thank you, Uncle! But of course you have heard the news – you know that poor Nada has two children to support.'

'Ah, Nabeel,' his uncle responds, 'you will be fine. Your luck has always been good.' They both laugh. Good old Rashid, straight to the heart of the matter.

Nabeel brings everyone together round the bed and announces that the baby will be called Yamam. 'It means dove and, yes, it is a new name, a modern name, but Nada loves doves and so do I. So Yamam it is.' They had discussed many times how they wanted a name that was entirely new, one that signified the beginning of their own tradition.

Sitting next to Nada, observing the scene of joy, he hears the clear, unmistakable voice of his mother cut through the hubbub. She is asking Nada if she can take Yamam on the seventh day.

'We must get him to an Imam,' she says. 'He must be blessed. The shrine of Moussa al-Qadim is close and we can plead for him there. We could be there and back in an afternoon. It shall be a most auspicious occasion. My first grandson, no less.' Although they are not devout, Nada and Nabeel agree to Sabria's request.

145

Sabria claps her hands. 'Good! I will take my sisters. Aunty Makkya can read the Du'a and Aunty Noua and I will call.'

The baby, limbs jerking and twitching involuntarily, wakes hungry. Nada knows he is more helpless than she could ever have imagined. It will take all their efforts to keep him safe. 'Will the world be frightening for him, Dudi?' she asks Nabeel.

'Sometimes it will,' he replies. 'But we will take care of him. That is our job now.'

Fourteen Fils
July 1977

Nabeel takes the pale blue gabardine suit out of the wardrobe and holds it up to the window. What stunning workmanship. Flawless stitching. Buttonholes and cuffs perfectly aligned. He hangs it on the hook by the door. He checks for a clean white shirt, then puts out two ties, one pale blue, the other patterned, ready to make the final choice when he wakes in the morning. His shoes wait downstairs by the back door. A last shine before he leaves, and he will look every inch the respectable citizen. In the meantime there is dinner with Mama and Baba.

In the bedroom Nada finishes dressing Yamam in a pair of rompers, white T-shirt and ankle booties, then goes to brush her hair, making brisk strokes through her gleaming, shoulder-length tresses.

'You wouldn't think hair could cause so much trouble, would you?' he calls to her.

'Are we talking about yours or mine?'

'Mine, of course. I'm going to cut it. Can you believe it? They are finally getting me to cut it.'

In the past three years the Ba'ath Party's Ethical Police had chased him on three separate occasions in their efforts to get him to cut it short. Their crackdowns were becoming increasingly bizarre, intrusive and humiliating. It is not only him: they have taken to splashing red paint on the legs of women caught wearing short skirts and they trail men with shoulder-length hair, looking for opportunities to arrest them and bring out their scissors on the street. Once he had been forced to jump out of a first-floor window to avoid a squad of the khaki-shirted killjoys. They had watched him drop to the ground, hoping no doubt he would break a leg, then chased him as far as the Tigris. He might have been forced to jump in, had a man not opened his door and let him hide in his house. It would all have been noted in his files at the militia HQ, along with his many other crimes.

'Nina,' he leans over his wife, using his pet name for her, 'can you believe it? After only a year as an Enemy of the State, they are going to let me work again. Ha! Tomorrow I will be a legitimate citizen once more!'

Nada fixes a grip at the side of her fringe but says nothing. It has been a difficult year. Even the Writers' Union and the executive committee of Iraqi journalists have snubbed him. Once he had been the talk of literary society with numerous friends but now the same people shun him: 'We like and respect you but we cannot support you, nor do we have the freedom to speak to you any more. We cannot overturn the decision of His Excellency the Deputy.'

'*Will not*, more like,' he had complained to Nada after another had disowned him. The most crushing blow of all had been the response of his publishers in Beirut who, without warning, had pulled out of printing a second volume of his latest work just weeks before it was due to go on sale. Publication, finally, of *The Poets Satirise the Kings* in Iraq would have made bearable all his other trials.

To know that his voice was being heard would have kept him buoyant.

Then, when all had seemed utterly lost and Nabeel had nowhere left to turn, the Communist paper *Tariq Ashaab*, sailing alone against the tide of complicity, had saved him. They suggested he write under a *nom de plume*, and he had, producing poems and articles under a host of pseudonyms. Of late the hitherto unknown Abu Yamam, Sahafi and his favourites Noon and NY have all made stinging attacks on the Ba'athists.

The editorial board at *Tariq Ashaab* have championed his cause, and through their endeavours he has been granted a meeting at the Secret Police HQ. Although he is not a Communist, the regular committee meetings they are obliged to attend with the Ba'athists have allowed respected voices to speak out on his behalf. 'They obviously need me,' he tells Nada. 'Few will speak out against His Excellency the Deputy or the Party now. And it is more important than ever that they should. I don't know of a single writer out there who hasn't been tortured or bribed. Even Hameed, who has always been a diplomatic voice, is under pressure now. Maybe I'm naïve but I think al-Jawarhiri will help me write again.' A powerful force within the Iraqi establishment, the poet al-Jawarhiri, who is the honoured President of the Iraqi Writers Union, has been petitioning Saddam for legitimate status to be restored to Nabeel.

'Let us hope he can,' Nada says. If the Secret Police are now monitoring Hameed's work, Fazia, his wife, would doubtless be in the same position as her soon. Supporting one's husband through isolation, persecution and arrest seems to be part of married life now. 'But you must not count on it. You know they may just be rubbing salt in the wound . . . or worse, Dudi.'

'I know. But just for tonight let me enjoy believing that things might change for the better.'

With Yamam on her hip, Nada rattles the car keys at her husband. They must go now for dinner with Sabria and Yasin.

'You are keeping me from my grandson,' Sabria tells them every time they visit. 'Yamam and Nada are strangers to me. How can you not feel guilty?'

Nabeel is grateful that his parents love Nada, but it is proving hard to balance all the sides of their two large families. They visit Yasin and Sabria once or twice a week, and still Sabria wants more. It is hardly surprising. She has lost one son and needs to keep her remaining family close to her. After a period of imprisonment for hosting a Communist rally, Jabbar has gone into voluntary exile to escape the Mukhabarat. He slipped across the border and has been living in France. And although Sabria had agreed with Yasin that Jabbar should leave Iraq until relations between the Ba'athists and the Communists had calmed down, it had been more upsetting when he left than any of them had imagined.

Nada and Nabeel shut the large iron gates, tumble into the Lada and drive the familiar route from al-Mansour to the house in al-Sayydia.

That night, although only the family are at the table, it is filled with small dishes. *Bamia*, rice, *mehshi* – stuffed auber-gines, vine leaves and courgettes – are spread out on floral plates. 'Where has it all come from?' Nabeel whispers to Nada. 'No one else has anything these days.'

'Aunty Sabria!' Nada calls, as Sabria disappears into the kitchen with Yamam. 'We are amazed at what you have found. But we are only *three* people and Yamam just a baby.'

Returning with a steaming bowl of *kubba* fresh from the oven, Sabria places it in the centre of the table and hands

Nada a spoon. 'The others will eat later,' she smiles, 'but you must have all that you want now. Do not hold back. To-morrow my table may be bare.'

Sabria knows it has not been easy for them. Recently the government stopped Yamam's milk allowance and Nabeel has been forced to find milk on the black-market. They are paying many dinars for the smallest tin. The previous month, Nabeel, Juma'a and Yasin had all had to search for it because Yamam's appetite had surged and they had run out more quickly than usual. It had taken two days to find some. That grown men could deny food to a baby!

'Juma'a will be sorry to miss out.' Nabeel does not want to dwell on hardship tonight. 'He would go anywhere if he thought there was food to be had.'

'Yes, but in these times, can you blame him?' Sabria hovers behind them, serving large helpings on to their plates.

Yasin has shuffled in from the reception room where he has been watching the nightly news and stands behind her. 'His Excellency the Deputy has saved us once again,' he says wearily. 'There is to be another grace-and-favour gift, *mak-rouma*. Frozen lamb from New Zealand in the markets for the next week.'

Juma'a calls the shortages the 'Ba'athist Policy of Crises'. The aim, as far as they can make out, is simple. By disman-tling the city's infrastructure, withdrawing food shipments, switching bus routes, withdrawing Baghdad's taxi service or intermittently closing the borders, His Excellency the Deputy ensures that people are unable to think beyond survival. Lack of food subdues people. Having done an inventory of every house in the country, the intelligence services calculated a strict allowance for each household to be purchased at authorised shops; sixteen eggs and a frozen chicken are distributed by one shop, onions and milk powder by another, fruit and vegetable from the next. Some weeks the food is there, others there is nothing. Stamps in a logbook expose those who try to obtain more than their share. Most people are so concerned with getting enough food for their families that all thought of politics and competing ideologies has evaporated.

The latest insult was a daily newspaper column and TV show, where, His Excellency the Deputy, told housewives how to cook rice or prepare meat. 'Presuming they have stocks of either! Can you imagine being told how to boil rice by that man?' Sabria and her friends had fallen about laughing at the impudence when the first article had appeared. 'I doubt he has ever held a spoon in his life, let alone put anything in a pan to boil.'

Sabria ladles more rice on to their plates. 'What is your news?'

'Mama, you saw us last week.'

Nada kicks him under the table. 'Dudi,' she whispers, 'tell her about your interview tomorrow. She will squeeze it out of you sooner or later.'

He follows his mother into the kitchen and leans against the doorframe. 'Mama, there may be some good news. *Tariq Ashaab* have put my case to the Ba'athists and I have been called in to the security headquarters tomorrow.'

'What?' She does not turn but continues filling the glass jug.

'They may overturn my blacklist status. They are saying I am an important voice and that Iraq needs independent writers. I would criticise the Communists as readily as the Ba'ath. With any luck I should be free to work and travel again.'

'And who are "they"?'

'Al-Jawarhiri, the poet, is leading them. He wrote to them on my behalf and the security forces have said they'll consider

it favourably.' Refusing to meet his eye, Sabria slips effortlessly past him back towards the dining table.

'And what about your other poet friend, al-Kamali?' She
huffs irritably. 'Did he not do this for you and fail last
December? Do you not think there might be another reason
behind this visit? Should you not be worried about walking
into that building again?'

'Al-Kamali failed because he had no influence. I asked him
to pass the request to His Excellency the Deputy, but he said,
"Nabeel, I was once minister of culture and a Ba'athist leader
but I don't get on with the deputy and he doesn't like me much
either. If I ask him this favour he is as likely to arrest you as he
is to grant your wishes." With al-Jawarhiri it is different. He
is respected everywhere. I have a real chance this time.'

'If you go, be it on your head.' This is not the reaction he
had wanted.

Sabria places the jug on the table and, pushing a pink radish
on to Nada's plate, looks up at her son. 'Do you really think
anyone can help? How long can you go on like this?'

'Mama, if nothing happens then Hameed says the Communists will find me work . . . in Sofia.' He puts a handful of
kubba on to his plate. It is the first time he has ever mentioned
leaving Iraq. 'The Bulgarian newspapers are short of writers.'

Sabria is about to scold him for even considering exile but
realises there is no need: without a passport he cannot go
anywhere. 'No more, Nabeel! Please, let us talk of happier
things,' she commands, with an imperious wave of her hand.

It is just before nine when he approaches the looming edifice
of the intelligence headquarters and pulls off into a side-street

to park the car. He has chosen a quiet one, far away from the patrolling guards. He will walk the rest of the way. The car is new, ordered nearly two years ago when he was still able to work, and he doesn't want its number-plate in their files. One cigarette later, he is at the main gate being frisked. From there he is taken straight to a holding room, somewhere deep in the building. He is ready for the long wait, but at the sound of the door locking behind him his heart begins to race. The room is windowless and, other than a single plastic chair, completely empty. The stark uniformity of the whitewashed concrete walls and strips of neon lighting are broken only by the steel-edged door. From a hole in the corner of the roof, a motionless black video-camera is trained on him.

He tries to occupy himself by strolling round the room, picturing himself wandering through the Souq al-Saray book market. Later, he slumps in the hard chair, his legs crossed in the most relaxed manner he can muster. He tries to think of some unfinished verse, images from some of his earlier poems. He doesn't want to give them the satisfaction of watching him wilt. Only after he feels the first beads of sweat on the back of his head does he sit up. Is it his imagination or is the temperature rising?

They have turned off the air-conditioning and the sweat rolls down the back of his neck and inside his shirt. He reminds himself it is all part of the strategy, part of the game. But such thoughts don't last long with the panic that sets in. This is supposed to be a good meeting and he is already feeling irritable and too thirsty to concentrate. His mouth is dry and he can think only of slaking his thirst. He is close to passing out when the lock turns and a uniformed man asks if he would like a glass of water. He can hardly move his tongue but he tells the guard he is not thirsty.

'No matter,' the man replies, as he closes the door, 'I'll ask again later.' Whether the man bothers to return is neither here nor there. Nabeel knows he will continue to refuse. He has not forgotten what happened to Cousin Abdul Razaq.

Abdul Razaq had been in his forties, living with his mother in a small apartment in Athawra City, the poorest part of Baghdad, when they came for him. Poor and uneducated, he had worked relentlessly to keep them both out of poverty, slaving at one of the tobacco plants, often working two or three shifts in a row. He had been a grassroots Communist, an old-fashioned member of the proletarian underclass, full of dreams of overthrowing the ruling élite. In publicly denouncing the National Front and proclaiming the Communists the 'lapdogs of the Ba'ath Party', he had become infamous in some quarters for his outspoken beliefs.

Yet despite his loquaciousness he posed no threat to the regime. Most people, family and friends alike, saw him as no more than a lone voice. Not so the authorities. His death was meant as a warning to the rest of the family that dissent, no matter how humble the perpetrator, would be crushed. They had murdered him slowly, in a cowardly way. He had been arrested one afternoon when he got in from work and taken for questioning. They left him to wait for many hours, then gave him a gold-painted glass of tea, laced with thallium. He knew nothing until it was too late.

Thallium works slowly, destroying the body gradually, until the vital organs collapse. There is neither antidote nor reprieve. For Abdul it had started with a stomach-ache. Walking back to his house after the Intelligence Service had let him go, he had begun to feel a creeping nausea. He had put it down to the stress of the experience and his relief at being discharged. A couple of days later, when he noticed his unusual fatigue and a tremor in his fingertips, he wondered if there was more to it. A week later, when his hair was dropping out in clumps and the shakes had set in, it was too late.

The doctors could do nothing. They performed blood tests and concluded that he had been poisoned. As his stomach collapsed in on itself, Abdul took to his bed, unable to speak, and waited for the end. Because he could not swallow he began to vomit, first the contents of his stomach and finally, when nothing his mother gave him would stay down, bile and blood.

This is the Ba'ath way. Nabeel knows that they still use snakes, releasing them into prison cells and that they lace food with poison. Or kidnap wives to lure their husbands to secret places. They are beginning to favour the clandestine approach. A few years ago the Secret Police had beaten Nabeel on the street. Now, 'accidents', 'suicide' or 'misfortune' are commonplace.

He guesses it must be after one o'clock when the door is unlocked again and the guard motions to him with his rifle. He is led across to the main building, past heavily guarded buildings and huts. Two young sentries, holding cigarettes under a date palm, watch him pass and he can taste the sweet smoke at the back of his throat.

They come to a huge black iron door on the far side of the main building. The guard unlocks it and steps inside, his machine-gun hitting the metal frame. Nabeel follows him along the dim corridor, which, as the weighted door slams shut, turns pitch black. At the end they emerge into a small concrete hall. In the centre is a chair, and in front of it a raised wooden platform. He is told to sit. Above him a single spotlight breaks the room into shadows. This is not a room for an informal discussion.

After some time a stocky little man with short, greased-back hair appears from the darkness, wearing dark glasses. He strides on to the wooden platform without acknowledging Nabeel's presence. His face is tanned and a thick black moustache covers his upper lip. A short-sleeved summer uniform shirt reveals nut-brown arms. He settles in a chair on the platform, pulls up the knees of his grey flannel trousers and opens a rust-brown file he has brought in with him. There appears to be a great sheaf of papers inside it. Nabeel gazes up at him but with the spotlight shining between them he cannot make out the man's expression. The opaque glasses hide everything.

'Your name.' The voice is clipped, neutral. It betrays nothing.

'Nabeel Yasin,' he replies.

'Your address.'

In the days preceding this appointment Nabeel has re-hearsed the answer to this crucial question many times, deliberating long and hard about whether to risk lying. Since the ID card system's fatal flaw is the absence of an address – it gives only a person's name, date of birth, occupation and the precinct from which they obtained it – the Ba'athists are obliged to make every detainee provide them with this vital piece of information. Although telling the truth is tantamount to signing himself over to them, he knows the penalty he will pay if he is caught lying.

'Only the fool has his answer on the tip of his tongue.' His mother's sharp voice rings in his inner ear. 'You should not be too hasty.' But this is no time for deliberation.

'Fifty, Fifty, al-Mansour.' He offers the same number for his street as his house, hoping that if he is caught, it will look like a simple clerical error on the part of the expressionless man or, at worst, a natural mistake on his part.

'Occupation?' The man speaks in the same dispassionate voice as he notes down the address.

'Poet and journalist.'

'Your political allegiance?'

'I am independent.'

The man looks down at his file. 'Our information suggests you are a very dangerous Communist. That doesn't sound independent.'

'I have never been a member of any political party.'

'Then you should sign a confession.'

'I don't need to sign.'

The man strokes his moustache. 'Not true. It says here you are a very dangerous man. You are against the Ba'ath Party and the National Front. You publish articles that denounce our policies and our government, and poems about resistance and identity. This is indeed dangerous activity . . . for all concerned.'

Nabeel says nothing. There is no right answer to a question like this.

'Are you married, Nabeel?'

'Yes.'

'To whom.'

'Nada Hamed.' He is careful not to give Al Hashimy as the family name, using her father's name instead. They may know she is a Sunni, but he does not want to inspire further irritation.

'Do you have a son?'

'Yes.'

'How old is he?'

'Sixteen months.'

'Ah,' says the man, putting down his pen, 'what does he do?'

Nabeel believes he has misheard the question or perhaps misunderstood it in the stress of the situation. 'I'm sorry? He is only sixteen months. A baby.'

'Yes, you said, but what is his job?' the man asks. 'What does he *do*? I asked you, what is his job?'

Nabeel tries to work out a response but is unable to come up with one that seems adequate.

'Tell me this, then, is your son a Communist, like you?'

'I am independent and, besides, the Communists are supposed to be your friends. You are in a coalition with them.'

The man laughs as if the idea is absurd. 'We are not in any coalition. This is not our job. We are the Iraqi intelligence service, not the Ba'ath Party.'

This expedient relationship has always been a means of covering the real working of the Ba'athists. By feigning lack of authority over the intelligence services, the Ba'ath Party allows the clandestine arm of the country to run riot. Neither side feels obliged to shoulder responsibility for the other's misdeeds. The complexity of the arrangement is growing; the administration supports a seemingly endless number of military and intelligence organisations: the National Guard, the Republican Guard, the Special Guard, the Secret Police, the Civil Intelligence Network, the Mukhabarat, the Special Intelligence force and the al-Jaysh al-sha'abee, the Ba'ath Popular Army. It seems that half of the country is set on interrogating and destroying the rest.

'Look,' he says, 'I am a poet. I can only say what I believe, what I see and what I think, as an Iraqi and a patriot of the true country.'

Since the incident with Tariq Aziz, Nabeel has acquired a certain standing among jailers and the police. His freedom from party loyalty prevents them defining him, and they are unsure what to do with him.

'OK. If you are the writer and patriot you say you are, I have an offer for you. Come and work for us in the Cultural Office.'

A Party job? The offer is offensive.

'You have the ear of the people,' the man continues. 'You speak with a voice they understand. You are a popular man. And you could help us reach everyone in Iraq. With full resources, support, the freedom to publish, you would be rich and well rewarded. It's an offer a true patriot would consider carefully. Many are doing it.'

'Propaganda is not my job.' Nabeel stands up to address the diminutive tyrant on the stage. 'I respect my work, I respect myself. That is why I am independent. I cannot belong to something I do not believe in.'

'Independent!' The man's tone ridicules the word. 'No one in this country is independent. Be careful. You will not survive on your own. Your Communist brother, Jabbar, has already had to run away. Learn from his mistakes.'

'It is your job to report. Not mine.'

'What do you mean? Do you think our job is dirty?'

Already many have sacrificed principles and let swollen bank accounts salve their consciences. And for Nabeel? At what point will his own principles cease to matter? 'I will reach people with my truth or not at all.'

Angered into action, the man pounds across the stage and back down the stairs. 'Prison is too good for you.' He grabs Nabeel's collar from behind, and pulls him roughly to the ground. Nabeel's neatly knotted tie and stiff collar, now soaked with sweat, cut into his neck as he tries to wrench himself free. But the little man has a trick up his sleeve, and as Nabeel makes one last effort to pull away, he feels something cold and hard against his temple.

'A poet, eh?' The man grinds the stubby revolver, pulled from the holster at his waist, into Nabeel's head. 'I call poets public enemies,' he sneers, through gritted teeth. When he speaks again his voice has regained its steely composure. He almost sounds reasonable. 'Do you know how much each bullet from this gun costs?'

Nabeel tries to shake his head.

'Fourteen *fils*. Each one just fourteen *fils*. What do you think of that, Mr Nabeel Yasin?' Coiling his finger further round the trigger, the man cocks the gun. Nabeel wonders whether there are men stationed behind the doors, whether he might be able to overpower the squat officer and grab his weapon. How far would he get in a place like this? But he knows the situation is hopeless. Running would give them the perfect reason to kill him.

'I ask you, poet. Your poems, your stupid words, are they worth more than fourteen *fils*?'

Through squeezed, shallow breaths, Nabeel whispers the question to himself. It is a good question, almost poetic. And unanswerable. How can all the words he has ever written be worth more than the price of the bullet that would take his life? Yet how can they not be?

'Let me hear the poet beg for his life.'

Only words are needed to end this, but he cannot find it in him to speak. In the dislocated twilight of the room, with the emblem of a gun muzzle cut into his temple, the prospect of dying seems simple. It will be easier for him, for Nada and

Yamam. The man holding him on the floor has all the power. He cannot see this changing. If he gets out of this room, won't he ricochet into other, similar, situations? The Ba'athists have the house bugged, informants are watching everything he does, visiting him at home to let him know they have seen him in this coffee shop or that club, talking to Tawfiq, crossing the bridge with Juma'a. It is no life for him or his family. Embracing the resolve that accompanies surrender, Nabeel says, 'I welcome death,' and closes his eyes.

The officer erupts into peals of laughter, pulls away the gun and stands up. 'Then you must go, you foolish man.' He reaches into his pocket and throws an exit pass at Nabeel. 'Get out. We will let you suffer a little longer. But one day my cheap bullet will find you. You may want to think over my offer because until you accept neither you nor your family will be safe.'

Slowly Nabeel uncurls himself from the floor.

'Go! Now! Before I change my mind.'

At the gate the tired guard, who had frisked him on the way in six hours before, is clearly surprised. 'You are leaving so soon?' he asks.

'My meeting is over,' Nabeel replies. He looks at the neatly trimmed lawns, the beds of flowers and shrubs, vivid fuchsia and indigo, lovingly landscaped around the stark concrete of the building behind it. It is typical Ba'athist perversity to surround a place of death with beauty. Reaching instinctively into his top pocket for his cigarettes, he remembers he left them in the car. Not long, he tells himself, shivering. He has emerged from this experience and is not sure how he survived unharmed. Bruised, yes, with a ripped shirt and chafing at his neck from where his tie has been pulled tight. But alive.

The guard flips the card over in his hands as if he is looking for some sign of fakery or deception, then stamps it 'Approved'. The barrier lifts and he nods to the road outside. 'Hurry! Before it's too late!'

Nabeel walks briskly back to the little side-street where he had parked the Lada. At the sight of its familiar dull blue sheen, and the headlamps peering at him, he almost cries with relief. In half an hour he will be at home with Nada and Yamam. He will embrace his wife, confess that she was right all along, take his almost-one-year-old and tell him how much he loves him. It had been a near thing. He turns on the ignition, revs the engine and pulls out on to the road. If nothing else, today has been the final proof, if any were needed, that there is nothing left to trust.

Absently accelerating along the street as he lights a cigarette, he hopes the road will bring him out on to the city highway. Looking up, he sees a high, sandy-brick wall at the end of the street. In his dazed state, he has driven the wrong way. He jams his foot on the brake – but nothing happens. He tries again. Nothing. The car hurtles towards the wall. He drags up the handbrake and turns the steering-wheel. The car skids, mounts the kerb and slams into the wall.

Silence.

As the dust settles, he is not sure what to do. Has fortune blessed him a second time in one day? If he had been facing the other way and driving towards the main road, things might have been different. He gets out and walks round the car. It is smashed and scraped, the windows shattered. What will Nada say? He is desperate to get home, away from this place, but he can't leave the remains of his precious Lada on the street – it will have been picked clean by morning.

He will take it to Christian Samir, the mechanic. His place isn't far away. Nabeel selects reverse and the car groans as it comes away from the wall. Slowly he noses out on to Al Nidhal Street. The late-afternoon traffic is heavy and vehicles pile up behind him as he creaks and kangaroos his way down the road. When he sees the sun-cracked blue and white sign for Samir's garage he turns off the road and, with relief, in to the courtyard. Samir, dressed as usual in an old blue overall dark with oil and dirt, runs out to greet his friend. 'Nabeel! Whatever have you done to your car?' he cries, the same jovial, friendly Samir as ever. 'And you look almost as bad. Sit down and let me get you something. Then you must tell me what's been going on.'

He waves at the chipped Formica table and disappears into the shop next door, returning a few minutes later with tea and cigarettes. 'Please, my friend, don't worry about the car. I promise I will fix it for you, good as new. It looks worse than it is. It's certainly a nice one – or should I say it *was* a nice one?' He moves to examine the bodywork, appraising it for damage. 'Where did you get it?'

'In Basra a couple of months ago.'

'How long did you have to wait?'

'Nearly two years.'

Samir whistles. 'You were lucky.' And he is right. Others Nabeel knows have been waiting for longer. And although people are forced to pay for half of the car when they order it there is no guarantee that their vehicle will ever arrive.

'So, tell me what happened?'

'I'm not sure,' Nabeel tells him. 'I had to go and visit the Secret Police HQ today. I parked my car a long way out but when I came back the brakes failed. No pressure at all.' He pauses, reviewing the event in more detail. 'Maybe I'd forgotten to change the brake fluid or some screw has come loose.'

Samir sucks in his breath and wedges the bonnet open. 'It can happen. Let's take a look, shall we?'

He slides under the car, and Nabeel hears the sound of pliers against engine parts. His diagnosis, when it comes a few minutes later, is breathless and urgent. 'Nabeel, you are a most fortunate man.'

He re-emerges from under the car with two pieces of fine black cable. A drop of red brake fluid quivers on one blunted edge. The ends have been neatly clipped. 'Someone has cut your brake cable . . .'

The Last Rites of Yasin
November 1978

Nabeel lies next to his father in the dark. In this room of shadows the only sounds, other than the rain drumming on the tin roof, are of the body creaking and sighing as the last pockets of air leave the old man's lungs. For the briefest of moments, Nabeel lets himself believe that Baba is alive. He sits up, lifting the blanket, waiting for the eyes to open or the faint twitch of an expression to play across his father's lips. But none comes. At Nabeel stares at him in the darkness, he looks as he always did when he was sleeping: cropped white hair, deep lines in his face, unruly eyebrows. Yet it is like looking at a stranger. Without the imperceptible signs of life, the unseen pulsing of the blood under the skin, he is looking at a dead man. The last vestiges of life are escaping. Baba has gone.

Closing his eyes, Nabeel tries to stay composed. It is hard. The overpowering smell of Tabac fills the air, burning his eyes and nostrils. It had been the only perfumed ointment in the house for Yasin's deathbed. The Communist doctor, Kadim, had promised to bring balm for his wounds but had come empty-handed, blaming the ever-worsening shortages. Nabeel had offered the Tabac in place of anything else to mask the growing stench.

Lying down again, Nabeel lets his thoughts spiral back into childhood, as far as he can go, to his first vague memory of Baba. His father is peeling a clementine, pulling back the skin with long, leathery fingers and smiling down at him. He can smell it now, the fragrant citrus perfume that had filled the room as a faint mist rose from the peel. He had been three, four at most, he thinks.

Suspended in the empty hours of the night, sorrow takes hold. In its own understated way, Baba's life had been good and full. Yasin had witnessed the end of the Turkish empire, the arrival of the British and the birth of this precious nation state, yet he had chosen to live beyond politics for his family. He had worked away from home for weeks on end, before, then travelling home on an overnight goods train, arriving in the early morning to the children's rapturous squeals. They had all loved him. Although he was quiet, he had somehow held the family together: where their mother was tough and determined, Yasin had been soft.

Keeping vigil, Nabeel wishes his memories were less jumbled and hazy, but it is hardly surprising: in a household of so many – his brothers and sisters, Uncle Rashid's two children, Aunt Makkya's two, Bibi and all the other visiting relatives – time alone with his father had been rare. He could just recall his mother sending him, aged nine, to collect a special vat of cream for the Eid al-Fitr feast. Through the pearly blue light of the morning, with the new moon still in the sky, he had scampered across the grassy fields towards the market, coins jangling in the pocket of his long trousers. In the distance the faint outline of a familiar figure formed and re-formed as it passed through the trees in the orchard. Shielded by peaches, plums and lemons, he had watched the figure draw closer. Then, when he was sure, Nabeel had dropped the bucket and run to embrace him. 'Baba!' he had yelped, holding his father tight. 'Baba, Baba, Baba.'

The storm is building again, making it impossible to sleep. This is one of the most dramatic he can remember and it has been raging since dusk. When Amel had telephoned and told him that Baba was dying, he and Nada had barely been able to get across the city. Every street was awash with water, great torrents gushing from doorways and across pavements, flooding in waves on to the tarmac. With the Lada's windscreen wipers failing to clear the deluge, they had been forced to creep along at a snail's pace. And, the city had been in the grip of yet another power failure. Without street signs or lighting to guide them through the darkened streets, the only illumination came from the flashes of lightning that ripped across the sky.

Nabeel hopes his mother is managing to sleep through the rain. She has nursed Baba through his last days without respite. When he, Nada and Yamam had arrived, Hiyjjia Moha, his aunt, Yasin's sister-in-law, had directed them straight to Yasin. He had barely been conscious. Hiyjjia Moha had stationed herself at his head and begun whispering to him, encouraging him to make the last rites. Sabria and Aunt Noua had sat on either side. The three, dressed in black, offered prayers and the words of the faithful: 'I bear witness that there is no god but Allah, and Muhammad is his prophet.' They had remained like that until the moment of Yasin's passing and then, on observing his face become still, they had clutched each other and wept loudly.

With Yasin gone, his mother's trials are only just beginning, Nabeel muses. She will need all the energy she can muster for the months of mourning ahead. She had wanted to stay awake and watch over her dead husband's body, but Noua had insisted she rest. 'There is nothing to be done until morning, sister. Let Nabeel keep watch for you.'

It is with some relief that, at the first sign of light, he hears the sound of others about the house and knows his vigil is over. Soon, the men will rent a coffin and transport his father's body to Najaf. There, they will bathe him, slowly and with tenderness, anoint his head with a oil and wrap him three times in a seamless white cotton kafan. After offering up their final prayers they will bury him.

First, he dresses and runs to the house of his father's nephews just a few streets away. Gathered in the living room, they embrace him, 'Long life to you.'

'*Albaqa fi hayatek.*'

'May the Almighty bring him to Paradise.'

'From God we came and to Him we will return.'

Nabeel holds close each of the brothers in turn. 'Please, pass the news on. I must collect the death certificate from al-Karama hospital. The family are at home and we should meet there. We will leave for Najaf as soon as I return.'

By the time Nabeel returns from the hospital the house is full. News has spread quickly and every aunt and second cousin is arriving to offer condolences. Sabria, protected by Noua and Hiyjjia Moha, embraces the line of visitors. In the kitchen Amel and Aqbal make coffee. It is served black without sugar, for life is no longer sweet.

With death comes obligation. During the next three days of official mourning, it will be their collective responsibility, at home and at the al-Bayaa mosque, to keep those who come to pay their respects fed and watered. They will receive them all, before Sabria begins her own journey, which will keep her in mourning for another four months and ten days. Only when the *Iddah* is over will she be free of the burden of grief.

'Remember this,' says Makkya. 'You will not be apart. At the Day of Judgement the Almighty will reunite you.' Whatever would she do without Yasin until then?

It is the men who are left with the duty of burial. Yasin's sons, Uncle Rashid and some of his many half-brothers, cousins, nephews and friends, some in dish-dash, others in trousers, loose shirts and suit jacket, drift out to the gate, leaving the women with Sabria. Nabeel, Juma'a, Jafar and Tariq lift Yasin, who has been laid to rest in a simple wooden coffin, and carry him out to a waiting taxi. They hoist their father's casket on to the roof and secure it with nylon ropes.

The journey will take two hours and they have yet to dig the grave, but they agree there is plenty of time to bury him before the ritual twenty-four hours have passed. 'We have the death certificate and it is all in hand. We are in good time,' Nabeel tells Juma'a. They are taking a quiet moment by the taxi and Nabeel is smoking a cigarette. 'We still have to call at the police station at al-Bayaa and get an authorisation stamp for the burial.'

Juma'a looks anxiously at Nabeel. 'Oh, brother.'

'I'm sorry. I know this is hard for you.'

'It could have been worse. I could have been still in there.'

They both sigh. Had it been Sabria's prayers that had brought about Juma'a's release in time for Baba's death?

'Not even the al-Bayaa police would make trouble over this. This is death, not politics. And, besides, you don't have to come in. I will do it.'

'*Yallah, yallah.* Let's go, gentlemen.' Jafar shoos the men into the waiting convoy of Ladas, Fiats and Jeeps lined up behind the taxi. With the women looking on, they set off on the 170-kilometre journey that will end for Yasin at the largest, most ancient cemetery in the world, Wadi-al-Salaam, the Valley of Peace.

◈

The al-Bayaa and al-Sayydia police station is set back off the long Tarmac road that leads out of Baghdad, across the Euphrates and down towards Najaf. The station is one of Iraq's most notorious. Juma'a has been imprisoned there several times. For him and his brothers it will be the first time that any of them have been there without having been arrested. Nabeel is not concerned: they may have removed his papers, declared him an Enemy of the State and black-listed him, but his father had never been anyone's enemy. Standing before the reception desk in his dark shirt and trousers, he peers anxiously round a towering pile of files and shakes the death certificate at a guard standing on the other side.

The guard peers at the sheet of paper and plucks it from him. 'Yasin bin Hussain, al-Sayydia,' he mutters, as he reads.

'We have the stamp from the hospital and everything is in order. He was my father . . .' Nabeel's throat contracts.

'Wait here.' The guard disappears through a plywood door and into the back office. He emerges with a colleague, who has an extra stripe on his shoulder.

'Yasin bin Hussain is the deceased?' His question has an air of excitement about it.

'Yes.'

'And *your* name?'

'Nabeel Yasin.'

'Nabeel Yasin. Nabeel Yasin.' The officer speaks as if he is greeting a long-lost friend. 'Ah, yes. Hello again.'

Nabeel's heart sinks.

'We know your family well, don't we? And, of course, who could ever forget you? Tell me about this man Yasin you want to bury. Who is he?' He holds the death certificate between his finger and thumb.

'He is my father. We are driving to Wadi-al-Salaam.'

'Where is the body?' The officer cranes towards the door.

'On top of a taxi. We just need the stamp and we will be on our way.'

The man wags his finger. 'A stamp! Oh, no, no, no, no, no. First things first. You will get your stamp soon enough but I need to know how this man died.'

'He died yesterday. He was old and—'

'I did not ask when or how old he was. I asked how he died.'

'He fell off the roof.'

'He fell, did he? And what do the hospital say about that? Do they believe your story?'

'Of course. Look, he fell from the roof. He was in hospital until four days ago. They sent him home to die. They signed the forms. It's all there on the death certificate. Call the doctor at the hospital and check.'

'Or maybe he came home and was killed . . . by you.' The officer lets a devilish smile of provocation play across his face.

'Why are you doing this?' Nabeel's collar is sticking to his neck. 'He was my father, why would I kill him? I found him and tried to save him. Do not insult me.'

Nabeel had heard his mother shrieking and had come running to find Yasin lying on his back on the ground. For some reason, he had been up on the roof in the night, lost his footing and fallen. Nabeel had lifted him into the car and, with Sabria wailing in the front seat, had driven to the hospital. The traffic had been at a standstill on the airport highway, full of cars, police and people waiting for the Arab Kings and Presidents who had flown in for the Pan-Arab summit. They were trapped in the gridlock, and Yasin had sat bleeding in the back seat. Nabeel had jumped out of the car and roared at the crowd to get out of his way. But it was too late. Yasin slipped into unconsciousness and never came round.

'I cannot stamp a death certificate if I think there may have been foul play.'

After a long pause Nabeel looks the officer straight in the eye and pleads: 'Please show us some mercy. We want to bury him, nothing more.'

'I don't doubt it. The faster the body is sunk into the earth, the faster you can forget the evil you have done. Am I right? But don't worry, there is no escaping us. We will dig it up again. As for mercy? You should have thought about that before. You are a family of Communists. That is a fact. And you, Nabeel Yasin, are an Enemy of the State, of President al-Bakr and His Excellency the Deputy, may God protect them. You are more than capable of murder.'

Nabeel walks across to Jafar, who is waiting on a chair by the door. 'I don't know how to say this, brother, but . . .' he hardly dares continue '. . . they say I murdered Baba.'

'What? Ignore them. They will give up if you show no emotion. Trust me, they will get bored of the game soon.'

'Baba does not deserve to end his life like this.'

An hour later two guards stride through the crowd of anxious family members gathered on the steps of the police station, parting them with their guns.

Jafar, Juma'a and Nabeel follow as they walk out to the taxi parked on the kerb. 'Yasin, are you in there?' The sergeant reaches up and taps the coffin with his gun. 'Once we see the body we will know that you murdered him. Bring the coffin to the ground and open it,' he orders.

For Nabeel this is too much. 'I am the reason they are doing this to Baba, so I should go. Even if they stamp the declaration, I think they will come for me at one of the checkpoints on the way to Najaf. They will radio ahead and it will begin all over again. We cannot risk any more delay. I will run, brother.'

'No! This is your father's burial, Nabeel.'

'This is the only way. It doesn't matter what they do to me but they should not humiliate the family. It is best that they think they have made me suffer. Then they will let you all go on in peace. Trust me.'

At the checkpoint Nabeel runs for his Lada, trying to outstrip the shame that follows him.

The Portrait
July 1979

Sabria's favoured poultry stall is just inside the entrance to the meat market in al-Sayydia. She has shopped here since the day they moved from al-Bayaa. Regardless of the shortages, she and Farouz, the ageing stallholder, have an understanding. Sabria gets the best chickens and he gives her the best price. On this warm morning in July, tipped off that there has been a delivery of frozen birds from the north, she has come down to get what she can before they all disappear. She arrives close to eight, well before the heat of the day has begun to rise. Once, the stalls would have been teeming with cages and carcasses, wood-pigeons, ortolans, boxes of dyed chicks, turquoise, green, pink, orange, stacked three high. Now stocks are permanently low. Peering beyond the few good birds, she is about to begin the bargaining ritual when she spots the unmistakable brown *thawb* and shambling gait of her sister Noua. '*Marhaba! Shlounk? Zein.*'

The two women kiss, then instinctively lower their voices to whisper. With Mukhabarat and al-Jaysh al-sha'abee informants on every corner you can never be sure who is listening. 'Sister, you look exhausted.' Noua stares at the creases round her sister's eyes and shakes her head.

'Is it Yasin?'

'It is not easy, but no. I have other worries.'

'Nabeel?'

Sabria nods disconsolately.

'What news? Tell me they have not taken him!'

'No, no, he is still in hiding. But the Eighth of February Brigades are coming almost every day.' She uses the family nickname for the intelligence officers and strokes her upper lip in imitation of the moustaches they sport. With seven different secret police directorates all looking for him, they cannot go a day without an arrest squad crashing through the gates. The other day one had arrived while another was leaving. Still, it is better to have him in Iraq than outside. Jabbar, in France, seems further away than ever.

'The militia are coming from every direction now, not just Karkh and Rusafa but Babylon, Karbala, Baakuba, even small places like Al Hindiya. It is unbearable. So many men who claimed to be his friend have fled to their home towns with their tails between their legs and given Nabeel's name as a Communist ringleader in exchange for their freedom. Nabeel is not even a member of the Communist Party! But the local police want a feather in their cap for arresting him. It's a sport.'

'Sister, are you surprised? You have brought this on yourself. I always said you have let your boys run wild.'

Sabria has heard this a hundred times from her sisters. 'There is nothing after hardship but repose.' She is saved from any further discussion on the matter by the arrival of Um-Ali, bustling through the crowd.

'Sabria, *marhaba*.' She reaches them almost out of breath and they kiss hurriedly. 'How are you both indeed? *Habibti*, I have been hearing things about that son of yours. He is upsetting everyone at the moment and now no one can find him. He has vanished!' There was no genteel preamble, no polite small-talk. But knowing the times they live in only too well, Sabria says nothing. She will not burden friends with her worries. Later, she will talk to her girls.

The truth is that Nabeel is fragile and life underground is making him ill. He is a casualty in a hidden war. Their country has invaded itself and is turning so many of its people into criminals. And it is not only Nabeel who is in trouble. Juma'a is back in custody, and Jafar, who has barely held on to his directorship at a local surveyor's office, has been in prison for several weeks. Only Tariq remains at home, continuing with his civil-engineering degree at Baghdad University, although he, too, is under constant surveillance. Even the girls are no longer safe. Two nights earlier Sabria had been forced to hide them from the Karkh Secret Police when they came for Nabeel. The men had barged through the gate, clamouring for Nabeel Yasin, shadow leader of the Communists. It was only Sabria's screams that stopped them: an army of neighbours had appeared in their dressing-gowns and somehow convinced them to leave. If they had entered the house and found her two perfect daughters, she knows what would have come next. There were horror stories every day.

'Well, I have news,' whispers Um-Ali. 'I have been visiting in Najaf, caring for my cousin. Anyway, her husband who works at the ministry, saw a huge fleet of bulletproof mini-vans being driven up from Basra. He says they're for the National Guard. What do you think they need them for?

'There is change coming. His Excellency the Deputy will take on the premiership soon, you can be sure of it. A friend of ours who works as a driver in the ministry swears that he has doubled his private militia in as many months.'

'Let us hope the tanks do not follow as well,' Sabria remarks wryly. It is a comment just bland enough not to arouse suspicion, but they should not be seen gossiping in public. 'Excuse me while I finish here,' she says, turning back to the poultry. 'How much for the ones at the back?' There follows much agitated waving of hands until the price is set.

'*Shukran.*' Sabria hands over the notes. 'It is always good to shade under your tree.'

Less than a week later, the rumours show themselves to be true. On 16 July al-Bakr announces his retirement, citing ill-health, and His Excellency the Deputy takes on the presidential mantle. Darker rumours persist, however, that al-Bakr is, in reality, being held under house arrest by those loyal to His Excellency the Deputy. And there is news of a bloody purge too. Thirty seven military and government men of the Ba'athist inner circle are murdered.

But the new president is unconcerned. Now in the office he has coveted, he wastes no time in aggrandising his appointment to the post. His first public act is to distribute tens of thousands of portraits to every institution, company, school and public body in the land. These forgiving likenesses, showing him in a suit with a beatific half-smile, are delivered by National Guard members with instructions to hang them in honour of their new leader. Where once the Imam Ali might have hung, it is now Saddam Hussein. Outside, murals appear on the side of buildings and in open spaces on billboards. Iraq is blooming with pictures of the new leader, on banks, hardware stores, clubs, stations and museums. He who is now to be known as His Excellency the President the Leader God Placed Him is everywhere.

Sabria detests them and averts her gaze when she passes one. With so many about, it is a relief to get home. She will stand before her portrait of the Imam Ali that hangs above the television in the lounge, and offer thanks that the creeping presence of His Excellency the President the Leader God Placed Him is not felt inside her home.

But even this proves insufficient to satisfy the new president's ego. A further decree is issued to the nation, stating that every home must display a portrait. It does not go so far as to specify where, but it is understood that the picture should be suitably lavish and displayed prominently. What vanity he must be possessed of, she thinks, as she watches the specially appointed presenter, a facsimile edition of the new president right down to the new grey Italian suit and 8 February moustache, give the people their nightly reminder. Each time she sees it Sabria strengthens her resolve never to allow him into her home.

One ordinary afternoon after this edict there is a knock at the door. Sabria is alone, preparing supper for those left at home, Aqbal, Tariq and Amel. The days of great family meals seem long gone and she misses her mischievous little grandson though, *Inshallah*, he, Nabeel and Nada are safe somewhere.

Although she tries every day to make the most of what little there is in the markets, it is a meagre offering. There are a few scraps of lamb. She bulks out the mince with pine nuts and lentils, squashing them into little egg-shaped balls. There are spices for the rice, some oils for a minty salad, a handful of garish pink pickles, and dough waiting to be slapped against the wall of the bread oven outside. It would suffice. Her feet begin to ache and she pours herself a glass of water. She has less energy now than she used to.

She glances at the clock – just past four. She hopes the knock heralds no more than a street pedlar or perhaps a friend. She rinses her hands, greasy from the meat, swishes across the pale stone tiles of the hall in bare feet and out to the gate. She pulls back the iron grille in the centre and peers into the face of a corporal from the National Guard.

She has barely drawn back the bolt before three officers push past her and into the house, shouting and pulling at their holsters. They barge past her into the living room, banging on cupboards, pulling up blinds and shouting to each other as they go.

She adjusts her hastily wrapped *fota*, stands back and watches them with weary resignation. Little fools, upstarts. One is young, not even the first whisperings of a beard, and skin as smooth as an almond. How could she take any of them seriously? Living in a climate of intimidation and random violence has taught her that it is sometimes best to bide one's time, let others expend their energy and anger. The greatest sadness, as she watches the trio of teenagers raid her house is how familiar it has become.

The guardsmen gather in the hall. Sabria stands framed in the doorway. 'Are you quite finished? Where are your manners? I don't think your mothers brought you up to behave like this.'

The baby-faced boy, the shortest of the three, lifts his face. 'You have no picture of His Excellency the President the Leader God Placed Him.'

'I could have told you that myself and you wouldn't have had to ransack the place, if you had bothered to ask,' she replies, drawing herself up to her full height and looking down on the diminutive captain.

'His Excellency the President the Leader God Placed Him is

our president, the leader of Iraq, the land that gave birth to civilisation.' The guard spirals off into a rote-learned speech. 'He is descended from Muhammad, the one true prophet. He will lead this country back to glory. And we, his people, will rejoice.'

'I haven't had time to get a portrait.' She gestures around the room. 'I have such a large family to tend and a household to run. I have to feed my family . . . cooking with nothing. Where do I get the time or the money to go about buying pictures to hang on the wall?'

'Every house must display a portrait of the president,' barks the guard. 'That is the rule and you know it well enough by now.'

She knows that many other houses do not have a portrait either: most of the people they know have ignored the diktat. In fact, it has become a running joke in the Yasin household. That man, that dreadful picture! What a fraud he was. 'Go ahead and arrest me but you'll also have to round up half the city at the same time.'

It is with surprise that she watches two of them disappear to their waiting van and return with a large framed portrait of the president.

'We make it easy for you,' the captain tells her, jerking his head towards the picture. 'We will give you one. A gift from His Excellency the President the Leader God Placed Him. You can hang it now, here in this room. It will be nice to see him there while you eat.'

Less than half an hour later the guards are back to check that Sabria has hung the painting. Finding it turned face to the wall, exactly where they had left it, the captain flies into a rage and grabs Sabria by the throat. 'I told you to get this picture up,' he spits, through gritted teeth, as he pins her to the wall. 'Do you *dare* defy me?'

Sabria wrestles herself free. 'That man's face will never hang beside Imam Ali,' she shouts defiantly. 'He may be your leader, but he is not fit to enter my house.'

'Then we will kill you,' the guard says simply, taking the picture of Imam Ali off the wall.

'If that is what you must do, just do it,' she snarls. 'Take a knife from the kitchen and get it over with. Then you will be able to tell your friends that you killed a mother because she had not put up a picture.'

'Old woman,' the third says, speaking for the first time. 'Why not just do as you are told? It is so much easier. Do as we ask. Then we will go.'

'Hang the picture,' barks the captain.

From where her will to defy them arose she could not say but in an instant she knew that she had taken as much as she was ever going to from this cruel regime. 'I will not do it,' she says, her voice steady. 'In this house I obey no one but myself, and the will of Allah. I will have my picture of the Imam Ali and only that.'

'Then you are a very foolish old woman.'

'It is you boys who are the fools, though you are too headstrong to know it. Do what you want. It does not matter to me.'

In the empty seconds that follow, Sabria wonders if they will beat her, behead her or shoot her. And what will they do with her body? They are hardly likely to report it. Enough people have already disappeared for her to know that these incidents become rumour and the facts are never discovered. She will be dragged out of the house and dumped by the road somewhere. Perhaps they will rape her too.

They go off into a huddle and she hears the clicking of their tongues, the rise and fall of their voices, but not the words. Eventually they break apart and turn to her again. 'Lady,' the captain announces, 'we have the authority. If you do not put the picture up, we will kill your sons. Starting with your firstborn.'

And, just like that, they have her. She will hang the picture, one in every room if they want, and string rows of twinkling fairy-lights around them, if they tell her to. She will dust the portrait and polish the frame until it glows.

She picks up the hammer and regulation-issue nail they have laid on the table, stands awkwardly on a chair and hangs the picture as they look on. Small bits of plaster fall on to the glass-covered table below, but eventually the nail is far enough in to carry the weight. She straightens the picture and gets down.

'Now turn and look at it.' She keeps her head bowed. '*Look* at it!'

She looks up at the picture. The frame is made from cheap moulded plastic and is badly sprayed in metallic gold and silver, with corners that are not quite flush. The portrait itself is hideous, printed in gaudy colours, bathing its subject in a saintly glow.

Crestfallen, she watches them troop back to their mini-van. The short one shouts at her, 'We're watching you, old woman. Just remember, it's your boys who will pay, not you, if that portrait comes down. You understand me, yes?' In the back of the van she sees row upon row of portraits, all identical.

When Tariq arrives home he is incensed. The girls cry at the thought of what might have happened. As they all sit round the dinner table, subdued, they wonder how much closer the regime will get. Now His Excellency the President the Leader God Placed Him is inside the house.

'Mama, we should take it down and burn it.' Tariq shakes his spoon at it. 'I cannot believe it is still up.'

'You will do no such thing.'

'Mama! Do you really want that man staring at us in our own house when we eat?'

'You will do as I tell you,' she shouts. 'Does the gosling teach the goose how to swim? In my house you abide by my rules.'

'So, he will stay?' Tariq looks at his mother in stunned amazement.

'He will stay,' she says resolutely.

And he does, watching over the family as they go about their lives. Whether they are discussing the household chores or plotting insurrection, those implacable brown eyes follow them everywhere.

The Third Relative
August 1979

Tariq, now a confident twenty-year-old, sits in the back of the Toyota Super looking straight ahead into the darkness outside. Flanked by two plainclothes intelligence officers, he shifts awkwardly in his seat in an attempt to alleviate the shooting pains in his torso. His arm and shoulder still burn from having been twisted hard, an unnecessary precaution given that he had made no attempt to resist arrest. They had flung him into the back of the car with such force that he'd slid right across the cream leatherette seats and smashed his cheek against the window. Now that, too, is beginning to radiate a dull pain.

As they drive through the busy streets of west Baghdad, down the wide airport road, the driver of the car hums irritatingly. The two secret policemen say nothing. Instinctively, Tariq reaches into the pocket of his tight-cut denims and pulls out a pack of Rothman's full strength. A smoke would improve things. Although he had known it was only a matter of time before they caught up with him, they couldn't have picked a worse moment. Jafar and Juma'a are both in prison, Jabbar has escaped to France, and who knew where Nabeel was? He hadn't seen him for weeks. The only man in the house was himself. Without her boys around her, Mama had worked herself into a state of exhaustion. What was that saying of hers? 'Bear sons and you will never be alone.' Well, since Baba died life had been nothing but hardship and misery for her, he thought.

The car jolts across the railway lines that run through the west of the city and Tariq's shoulder bumps the officer next to him. The dark, wiry policeman speaks to him with a northern-Iraq accent, so quickly that Tariq can hardly make out what he is saying. 'Do you know why we have taken you in, Tariq?' He does not pause for an answer. 'Because your brother is a traitor. And that makes you a traitor too.' His bony face is shiny with sweat in the close heat of the evening and his long teeth are bared. 'His Excellency the President the Leader God Placed Him despises you. He despises all traitors who seek to undermine his presidency with their lies and cowardice. I think you Yasins must have been born stupid. Why should you be allowed to roam free while your brothers go on committing crimes against the state? But no matter, we'll get you all eventually, throw you into prison, leave you to starve, or just put a bullet through your knees. We might even make you disappear. Will your mother find you in a back alley with your throat cut like a pig in the slaughterhouse? Will this be your future, Tariq? Remember, life is very cheap once you betray His Excellency the President the Leader God Placed Him.'

Despite his pounding heart Tariq keeps telling himself to stay cool and composed. So far it was all as Juma'a had said it would be. 'One will scare you, the other will tell you that you just need to play the game.' And here they are, one in each ear. The second officer digs a fat elbow into Tariq's aching ribs. 'If you tell us where Nabeel is hiding, we can pull over and you can be on your way. No one will know it was you. Just a name or an address. A contact, a place where he might be found. Think carefully, Tariq. There is no point in protecting him any more. We will find him anyway. If not today, then tomorrow or next week. It will be better for him if you tell us what you know. Better that he meets with us than a death squad. They don't ask questions. They have their orders to kill and that is what they will do – just like that.' He clicks his fingers. 'But you can save yourself and him.'

His partner pushes his angular face right up to Tariq's, revealing a row of dirty teeth. 'Does your brother think of you when he undermines His Excellency the President the Leader God Placed Him? Why protect a man who has no thought for your suffering? You are not even a Communist.'

Tariq tries to remember the drill, instilled in him by his brothers. *Say nothing until you get to the station. Answer the questions politely. They are less likely to kill a man they respect. They are less likely to kill if they are not angered.*

'Anyway, you can't run. You're clever enough to know what would happen if you did. There are still others in your family who can be punished too. We will see to it that their treatment is harder than you could ever imagine.

'And with your brothers in prison and you here with us, your sisters will be alone at home, with no one to look after them, should anyone . . . visit the house unexpectedly.' His skin is bathed in a greasy layer of sweat, which glows each time they pass a sodium streetlamp. 'Let me give you a piece of advice. There is nothing we won't do to get the information we need.'

Tariq wants to dismiss their words, the clichés of intimida-

187

tion, but he knows he cannot. In this city, and probably across the entire country, it happens all the time.

'How old are you anyway?'

'Twenty.' Tariq flicks his hair out of his eyes.

'Twenty? Ha! Too young to ruin your life.'

The car journeys on in silence.

Tariq knows what he *should* be doing; waiting till he gets to the station, but his resolve is being eroded. Jafar and Juma'a are made of stronger stuff than he is. Tariq would not take well to prison life. Juma'a is a seasoned prisoner. When they had dragged him away in a midnight raid on the compound earlier that summer it was for Juma'a's eleventh stretch inside. At home they do not talk about it much, although everyone's thoughts are on how he must be suffering. Somehow he avoids being killed. After months in prison the previous winter, his captors had simply driven him to the outskirts of the city and pushed him out of the car. 'Touch your blindfold before we have gone and we will shoot you.' They whipped the back of his neck with a gun and sent him reeling to the ground. When he came to, he pulled back the strip of thick cloth that had been tied round his head for the past two hundred days and let in the daylight. It was half an hour of agonising pain before he could make out even a rough silhouette.

Battling the fear they have planted in his mind, Tariq reaches for the cigarettes at his side.

'Rothman's. The best.' He holds out the packet to them, they take one each and he helps himself. He shifts down in the seat as the fat guard reaches over with his lighter. Then all three sit back, puffing on their cigarettes, filling the car with soft blue smoke.

Casting a glance out of the window, Tariq tries to work out

where they are heading. The car is moving towards the Tigris. In the distance he can see al-Jomhurria Bridge. They will cross and then, he has no doubt, start north towards the main security headquarters in al-Rusafa. These two must be officers of the élite Republican Guard, a more select band than their commonplace cousins in the National Guard. In twenty minutes, perhaps less, they will arrive, strip him, humiliate him, beat him and apply burning cigarettes. Or maybe they will kneecap him. Was he really going to follow Juma'a's instructions to the letter and wait for them to set on him? Noble though it is, this is not Tariq's way of doing things.

He catches sight of himself in the rear-view mirror, the long face and bulging eyes, the wild shock of wiry hair, the wispy beginnings of a moustache. Maybe, with Allah's help, he will be able to think quickly enough to save Nabeel and himself.

'Look, I know you want Nabeel and I know he is my brother in name, but I don't know where he is,' he blurts out. 'Really, I haven't seen him for months. You can do what you like to me but I don't know where he is and I don't *want* to know.'

'Ah, everyone says this.' The fat one guffaws. 'Of course you know where he is. He is your brother.'

'No, that's not true!' snaps Tariq. He feels himself slip instantly into character – Nabeel has always said acting is his forte – delving for a story so believable in its detail and emotion that they will be forced to believe him. 'You don't understand,' he starts solemnly. 'Nabeel isn't my brother.'

They turn their heads. 'What? You are Tariq Yasin, no? Nabeel *is* your brother.'

Tariq nods. 'We were born to the same mother. But that accident is as far as we go. Since he married that woman he has been nothing to me.'

'You are lying,' counters the fat one.

'How dare you call me a liar? How can you know what has passed between me and my brother?'

'Foolish, foolish boy, we have pictures of you in your garden and on the bus together. Talking, laughing, reading banned literature. We've been watching you for a long time. We know when you eat, when you shit, when you reach for your favourite friend under the linen.'

Tariq shakes his head. 'You do not know as much as you think. She is beautiful on the outside, yes, but inside she is poison. And she wormed her way into our family like a snake and persuaded him to marry her. She even denies our mother time with her grandson. She is high-born, and looks down on our family. She came into his world, with all her petty snobbery, money and riches and took him.' He stubs out the cigarette in the ashtray. 'Do either of you know what it is like to have your life overrun by a person like that? It is like opening the door to Satan, a terrible, irreversible moment of evil.'

'What did she do that was so terrible?'

He pulls out another cigarette and offers the packet round once more. He has them hooked with the promise of a tale seething with internecine wrangling and family feuds. 'She said my mother was no more than a peasant. We were not good enough for her, a spoilt little rich girl from al-A'adhamiya who has never done a day's work in her life. They probably live in a big house with good furniture and servants. But I do not like the petty bourgeoisie.'

The two officers look at Tariq, as if urging him to finish the tale.

'We confronted him. We said, "It's your mother, or her." He loved Mama, you see. And he was her favourite son. But he chose that woman. And, believe me, now that he has placed her above his mother there is no way back for him. I spit on the man who shames his own flesh and blood. He will never be my brother again.'

Looking almost sympathetic, the fat guard flicks his ash into the grey plastic ashtray in the car door. 'It is a bad situation. I can see that.' Even the thin one is silent. With any luck, they now see a young man deeply wronged by the brother he no longer sees.

On the other side of the bridge they hit the tide of heavy evening traffic, Ladas, lorries, police motorcycles, white presidential mini-vans. As the car slows to a crawl behind the chain of red taillights inching towards the pale lamps of al-Tahreer Square, the fat policeman leans across to his partner. 'Hey, Abdullah, you hungry? Bet you're hungry too.' He looks at Tariq. There is genuine bonhomie in his voice. Tariq is not hungry – he has never felt less hungry in his life. His only interest is in delaying the proceedings long enough to give Nabeel and Nada the chance of escape. 'I could eat something,' he ventures. After all the lies he has told about his brother and sister-in-law, may Allah forgive him, what harm will one more do?

They order the driver to park up. A minute later all three are walking through the square.

Al-Tahreer is teeming with men, eating, drinking and talking at the food stalls, which have been wheeled down from Athawra City by the city's poorest. Each day, they are open for business by the time dusk falls. Men squat over dominoes and backgammon, or contemplate matters of importance over a smoking *narghila* pipe. The still air, thick with the smell of stew, soup and the spicy wafts of tea, cardamom and tobacco, is overwhelming. Streetlights and lanterns strung through the trees of the outer perimeter shine like beacons against the low iron railings round the square, illuminating those beneath with their dark yellow circles. Elsewhere, shadows move and break, and little glimpses of white appear briefly in the moonlight, the groups of men identifiable only by smoke or the hum of conversation. Over the years Tariq has been here many times.

The policemen nod at a group of men clustered under the leafy darkness of an orange tree. Tariq realises that they, too, must be plainclothes intelligence officers, secret police, perhaps, or Mukhabarat. There are spies everywhere! The 'speedy-hands' informants, who rush to note down all that they have seen, then pass it on for advantage of one kind or another. The square appears to be a huge clandestine club of greedy little traitors working for the regime. He can see why. In the summer darkness, when it is cool enough to eat, this is the perfect place to watch ordinary people, to blend in with the crowd and listen for a small piece of information that may lead to someone's arrest or disappearance.

The fat one, now panting like an old dog, spies an empty stall and waves to his partner. Ignoring the stallholder, who is still clearing white china bowls from the table, they settle into small metal chairs, flicking their cigarettes into the darkness. 'Three stews and be quick about it.' No sooner are the bowls before them than the two set to work scooping it into their mouths with great folded chunks of bread. Tariq forces small pieces into his churning stomach. Abdullah waves wildly at him, stew spraying from his mouth on to the tablecloth. 'Eat! Eat, Comrade.' He looks like a snake ingesting a rat as he pushes palm-sized pieces of moist pitta down his straining gullet. What pigs, they are, these Ba'athists. Tariq suddenly finds himself overwhelmed by the absurdity of it. Here he is, a prisoner en route to an interrogation, having a meal out in a city square with his captors. This is one story his brothers have never told.

Tariq has been waiting for his first arrest ever since he can remember. Watching his brothers and their friends dragged from the house, listening to the tales of punishment, cruelty and survival on their return, he is now about to undergo initiation into the great tradition of the Yasin family. But this is like nothing he could have imagined. They don't even use handcuffs. It is like one of those Beckett plays Nabeel is always quoting where nothing makes any sense. The two police are gossiping about their superiors at the station, slapping Tariq's wrists when one makes a joke that they clearly assume Tariq is in on. And while he struggles with the stew, the fat one decides they should stay for tea and ices.

With their stomachs full, the unlikely threesome drive on to the militia's headquarters. Tariq has given them the name of an old safe-house that he knows is no longer used and is pushed into a cell with thirty other inmates, all fresh arrests. An hour later he is released.

'Remember, if you have lied we will be back for you,' the fat one calls, as Tariq is marched through the station towards the door '. . . or your sisters.'

'Don't worry, my family all think like me now. We don't know what Nabeel is doing now and that is how I hope it stays.'

But even as he says it he imagines his mother at the house, watching from an unlit window, awaiting his return. And somewhere across town, Nabeel and Nada will be bundling the sleeping Yamam into the Lada and driving into the night. All of them are in motion, moving across the great city trying to stay one step ahead of their opponents.

Tariq may be charmed but the Ba'athist machine is not so often or so easily outwitted. Just weeks later, in Babylon, Uncle Rashid is swept into the black heart of the intelligence service's ruthless quest to seek and destroy their enemies.

Rashid, Sabria's elder brother, had retired to Babylon to get away from the heat and hustle of Baghdad. 'I've worked hard,' he said, 'and now I intend to live out my days without any trouble.' And he *had* worked hard. After training as a carpenter he had set up his own business and was soon in demand. He had married and his beloved wife bore him three sons, Amir, Kamil and Bulbul, and they had all lived together for several years. But this time of happiness came to a cruel end when she and Bulbul died. By taking them in Sabria had saved them from a life he dared not contemplate and for that he was grateful. Her boys had been as brothers to his sons, their close childhood bonds lasting into adulthood.

Now, in one of the old houses in the town, close to the Euphrates, he passes his days uneventfully, with just Amir and Kamil for company. At least, that's how life is until the August morning when he wakes to the thud of fists on his thick wooden door. Five militiamen wrestle the old man out of the house in his nightgown and bundle him towards their mini-van. Rashid has just enough time to brush his thumb and forefinger down the stretch of skin between his nose and mouth, making the moustache sign for a secret policeman to Kamil, who stands, terrified, in the shadows. Kamil knows the routine well enough. He must catch the bus to Baghdad and tell Aunty Sabria. The moment the mini-van is gone he dresses and heads for the bus station.

Rashid finds himself in an unventilated room with rough concrete floors, peeling white walls, and a disused air-conditioner wedged into a gap in the bricks. This makeshift hollow passes as the detention room at Babylon's central police station. Sitting at one end of a long, cracked wooden table, he listens as the two officers fire accusations at him. He is tired and hungry, his ample stomach growling as he shifts in his chair.

'You are friendly with Nabeel Yasin. We have heard you talk of him and his family. No one will ever know what has been said between us here, you can be certain of that.'

The thrust of their argument seems simple enough; they have discovered he is close to the Yasins and now they want him to reveal where Nabeel is hiding. But what can they do? Beat him, torture or kill him, even? He is old anyway. Let them do their worst.

Rashid looks at them and is astonished by the hatred in their faces. They have never met his nephew Nabeel, nor, he imagines, read any of his poetry. Of course, in answer to their questions, he knows where his nephew lives. He has been several times to the rather splendid new house he and Nada live in but he will not tell them this. Why should he? What right had they to ruin a good man's chances? His own children's exploits have never caused him trouble – for which he feels immense gratitude – but Nabeel is still his family. And is a man's duty to his own blood not absolute? For the love given so freely to Kamil, he owes Nabeel a huge debt.

Twisting the tasselled end of his white headdress into the nape of his neck, he rises forward in his chair and looks them both in the eye. 'Look, I am an old man, nearly seventy, and I don't see my sister any more. She and her family live in Baghdad. It is a long way for a man like me to visit. I have lived in Babylon for many years now,' he insists, affronted to be justifying even the most basic facts about his life. 'Last I heard my nephew is married and working, no longer living at the home of my sister. As for having talked about him, well, many talk about him. He is the most famous son in our family and I am a boastful old man. I can't say I have much understanding of what he writes.'

As they walk out and leave him, he thinks of his sister Sabria. At the last visit he made to Baghdad, a few weeks after Yasin's disastrous funeral, Sabria had been consumed with anxiety over the safety of her sons rather than mourning her husband. He clicks his tongue with sadness and reproach. She deserved respite from them and the troubles they seemed to leave in their wake. All that education and sacrifice, yet look at how it had all turned out! How many visits to prison will it take them to realise that those carrying the guns have the last word? There is a life to be lived beyond the struggle against the Ba'athist foe, if they knew how to find it. They seem to enjoy poking sticks at the hornets' nest even though they have been stung.

When the officers return it is with a heavily built third man. Looking at his rough, hardy hands, Rashid wonders if he, too, was once a carpenter. 'Old man, we think you are lying,' the first policeman says, enunciating slowly into Rashid's face. 'I will ask you again, where is your nephew, Nabeel Yasin? And this time be very careful how you answer me.'

'I do not know. As I said, we do not live in the same city, and I do not see my sister any more. Why do you come to me? I am just his uncle.'

With a nod from the first man the third walks to Rashid and punches him with full force against the side of his face. The old man slides off the chair and on to the floor.

Gingerly he touches the side of his head, which is already swelling. Each time he makes the same answer he is struck again. Laid out on the floor half conscious after the fifth blow, he wonders why Nabeel is so important to them. Can a man who writes poems called *The Meadow* and *Picnic* be a genuine enemy of this new president?

The big man hauls Rashid off the floor and back on to his chair. There is a file open on the table in front of him. There, in thick black ink, are the names of his two boys. 'Now,' the senior officer strokes his beard, 'I think maybe it is time we talked about your sons, Rashid.'

Rashid rests his elbows on the table and leans forward. An image of them trailing Kamil to the city flashes behind his swollen eyes. They have had him all this time.

Given impossible choices, people make terrible decisions. Rashid knows this. And although he loves his sister, and adores Nabeel, his own sons are the dearest things in the world to him and all he has left of the life he began with his wife so long ago. He would gladly have bought Nabeel's freedom by taking the punches himself, but he will not risk the lives of his own children, especially Kamil. His innocent son would never understand such suffering.

When he speaks it is clearly and with detail. 'Captain, I don't know his address but I could *show* you where I think he might be. I'm certain I should know it by sight. I went there once a few years back.'

In stark contrast to the winding, narrow, overhanging mews of the Old Town, the streets of Baghdad's modern districts are built on a geometric grid system, a reminder of the rapid growth of the city, of riches gleaned from oil, sulphur and phosphates, and the influence of the West. The neighbourhood of al-Mansour is one such district. Studded with lavish villas and houses, inhabited by the *nouveau* well-to-do, it is the embodiment of the country's modish aspirations. Many Ba'ath loyalists, fat on backhanders and underhand dealings, have settled in this prestigious area. And it is here that Nabeel and Nada's wedding mansion, the fifty-fifth house on the fiftieth street, is to be found. That it has remained undiscovered by the secret police is one of the greatest miracles of all. Despite the extraordinary interest in his movements, the address he had given that day at the security headquarters had remained on his files. They had assumed that he still lived at home with his new bride. Besides, who would ever believe that the dissident poet, the educated son and working-class Enemy of the State would be living in al-Mansour? Individual branches have tried, during that time, to unearth a new address, but in a district of hundreds of streets and alleys the possibilities are endless, and although every so often a bemused family has found their home ransacked not one branch of the militia has yet arrived at al-Mansour.

Sitting in the back of the Peugeot 404 passing over the Euphrates, with his swollen, calloused feet half out of his ageing black sandals, Rashid hopes that Kamil will have warned Sabria. He will stall them, of course, with the befuddled-old-man routine but eventually he will give them what they need. There is a chance that the sight of a white Peugeot crawling the streets, a car that everyone knows is favoured by the secret police, may alert Nabeel and give him time to escape. But as they turn speculatively into the fiftieth street, Rashid knows the time of his betrayal is upon him.

Scanning the lines of perfectly spaced houses, the dusty palms peeping above high stone walls and the long Japanese and German cars on concrete driveways, Uncle Rashid twists the white *misbaha* beads in his pocket and makes a series of short, silent incantations. 'In the name of God the Merciful, God the Compassionate. There is no God but He the Wise.' The flat line of the al-Mansour roof looms ahead and is gone as they drive past the first time. He looks round and makes a vague backwards motion with his hand, 'I think that may be it,' then lowers his eyes and sinks into the depths of ignominy.

But as the car draws up to the gates he can see only rubbish, blown in on the hot *sharqi* winds of summer, lodged in the corners of the steel gates. Edges of newspaper flutter and a thick film of dust covers the railings. There are no tyre tracks in the dust. The house is deserted.

'Are you certain this is the place, old man?' An officer jabs Rashid with his elbow.

'Yes. May God have mercy on me, it is the place.'

'Be certain, old man, because if you have led us on a wild-goose chase you will feel ten times the pain.'

'Yes, yes. I can swear in the name of . . .' He pauses to wonder if, rather than swearing in the name of Allah, or the Imam, it is now required of him to make vows in the name of the president. But by the time he has finished stumbling over his apologetic words, they are gone, two of the officers running from the car and scaling the wall. He hears them bang the glass of the French windows. He pulls at his white stubble, gets out of the car and shuffles up to the gate. There is no one here, of that he is certain. His heart leaps for joy. The garden is all but dead, the orange trees and shrubs dried by the winds to little more than brittle skeletons, and between the peaks of sand wedged against every doorway the last remaining curled brown leaves drift back and forth, rustling quietly in the breeze. Only the rhododendron lives on in the uncared-for emptiness.

◈

With the pallor of the sleepless, Nabeel slips into his mother's house in the dark.

'Uncle Rashid!' He embraces the broad frame. 'I heard you were here. Still managing to eat well, I see. I came as soon as I was able. It is not easy to move at the moment. Nada sends her blessings to you.' He stands back to survey him. 'But what of you? Mama told me the police took you in Babylon.'

'Yes, and, *inshallah*, never again.' The old man sighs as they settle into armchairs. 'I sent Kamil up to warn your mother. Did you see him?'

'I wish I had been able to. How is he?'

Pulling awkwardly at his headdress, Rashid says, 'He is well. Working hard, *inshallah*. He gives me no complaint at any rate. He misses you, nephew. Ah, well.' He pauses. 'But you are in hiding, I hear. For how long now?'

'Tsk, brother,' Sabria scolds. 'He has been away since the Communist paper closed in April, almost five months now. And you,' she shouts after Amel, who has turned from the doorway to go and brew some Turkish coffee, 'bring some cardamom pods.' Nabeel always liked to carry a few in his pocket, occasionally chewing one before a cigarette, to enrich the taste.

'So where are you staying? There cannot be too many places they have not searched.'

'It is true. We are running from here to there, moving with our sixth sense.' Nabeel reaches for a cigarette from the box on the tabletop. He smokes constantly now. 'For the moment we are hiding in the house of Behija and Hamed, Nada's parents. They are very well respected people. I don't think the police will think of searching their place, but you never know. Anyhow, we leave there tomorrow. These days, everyone you meet is a speedy-hands. Some are still stupid enough to parade about in their uniform, but most look like you or I. They listen outside garden walls and make deliveries to the house. Can you imagine all the games we have to play to keep Yamam quiet? And until today not even I had set foot outside for two weeks. But we have word they are going to raid houses in the area so we must move on.'

'To where?' Rashid asks, sucking in air through the large gaps where his teeth once were, hoping that the couple do not plan to return to al-Mansour.

'Do not concern yourself with such details, brother,' Sabria says, retrieving a covered plate from the console sideboard. 'We know how you have suffered already and none of us wants you to be taken in again. If you know nothing, you can give nothing away.' She removes the upturned glass bowl that has been acting as a lid and places a plate of dried fruit and sweets on the table between them. 'Last month they were almost caught in a public taxi.' She nods. 'It is all getting very exhausting.'

Shifting uneasily on the brown cushions of his chair, Rashid reaches across the table for a sweet and waits for the chance to make his confession. The taste of the sweet rosewater and sugar syrup is unbearable. In all his life he has never kept anything from his sister.

'Sister, Nabeel, please listen. There is something I must tell you. And please do not interrupt me until I have finished.' Rashid looks as though he is about to pass out. 'You must not go back to al-Mansour. A terrible thing has happened . . .'

But before he has managed to fully explain, Sabria is on her feet, swiping at him with her hands, ash from her cigarette flying on to the table. 'Brother! You have betrayed me! Nabeel! Amel! Listen to this man. Brother, uncle, traitor! How could you? You are afraid of a little punch. It is disgraceful. Shameful! Get out of this house and pray that you have not passed a death sentence on Nabeel.'

Rashid, head in hands, begins to sob gently. 'Sister, maybe I am all of those things but understand that even though they hit me very hard and even though I am old, that was not the reason I had to tell them. I did not care if they killed me.' His hands quiver as he raises them in surrender. 'They were going to kill the boys. They had already seen Kamil and they were coming back for him. They told me they would find them and torture them. And I saw the names in their files. You know Kamil. He could not defend himself against a fly. How could I let someone hurt him?'

'And my Nabeel?' Sabria hisses. 'To protect your own sons you try to sacrifice mine?'

Tears stream into the fleshy pockets beneath Rashid's eyes. 'Sabria, Sabria, it was an impossible choice. I delayed them as long as I could but what else was I to do?' He drops his face into his hands and cries, 'Sister, the boys are all I have. Would you ask me to sacrifice them too?'

Sabria slams her hand on to the table. The brass teapot jumps, spilling some of its contents. 'I understand you, but I *cannot* forgive you. That is all. Two of my boys are already in jail, another banished and the fourth in hiding, and you do this to me! I brought five sons into this world and now I have only one left with me. Tariq, only just a man, and now they are after him and the girls. You are my family, Rashid, someone I should have been able to trust with my life and the lives of my children. And you have betrayed me.'

Nabeel knows he must intervene. It's as if all the resentment, frustration and anger that has built up in her over the years, the pain of the imprisonments, the beatings, the death of Yasin, whom she has never had the chance to mourn, is being discharged at her brother in one huge ugly torrent. 'Stop, Mama! This is the Ba'athists' Third Relative Policy. They have designed it to splinter and fragment us, make cowards of us all. Just as they arrest Tariq for being my brothers, so they extend their net wider across the family, to uncles and cousins, nieces and nephews. "The suffering for one man's crimes shall be inflicted on the family until it is three relatives removed." This is what Saddam has decreed. Uncle Rashid did the right thing. What other choice did he have?'

'There is always choice, Nabeel.' Sabria sits back defiantly on her chair. *'There are ways of getting what you want.* You use charm, cunning, bribes, lies, blessings and warmed pots of stew if you have to, but you do not betray your own.' She lights another cigarette and inhales furiously. She knows this is no longer true. Jafar and Juma'a, in separate jails, at the mercy of their adolescent prison guards, Jabbar exiled from her, Nabeel and his young family living in constant fear: her influence is waning, and with it, she admits, her hope.

'In the name of Allah, the Compassionate, the Merciful, I only gave them the address because I was certain you would not be there.' Rashid looks at Nabeel imploringly. 'I knew you would not sit and wait for them to find you. He is not a fool, that nephew of mine, he will have disappeared, I thought. And I was right, for you have been in hiding all this time.'

'Uncle, Uncle.' Nabeel comes round the low wooden coffee-table to embrace him. 'This is a test of our family. We cannot let them divide us up and pick us off one by one. This is their intention. You know that Saddam Hussein has said that he will not rest until every last person in Iraq feels the hand of the Party.'

Getting Away With It
October–December 1979, January 1980

Nabeel and Nada have come to dread the sound of the doorbell. Family rarely use it and, these days, they do not expect people to come calling at night. When it rings with short, urgent bursts that October evening, they are immediately on alert. Nada scoops up Yamam and pads silently to Sabria's room. Wrapping her arms tightly round his little body, she lies down on the bed and tucks his head under her arm. His shallow breath is warm on her neck and she prays that her pounding heart will not wake him. Although she has tried to protect Yamam from the worst of it, she knows he is becoming more unsettled as the weeks pass. Even when they are alone she is distracted. The ever-present threat of separation from Nabeel or her own family sits ominously in the back of her mind. She shuts her eyes and hopes for the best.

Nabeel tiptoes into the room, turning to wait with his ear to the door. He looks back at his wife and sleeping child. She starts to speak but he puts a finger to his lips and shakes his head. They hear Sabria coming from the gate, talking, and then a man's angry voice.

Nabeel's heart surges and his legs go weak. He holds the doorframe and listens. Looking at the window, he plans an escape route through the garden and over the wall. Or would that be playing straight into their hands as they stand out there, lined up round the walls? He hears his name spoken. And then, as suddenly as it had arisen, the fear falls away. 'Nada, relax. It is only Rashid Falahi the carpenter.'

Sabria comes for him. 'Rashid Falahi is here to speak with you. I don't know what you've done but he is furious.'

Rashid Falahi, his old friend and sparring partner in all things learned and literary, is led into the living room where he stands perfectly still, fingering the edging of his tunic. Sabria disappears into the kitchen to boil water for tea, talking as she goes. 'Thank goodness it's only you. I was saying only last week that we hadn't seen you in a very long time.'

'Forgive me, Aunty, please, but I have not stopped for tea and chat,' Rashid interrupts, his voice raised for Nabeel's benefit. 'I have urgent business to discuss with Nabeel, should he decide to show himself.'

Nada clicks her fingers at her husband. 'Dudi,' she hisses, 'he's really angry. What have you done?'

Nabeel ignores her and walks out into the living room. 'Comrade! It's good to see you.' He goes to embrace his friend but Rashid steps back.

'You have caused me great upset and made me look a fool.' Rashid's face glows with indignation.

'A fool? Over what, exactly?' Nabeel asks, though he knows well enough.

'You insulted my contact Abo Hameed. And you insulted me. You reject all my efforts to get you out of danger and you have made me look ridiculous in front of a Party deligate. Should I go on?'

'Rashid, I have no argument with you. It was *my* decision

not to go through with Hameed's offer, and I will take the consequences.' He walks across to the radio and tunes it to static, raising the volume and pulling Rashid towards him with a tap to his ear. 'Listening devices.'

'How can you doubt me, Comrade?' whispers Rashid, shaking with frustration. 'Have I not been a loyal friend?'

'Rashid, my intuition is all I have to rely on. I get a feeling about a car in the street so I bend to tie my shoelaces as it drives past. Later I see the same car pull someone over and they turn out to be plainclothes police. I get a feeling that this road will take me towards trouble so I walk a different way and I find out they have blocked that road and are checking everyone. Small things, Rashid, details, but I have learned to trust that inner voice. To me, there was something not right about Abo Hameed.'

'Are you saying he is not what he seems? Your mind must be going. He has been my contact for so many years I cannot recall when we met. The whole operation has run perfectly well until now. Do you think because you are the great Nabeel Yasin, the poet revolutionary, that you can doubt me?' He shakes a fist. 'You have offended us both.'

'Rashid, I am sorry, but this is no time to trust anyone, no matter who vouches for them. Anyway, he was an idiot, a loose-tongued fool.'

'There you go again. When will these insults end? Perhaps you will look back on this moment from your prison cell and wish you had chosen differently.'

'Come on, do you not remember how he spoke? "By the way, I am from the Party and if you ever need to leave Iraq illegally just come and see me."' Nabeel mimics the man's conspiratorial tone, and laughs contemptuously. 'This is not a *film noir*. He knows the city is bugged and yet he forced me to lie. "I do not plan to leave Iraq but if I ever do I will go to the consulate, get the proper stamps and papers just like a good citizen." Imagine if I had accepted his offer. I would have been arrested quicker than that.' He snaps his fingers in the air.

Nada turns from the door where she has been listening and stares back into the room. She is close to tears. She looks at the neatly folded clothes on the table in the corner, the small pile of papers and keys, then at Yamam. Her husband has been six months in hiding. Six months of living in tiny dark rooms, pacing, smoking and worrying. And it is taking a terrible toll. From the way he is with Rashid, a thoughtful, loyal man, she can see how bad it has become. The anger, the paranoia, the tension in his voice belong to a different Nabeel. The authorities, if they could see him, would be rubbing their hands with delight. He has made his own jail. 'They have silenced me. I can't think about writing or poems.' Instead he occupies himself with obsessive vigilance. Every sound, every taxi that passes the house and voice on the street, then every silence, is endowed with malignant possibility. And the days blur into nights and back again without separation.

It has been a strain for her too. Still working at the ministry, she is leading a double life. She clocks in and clocks out, ducks small-talk with her colleagues, and while Yamam stays with her mother, Nada maintains the pretence that life outside work is as usual. Sometimes Nabeel is there when she returns, or has left a message, but mostly he is not. He moves from place to place, relying on a network of trusted family, friends and comrades to warn him should the militia come snooping. When she does see him she wants to ask where he has been but she knows she can't. They have agreed that it is best if he does not talk about it. 'You should not be at risk,' he says to her repeatedly. 'I do not want them ever to come for you instead of me.' For Nada, this is the hardest thing of all to bear. To be unable to share with him even the most ordinary and incidental details of daily life is breaking her apart. He has become a stranger.

She longs to sit out in the fresh air with him or snatch a minute in the darkness of the night to look up at the stars. She longs to hear him sing. She has tried before to persuade him that they could slip outside while Yamam sleeps, but he won't go. 'There are men with cameras on the roofs. Night-scopes. You know we are being watched,' he reminds her bitterly. This, she knows, is not paranoia. Intelligence and surveillance are strangling the city, bringing social contact down to the barest and most practical exchanges. Saddam Hussein has wrapped so many security agencies round himself, each layer busy digging for information, that most people dare not say anything. And people are folding willingly into the Ba'athist ideal every day. It is easy to spot the converted. They have been rewarded with Mercedes-Benz cars, houses in gated complexes, cash and servants. The country has a new élite, as corrupt as any that has gone before. The great sadness is that so many were once friends.

The idea comes suddenly to Nabeel. Even after he settles Nada into a chair to tell her, he continues to pace the room while it forms in his head. Then, kneeling on the rug in front of her, he tells her his plan. 'I have been thinking about everything in the wrong way, looking for ways to sneak out of Iraq, talking to smugglers and hiding on fruit lorries in a *dish-dash*. Yes, I am outside the regime. But what if we were to behave as if I wasn't? What if we act as if we are part of the system? We are educated, we speak well, and wear the right clothes. We could get the money together, act confidently and—'

'Dudi, Dudi, slow down.' Nada is tired and reluctant to get into another unlikely escape fantasy. She has to work in the morning. 'How on earth will confidence help us at the borders? We probably won't even get to a border. There are roadblocks and patrols everywhere, and they search every car.'

It is true that in the last few months army recruits have begun to prowl the city streets day and night and there are new checkpoints on the main highways and in and out of every town. Even ordinary vinyl suitcases and canvas bags are being opened at border crossings since it has become common practice to hide people inside them, arms bound to their bodies to make them fit.

'Syria, Turkey, Jordan, Kuwait, there is nowhere left to cross any more, Dudi, no matter how much money you have or how confident you look.'

'Exactly. There is nowhere left to cross by *land*. But what if we fly? If we act like an ordinary family going to visit relatives abroad, we could go to the airport and get on a plane. You have a passport with Yamam already on it. We could try to get the permits, I could get a fake passport and papers, buy the plane tickets and we can fly away from all of this.'

Nada is astonished by the absurdity of this latest scheme. It is so typical of Nabeel to ignore the practicalities. How is he proposing to fly out of Iraq when he can't even be seen outside the house?

'I know you are not taking this seriously, Nina, but you must! I am serious. The point is,' Nabeel goes on, 'that if we are really bold we become invisible. They expect us to creep around like criminals. So let us do the opposite. I will use some of my contacts, and Juma'a knows some people who might help.'

She begins to laugh. Who knows if it would be possible? But for the first time in months her husband is optimistic. The practical problems are enormous, she can see that, but of all the many escape routes they have been offered, this seems to make the most sense in some way that she cannot yet grasp.

'It is our good fortune I didn't take up the other offers. I should thank your father for making me promise not to let you go ahead of me to a strange land. We should go together or not at all.' Nabeel takes another cigarette from the crumpled packet in his pocket, lights it and draws on it long and hard. 'It's Fate. Fate is edging us to the right choices.'

After they have told their families, Nabeel and Nada set about planning their escape in earnest, recruiting help from those they trust most. There are many obstacles, not least the travel permits, money and passports, which all have to be signed and stamped before the tickets can be bought.

'Cousin Hussein works at the Iraqi Airways office downtown,' Juma'a tells Nabeel when he learns of the plan. 'He may be sympathetic. I will go to him. A passport will be more difficult. There are not many who can make a convincing forgery.'

Because she is not blacklisted, Nada finds it easier to make her own preparations. With the help of Selwa's husband's nephew, who is in the military, the remainder of her unused maternity leave is approved. Exemption from work means she will be ready to leave the country when the time comes without drawing attention to herself.

To get a passport she needs documents which are in a chest

of drawers at the house in al-Mansour and she, Nabeel and Juma'a drive back to retrieve it one evening. It is the first time they have been to the house in many months and in the dark they creep through the creaking rusted gate into the familiar garden and up to the front door.

'Dudi, look.' Nada grabs Nabeel as they step across the threshold into the hall. 'Everything is the same as it was when we left.'

The table in the hall, the glass vase and a small stack of books are untouched. In the living room she can see their favourite leather chair, as she left it, pushed close to the window to catch the sunlight. 'It is so beautiful.'

'We have hardly lived here at all,' Nabeel says wistfully as they wander through the unlived-in rooms. 'But when we come back, we will begin again. Don't you think?'

'Come on, come on,' Juma'a interrupts. 'Just collect the documents you need, some clothes, and let's go.'

Nabeel climbs the stairs to the bedroom as Nada opens the juniper-wood chest of drawers and looks for her papers in the hall. The stairs are dark but they dare not light the house. They will have to make do with the streetlight outside the living room.

'Should we really take everything now? Maybe we can come again when we know a little more.' Nabeel can't decide what to take because they don't know where they will go or for how long. Certificates, legal documents of ownership for the house and car would all be useful. Their plan is to escape to France, but even this cannot be certain. It depends what tickets Hussein can get for them, if any.

'Take warm clothes. Anywhere in Europe will be much colder than it is here,' Juma'a reminds them. 'There might even be snow.'

They push sweaters and leather shoes, vests and the thickest woollen jackets they own into a suitcase.

As they rush about the house, Juma'a watches from the window. The curtains are drawn but at the slowing of a pair of headlights in the road beyond the driveway he claps his hands and shouts to Nabeel, '*Yallah, yallah.* We must go. If it is the Mukhabarat we have only seconds.' They skid down the stairs, grab Nada and throw the suitcase out of the back door. Hurrying across the grass, Juma'a in front, Nabeel at the rear dragging the case, they drop to the ground in a shadowy corner beneath the wall of the neighbouring house. Behind them they hear the car slow and the door open. Crouching next to each other in the darkness, they wait as footsteps approach the gate and crunch down the pavement alongside the wall behind which they are hiding. Above their own breath they hear him, walking slowly, pausing to look into the shadows, his shoes heavy. Thankfully he is alone. Huddled in the moonless night, all three know that they must remain still although every instinct tells them to run.

Pacing along the front and sides of the house several times, the lone informant eventually returns to his car and drives off. Only when they are certain he will not return do they get up and run silently the half-block to where Juma'a parked the car.

'You have all the documents. Do not return here,' insists Juma'a. 'Someone must have seen us go in. They will be watching this place from now on.'

Autumn brings a reprieve. Following a series of grenade attacks across Baghdad in July, militants from the Shia'a Da'wa Party, emboldened by the Islamic Revolution, make several attempts to destabilise the country and overthrow the new president. With an arsenal of weapons and an active, zealous leader in Muhammad Baqr al-Sadr, Saddam Hussein is forced to turn his attentions and most of the secret police resources away from annihilating the Communist Party and its sympathisers. Nabeel is able to emerge from hiding for just long enough to pursue in earnest their escape plan. During the autumn weeks he chases up endless leads in his search for a passport and papers, but no one can help. Juma'a comes to his rescue with the boldest and riskiest strategy yet. 'It is a long shot but I have a friend, Khider, who says his nephew will try to help you. Of course, he can't promise anything . . .'

'Is he to be trusted?'

'Khider is an old comrade,' says Juma'a. 'I've known him for twenty years and he's a man of his word. I trust him.'

'What does his nephew do?' Nabeel asks, as they sit in the darkened back room of their mother's house.

'He works as a Customs liaison officer.' Juma'a's voice is gruff and serious. 'At the Customs House near the airport. He knows people. He told me that your best chance is to apply for a passport like everyone else and hope you're not caught. He can get you the application form. It will cost but he will do it quickly. You have to fill it in, get the photos and the official certificate of identity, then I'll tell him you're ready and he'll tell you when to take it to the passport office in al-Rusafa.'

'But how will I get the stamp?' He knows it is impossible to get round the blacklist.

'Calm down, brother! I'm coming to that. He has a contact who will remove the page in the ledger that bears your name. We don't know when the contact will be able to do it and it can be only for one day or even, perhaps, a few hours. He cannot risk being caught trying to do it a second time. So, you will have to go there often enough to be sure you don't miss it.'

'What? I must keep returning there and hope that one day when they open the book my name is gone?'

'That seems to be what he's saying. If you see your name or think you've been recognised, you must try to walk out. It's risky, but now that the secret police are dealing with other things, you stand a chance. Anyway, what alternative do you have?'

A week later, having borrowed the money to pay Khalid, the two brothers arrive at his tiny office on the airport ring road to pick up the prized passport form.

'It is important you meet him,' Juma'a insists, as they walk, heads down, shielding themselves from the windows of the nearby office blocks. 'He knows who you are and is honoured to be able to help but you should show your gratitude. He is putting himself at considerable risk for you.'

Surrounded by filing cabinets and piles of Customs forms, Comrade Khider is a big man with a large moustache. Sitting behind a metal desk, he turns slowly on his swivel chair. In front of him, among the vast quantities of paperwork, is the form. 'They'd put me in jail for this,' he says, pushing it to Nabeel. 'By the way, what was your grandfather's name?'

'Hussain. Did you know him?'

'No, of course not. When you fill in the form, add his name to your own. This will give you some protection if your name hasn't been removed from the blacklist. If they ask, you tell them that you're not Nabeel Yasin but Nabeel Yasin Hussain. Answer to that name only, and remember, they may try to trick you.'

Over the many visits he makes to the passport office Nabeel learns to control his nerves. Open between eight and noon each day and situated in a large grey building on Fifty-Second Street, the heartland of the Mukhabarat, it is the embodiment of a bureaucratic government office. Air-conditioners hum and drip in the corners of the rooms, and although a queue system is in operation, no one seems to pay much attention to it. Streams of people barge and push their way from line to line arguing at every name called out. Can all these people really be planning to make trips in and out of the country?

At the first attempt he arrives in his crisp linen shirt and grey suit trousers, looking ahead at the line of glass-fronted booths and the industrious police clerks seated behind them. Instinctively he checks for a separate exit, but there is only the door by which he came in, guarded by two officers armed with automatic weapons. He ambles up to the reception booth and joins the queue of people that reaches back into the middle of the room. Lighting a cigarette he waits until he is called. Then taking a deep breath he approaches the desk, smiling confidently.

The passport officer, a pale adolescent with slicked-down hair, flicks distractedly through the application. 'Wait here,' he drawls wearily, spinning round in his office chair and pulling down the large black book spread across the central filing cabinet. He hauls it open and Nabeel can just make out a list of names and their suspected crimes. The officer runs his fingers down the pages, moving from list to list, checking to see if Nabeel Yasin Hussain is among them.

'Nabeel. An unusual name, no?' Nabeel cannot speak. 'Ah,' exclaims the officer triumphantly. 'We do have a Nabeel Yasin . . .' He reads the entry and stops at the words 'a writer, at a Communist newspaper . . .' There is a note of sarcasm in the young man's voice as he looks up. 'Is this you?'

'No.' Nabeel pulls back his cherished application form

from the clerk. 'You can see, I am Nabeel Yasin Hussain.' He points at the page and the officer looks at him blankly.

'Hussain? Oh, yes, well, I'll have to check. This Nabeel Yasin will certainly not be going anywhere soon.'

Though this officer appears to believe he *is* Nabeel Yasin *Hussain*, Nabeel can see that the cabinets behind are solid with files and that it will take only a little digging to reveal his true identity.

'I have just noticed there is a mistake on my form,' he says. 'Let me take it. I should check it again. It must be correct.'

The officer inclines his head. 'As you wish.' He leans forward to call the next man in the queue.

Nabeel walks coolly through the exit and flags down the first passing taxi.

Over the next few weeks he returns many times and gets no further. On his third visit he spots his name on the list before the clerk does and tells him he has left his car unlocked. Another time he senses he is being watched by two plain-clothes men behind the security glass at the far end of the room and pretends he has to find a bathroom. On his sixth visit he brings his cousin Khazaal with him. 'Just come as my companion,' he had said. 'It will give me someone to talk to while I wait. You don't have to do anything.' This proves calamitous. When the officer clicks his fingers to draw Nabeel's attention to the page in the black book where his name appears and asks, 'Are you a Communist writer?' Khazaal freezes. The room seems, for an instant, perfectly still, stamps held in mid-air, papers suspended between one filing cabinet and another, mouths open, cigarettes dangling on lips. In that moment of horrified silence, Nabeel is aware of only one thing: Yusuf turning and breaking into a sprint. Left alone, he has no option but to join him. He grabs the form and runs for the door, head down like a charging bull. The guards look on as he sprints past them, and although they pursue him into Fifty-Second Street they lose him in the throng. Nabeel finds Yusuf in the shadows of a closed shopfront half an hour later. 'I heard the word Communist and thought we were done for. I'm sorry. I let you down,' Khazaal tries to explain his panic but Nabeel breaks into riotous laughter and puts his arm round his cousin's shoulders. 'This is quite a situation, don't you think? Come, I must hide before someone else round here sees me. There are many speedy-hands about.'

Nabeel jokes with Nada that visiting the passport office has become his new job. 'I have been so many times I should have my own security badge and a little glass booth.'

'You have to keep going, Dudi.'

'But for how long? It seems pointless. The more times I go, the less I understand how Khider's contact *can* remove my name. There are pencil markings here and there. But to delete a whole entry? What will he do? Pull out the entire page, or pencil over another entry? And one of these days I will be caught. Several of the Customs officers recognise me, I am sure of it.'

'It is a government office. They see hundreds of faces every day. They won't remember you. Just go one more time, Dudi. Then maybe you and Juma'a can go back to Khider and find out what has happened.'

Nabeel returns once more for Nada's sake, but as he approaches he senses something out of the ordinary. Today there are two men at the door whom he knows to be plainclothes Mukhabarat. Avoiding their gaze, he crouches to do up an imaginary shoelace, then pads as calmly as he can across the carpet, unwrapping his navy blue scarf. 'Cold today.' He chances chit-chat with the man next to him. The man nods and smiles. He sits down and chain-smokes five cigarettes.

When he is eventually called he walks briskly to the booth and pushes the application form towards the officer, far enough in for the details to be seen but close enough for him to retrieve it and run if there is trouble. The officer pulls the application form right through and, without looking at Nabeel, takes it to the logbook. He checks the name and starts running through the list, turning page after page. The names roll by. He gets to the final page and, having failed to find what he is looking for, shuts the book and scores a lazy signature across Nabeel's form.

Nabeel cannot believe what he is seeing. It plays out in slow motion: the officer reaches for a pair of scissors and starts to cut his photographs down to size. And then, without looking up, he reaches into the drawer at his side and pulls out a crisp, green passport. Carefully prising up the plastic leaf, the man places the photograph, and the government date stamp, in the top left-hand corner. Looking back at the form, he inks the details into the title page. Leaning against the counter, Nabeel feels light-headed. This wonderful man is making out a passport in his name. He is marking it with the huge rubber stamp of validation and scribbling his signature across the middle. When, at last, the man hands over the document, Nabeel feels his fingers at one end of the little green book connect with the officer's at the other, and then, suddenly, it is his. He slides the passport into his top pocket, walks down the line, past the armed guards and out on to the street. Only after he is tucked into the back seat of a taxi does he dare pull out the passport and take a look.

'Dudi!' Nada shrieks with excitement, as Nabeel produces the passport from behind his back.

'What now?'

'Let's hope Hussein can get us the tickets.'

Nabeel's cousin Hussein has let it be known to Juma'a that he will help on the condition that it is treated like a normal business transaction. That way, if they are caught, it will not look as if he was involved.

'I can't be sure but, *inshallah*, I will try to find a cancellation, a late booking – something will come up. You must be ready to go immediately. If a cancellation comes I will book you on to the plane.'

Nada twists a strand of hair round her fingers.

'Nada, it will be OK. Let's carry on as normal until Hussein calls. I have told the neighbours he will ring and they will come and get me. I'm going to sell the car, get rid of everything I can.' He leans in to hug her but her head is buried in her hands.

'Do you think it will happen, Dudi?'

Over the next fortnight the couple gather together all the money they can. Nabeel begins by finding a buyer for the Lada in Farouk, a literature teacher at Juma'a's school.

'The market price is three thousand,' Nabeel tells him when they mert, one night behind the house.

Farouk, a taciturn individual, wanders round the car and shakes his head. 'I don't know, Nabeel. I have only two thousand. I cannot stretch to three but perhaps—'

Nabeel interrupts before he has a chance to finish: 'OK, OK. Take it for two thousand. But I want the money in cash tomorrow.'

Farouk is delighted. He had expected the bargaining to continue for days.

Nabeel makes a list of all their family, friends and acquaintances for Jafar to inform when they have gone. Few are left. Almost everyone they know has been arrested at some point, Jassim, Khalil, Yusuf, taken from their homes, imprisoned and tortured. Others have disappeared, some into exile, others to who knows where? Although it is a sharp reminder of why they are leaving, the brief list pricks his conscience.

'Nada, why have I been spared arrest and others suffered so much? I am not so clever. I am not a hero. Perhaps we should not really be trying to leave. Should I not just fight on until Saddam is gone?'

Nada sees the guilt in his eyes. She knows he wants to stay but if they do he will die. Because they *will* get him in the end. After all the years of injustice, of fighting for reinstatement, the months spent hiding in tiny rooms, ducking into cellars and inside wall cavities, he still feels culpable.

'Your friends call you the Last Man Standing. Leaving is not a betrayal, Dudi. You have fought them for long enough. Let us try to have a life together where Yamam can be with us both. And Sabria, Tariq and the others will be safer if you are not here. My family too.'

Civil Intelligence had recently found Hamed and Behija's family. Only a clerical error, a misspelling on a detainment form, had saved them from interrogation. 'No, no,' Umaima had told the militia that had come to their door, 'we are not the Ahmeds. We are the Hameds.'

After days of waiting they are both almost grateful to be plunged into the confusion that ensues when Juma'a comes home with the news that Hussein has secured them the plane tickets. 'We are to go there at eight tonight with the money,' he tells Nabeel.

Nada's knees buckle and she cups both hands over her mouth to stifle a gasp.

'Are they for France?' Nabeel asks.

'I think so, brother. Paris.'

'And when do we leave?' He is feeling light-headed even to be talking about the possibility.

'We will know tonight.'

The two brothers drive into the city to pick up the tickets. Dressed casually, they park and walk down to Sa'adun Street. The lights of Baghdad's newest shops burn brightly and, amid them, the neon Iraqi Airways sign. Inside, lit up behind the glass, sits Hussein, at his customer-service booth, talking on the telephone. He is alone. In front of his desk are two leather chairs. As they walk through the door, he gestures for them to sit and finishes his call.

'*Marhaba.*' He leans across and kisses both men. 'How are you, gentlemen,' he says, addressing Nabeel as though they have never met. 'Can I get you tea before we talk?' Although no one else is in the shop and all three would like nothing better than simply to do the deal, they know that they are visible from outside, and that even if they are not being observed, someone will almost certainly be listening in. It will not do to hand over an envelope hurriedly, or to whisper as if they are afraid of being caught out. If there is anything important, Hussein will write it down for them. Tonight they will discuss, for the benefit of the listening devices installed throughout the building, tourist tips for Paris, check-in and seat allocation. Like most people, Hussein has long since given up searching for bugs. When he first discovered one inside his telephone receiver three years ago, he had searched the whole building from the phones to the bathroom and pulled out nearly twenty more. Returning the next day, he found every one had been replaced. He never bothered looking again; it is easier to assume that life is lived under scrutiny. For this reason no one speaks of family or mentions any names. Even when he hands over the printed itinerary, flight coupons and travel pouches, he maintains the neutral veneer of an agent with his client.

'The flight leaves tomorrow morning, as you know, at eight, and you will be in Paris for a late lunch. I recommend you check in a few hours before departure. The checks at the airport are time-consuming. Have a wonderful time. You are on business?'

'It's a short holiday with family,' says Juma'a.

Nabeel says nothing. All he can think about is that it is only fifteen hours before they will try to leave.

With the tickets safe, Juma'a and Nabeel go into the *souq* in the Old City to buy two large travel bags. Nabeel has decided that they should look like seasoned international travellers off on holiday and suggests they buy two smart black canvas cases. They pick the two largest in the shop, then return to the car. As he carries them along the thronging alleyways, he feels sick with anticipation. After months of transporting his possessions in a worn carrier-bag, it feels wilfully irresponsible to be holding the two largest cases in the shop. What on earth they will fill them with he doesn't know. Nada, he is sure, will have a clearer idea of what they should take.

'I want to say goodbye to Tawfiq.' Nabeel grabs his brother as they walk towards the car. 'He is just round the corner from here. Please, I should say goodbye.'

'We must be quick,' warns Juma'a.

'Yes, OK, but I must see him, brother. He is my best friend and he would never forgive me if I left without saying farewell.'

Tawfiq is standing beside his workbench, engaged in frenzied stitching. For once, the shop is empty. He sets down his needle and embraces his friends. 'Brother! You are here, once more, at my shop. Come in. You look grave. Tell me, do you have news for me?' He can see from their faces that there is news. Here in Baghdad there is always something. 'Please do not give me bad news.' With little steps he dashes to the back of the shop and turns the tape of folk songs over in his machine, songs from the iconic Fairuz. 'You know why,' he whispers.

Nabeel sighs and whispers into his ear: 'I come to say farewell. We have tickets, Nada and I. We are leaving tomorrow, brother.'

Tawfiq gasps. 'No, no. Brother, do not abandon me.' His round eyes fill with tears. 'Where do you go?'

Nabeel reaches over to the counter and writes in clear letters: Paris.

'Ah, Camus, Proust. I envy you, brother. Please, let us have tea. Quickly, quickly now. If you must abandon me, you will at least take tea before you go.'

As Nabeel watches his friend dart about in his embroidered cap he feels the loss already. They have been friends all his adult life, sharing time and ideas, argument and a passionate love of words. Tawfiq is a true member of the brotherhood, the most loyal of men, an honest companion in a dishonest time. 'Brother Tawfiq, you have been good to me.'

'Likewise. And please, though I have tried to persuade you not to run off, do not think any more of it. I understand. I want you to be safe. You will be better off in that great city, with street-sweepers, writers and artists. But when you return we can sit with our children at our feet and you can tell me everything I have missed. Ah, I will envy you for your European travel but I will hang on your every word.' He takes Nabeel's hand with a flourish. 'If you had warned me I would have made you something to take with you, trousers or a suit perhaps. It will be cold there.' He pauses and looks down. 'I will miss you greatly, Nabeel Yasin.'

'I need only your blessings. Besides, I have nothing to give in return.'

'But that is not the case. Remember,' his eyes dance mischievously, 'I have your poems.'

At home, Nabeel takes Nada aside, embraces her silently and shows her the bags. Sabria is in the living room, feet under her, on the russet-patterned sofa, watching television.

'Mama,' he says, and crouches before her. There is no point in trying to break it to her slowly. 'We have the tickets . . . We fly tomorrow.'

She grips his wrist and emits a small wail.

'Hussein has been a good friend. We go directly to Paris. And we will see Jabbar.'

Sabria raises her eyes to his, and he knows she is about to

ask the one question he has been dreading. 'How long will you be gone, my son?'

'Not long, Mama, I promise. Just until it is safe again.' She grips him harder. And, although he has no idea of how long they might be away, he accepts that, for her sake, he must put a time on it. 'A few months, six, maybe.'

She gets up and disappears into her room, closing the door behind her.

That night no one sleeps. Nabeel, fearing that the whole thing is an elaborate conspiracy, sits by the window, poised for any sound that is out of the ordinary. Nada sorts through their clothes and possessions, placing only the essentials in the bags. The girls cuddle Yamam and everyone is quiet, knowing they are on the cusp of change.

'It will be great to see Jabbar, and meet his fiancée,' Tariq says, in an effort to sound positive. 'I can't wait to find out what she's like. The playboy has settled down at last with a Frenchwoman!' They laugh nervously. For while they talk about it as though it is little more than a family vacation, none of them knows if Nabeel and Nada will even make it out of Iraq. This might be their last night ever as a family.

Knowing that her place is with Nabeel, Nada had said farewell to her family that afternoon. Her mother, tipped off in a coded telephone call that Juma'a had made from a neighbour's house, had rounded up her three sisters and they had come together for a final meeting. All five had sat on the sofas chattering together tearfully while their children played without any idea of what was coming. Although Nada had promised her mother it wouldn't be long before they saw each other again, Umaima glimpsed a more lasting separation. She had caught Nada in the hallway and pressed a tiny gift into her hand. 'Take it, keep it. When you see it, know that we are with you.' It was a beaten-silver pendant: it had been Behija's and before that their grandmother's, a most precious thing. Umaima hadn't let her cry. 'Ssh,' she had said, pressing a finger to her lips. 'It is a little something to remember us by, nothing more.'

Her father had come to sit with them too. They had talked little but he had held her close and she had promised to return as soon as it was safe. Now she clutches the pendant, which is strung round her neck.

It is a relief when the sun appears above the horizon that January morning and the bewildered family, overcome with nerves and fatigue, head out to the car. As the sparrows and sandpipers chatter in the trees, Jafar and Nabeel pack the car. Nada drags a bleary-eyed Yamam into a pair of navy blue trousers and a checked shirt, and Sabria straightens her crumpled *fota* until the pale weave running along the edge of the cloth disappears. Amel, black smudges under her wide brown eyes, takes hold of her mother's drooping shoulders. 'Mama, please, this is the right thing. We will know soon if they have made it . . .' She tails off. 'Look at us. Look at Nabeel. None of us could get through another month as things are.'

When there is nothing left to do, Nabeel takes Jafar aside. 'Please, do this for me. Go back to the house when you can. I have hidden some notebooks and pictures already, but there are more papers that should be put away. The box is hidden in the storeroom on the roof.'

'Don't worry, I'll go for you. We'll make sure everything is safe.'

'Thank you.'

'And, Mama, there is something I need of you too . . .' There is a lump in his throat. 'Promise you will do what I am

Sabria & Yamam

Aqbal, Jabbar, Nabeel, Amel & Yamam

about to ask.' Her eyes have already dropped to the ground as if she knows it will be impossible. 'When I am gone they will come for you. They will bully you and try to wear you down. They may try to punish you. If there is any trouble I want you to renounce me as your son.' He puts his arm round Jafar. 'You too, brother. There must be no retribution for anyone because of my actions. It's the same for Nada's family. Don't let pride be an obstacle to your survival, Mama.'

'I could not live with that lie, Nabeel. I would rather face it in truth,' Sabria protests. 'We are proud of you, my son.'

'Mama, please, give me your word!' he implores. 'This is no time to argue.' He looks straight at her, then wraps his arms round her. There are no tears. So much has passed between them all in recent days that to give in to emotion now would risk a deluge.

'Make a prayer for Yamam, Mama,' he begs. 'Just until you see us all again.' And then, without waiting for a reply, he ducks into the waiting car.

Sabria watches it pull out of the gate and, as it turns slowly on to the asphalt, she drops to her knees with her head on the ground. Looking back, Nabeel sees only the bent black figure of his mother, crying into the stones.

BOOK II

A Long List of Cities
September–October 1980

When the train pulls into Leipzig it is three hours late and they have to run, with all their cases, to make the connection to Halle. Nabeel shouts in Arabic to the platform guard, who is waving his flag. It is still instinctive to speak it. Although he learned English at school for ten years, the languages of Europe are strange to him. Of course both he and Nada have tried to pick up a few phrases during their search for a city that will take them in: Paris, Prague, Damascus and latterly Beirut. It is surprising how few words they need to make themselves understood.

The local train is slow and ponderous, scheduled to stop at every small town along the way. It could almost be an Iraqi train, Nabeel thinks, as he gazes at the hard seats and wooden-framed windows. Nada wraps her arms round Yamam. 'Not long now, little boy. This is the final little stretch and then we will be at Halle with Hameed and Fazia.'

She smiles at Nabeel. The idea of seeing friendly faces from home has induced in her an almost giddy sense of well-being. Hameed is an old friend of Nabeel's, a writer too, and Fazia, his wife, and Nada are as close as sisters.

'They know what it has been like and they will look after

us. We have stayed with so many people, having to whisper and hand over our papers. Remember all those houses and hotels, during our time in Syria, all those people saying you were a show-off because you'd stuck it out in Baghdad and shamed them into feeling like cowards? No,' she pulls out her cigarettes and offers one to her husband, 'this is going to be the start of something better.'

She gives Yamam an apple. They have been travelling now for more than forty-eight hours and are so exhausted that they can do little but stare at the rolling countryside passing by. She pulls open the tiny vent and blows out smoke towards the ripe golden fields that are nearly ready for harvest.

'Mama? How many hours have we been on the train?' Yamam asks, ready to impress his mother with his skill in counting.

She flicks ash off her cigarette. 'I don't know. But we might be able to work it out. Let me see, we left Beirut three days ago and there are twelve hours in the day so that is . . .?' She looks at Yamam as he vainly tries to count on his fingers. 'It is more than you can count — isn't that so?'

Nabeel ignores them and begins to scribble in his notebook. Half dazed from yet another protracted journey, his thoughts come uncensored and free. All his best work starts this way, in a swift, honest moment of creation. Of course, he may spend days, weeks, months even, in perfecting it, but isn't that the same for other artists? The flat land to the south-east is greying as the September sun tips westward, and although he wants to explore the newness of the world in which he has found himself, its seasons and textures, he is often pulled back to the place he has left. The last time he wrote anything of note was the morning they left Baghdad.

Sitting on the plane, holding Nada's hand, he had been

almost unable to comprehend what was happening. He had not even let himself believe they would be free until the plane was out of Iraqi airspace. Even then he half imagined that it would be ordered to turn round and take him home. They had held on to each other until their knuckles turned white and then, as the sun streamed through the windows, he had scrawled some verse on the back of his boarding card. It was a memory of the sunset he had witnessed the evening before. As he and Juma'a had driven to pick up the plane tickets, the sun's gold heart had bled across the sky, pink, purple and red. Was it his last Iraqi sunset?

The train stops at a small town, and passengers bustle on and off with bags and boxes. After the express service between Berlin and Leipzig, it is like stepping back in time. The ticket collector walks through the carriage between every station, clipping stubs. Several stout women in sensible skirts on the opposite side of the carriage nod vigorously to each other and hold up their tickets as he passes. At the sight of a herd of cows and a giant yellow haystack, Nada shoos Yamam back to the window. 'Look.' And with this image comes inspiration. That is what he wants to say: 'When summer is ended, there is only darkness on the horizon.'

It had been a little over two weeks earlier, in the searing August heat of Beirut, that they had received a blue airmail letter, forwarded by Jabbar from France, postmarked Halle. 'But that is the DDR,' Nada had said, scrutinising the postmark and stamp. 'We don't know anyone there.'

Nabeel had sliced it open and inspected the paper inside carefully, to be sure it was not poisoned, then removed it. He read the scrawled writing and burst into laughter. 'It is Hameed and Fazia! They have escaped Iraq, too. They are in Halle and they want us to visit.'

'Let us go right away. There is nothing to hold us here and I do so need to see a friend. Please can we go now?' Nada had beseeched, and she rarely asked for anything. 'Let us go now. We need to see real friends, and have the chance to discuss our future in confidence.'

Nabeel had gathered all their remaining cash and booked tickets to Prague that afternoon. There was nothing to keep them in Beirut. The search for work had led them back into a war zone. Nada had implored Nabeel to leave as they sat in a flat in the centre of the city, bombs exploding in the distance and gunfire piercing the night. 'So, they are not after us personally, but we are still prisoners here.'

From Prague, where with Hameed's help they secured a DDR visa, it was on to Leipzig by train.

As the pretty agricultural land disappears, replaced by grey concrete blocks of flats surrounding Halle and the Saale river, Nada's excitement bubbles over. Nabeel knows that everything has been hard on his wife, who has always had her sisters and friends around her. Now, because of him, she is alone. He has always enjoyed solitude. He needs it to write. Still, he was looking forward to seeing Hameed and Fazia. In nine months of exile it had been impossible to know who to trust.

Of course, it had been fine with Jabbar and his new French wife, Sylvienne. On the night they had arrived in Poitiers, they took a taxi from the station to an address that Nabeel had memorised. Jabbar had pulled open the window and stared, bleary-eyed, at the sight of his brother in the street, surprised and elated. But after two months the authorities had refused to extend their visas, so they had moved on to Prague where some of his old Communist friends were living, then after short sojourns back in France and Damascus, to Beirut.

Nada & Yamam in Prague

Finally, in the late afternoon, they step on to the platform at Halle and into the waiting arms of Hameed and Fazia. Nada cannot contain her relief.

The cries of the two women echo down the platform.

'*Habibti*, this is a wonderful moment! I never imagined I would be so happy to see you.' Fazia grabs her friend's cheeks and they fall into each other's arms.

Hameed, in a car coat, raises his eyebrows at Nabeel. 'Comrade, I think they are pleased to see each other.' The two men embrace. 'Good journey?'

'Let us say it has taken a while.' Nabeel chuckles. 'At least there is something good at the end of it. When I returned to Paris from Prague the first time they detained me in a cell with drug-smugglers and thieves. Nada was outside in the airport arrivals lounge and had to wait all day for me!'

'Just like old times then.' Hameed winks.

They drive through the city, along the modern boulevards and past the geometric monuments built by the Soviets.

'I am afraid it will be a squeeze. Our apartment is small,' Fazia tells Nada, 'but there are advantages to living at Hotel Hameed.'

Nada shrugs. 'We have lived in so many places this year. It's a relief to be with people we know.'

'We are so glad you have come. When we heard you were living in Beirut I said to Hameed, "Will we ever see them again?" Nada, I have been so worried for you.'

'It's been a disaster.' Nada checks that Nabeel is engrossed in his conversation with Hameed. 'We have been failed by all of Nabeel's so-called friends, in France and in Prague. In Baghdad everyone promised we had only to come to Prague. Now we find all the Party members have jobs but there is nothing for us. That is why we ended up in Beirut. It was the only place he was offered work. We have spent everything on just living these last few months.'

'But, Nada, Beirut is a war zone. Everyone is fighting.'

'It is no longer the "Paris of the East", that's for sure. I told myself that we were safer in Beirut than we were in Baghdad but now we are out I have told him we cannot go back. What price a salary?' She taps his shoulder. 'Right, Dudi?'

'Our house is yours. You are welcome to stay for as long as you like.'

As September unfolds, and the looming spectre of Iraq's war with Iran hovers ever closer, the four friends find themselves talking constantly of home.

'Everyone knows it is coming,' Hameed says, trying to dispel the gloom.

'But now it is upon us,' Nabeel snaps. 'Look at the

news. There are border skirmishes. It will be official within days.'

'What about Mama, Baba, everyone we know? What about conscription?' Nada's image of her home and loved ones is threatened by the prospect of war. They have heard that Saddam's army is one of the largest in the world. Thousands of tanks, hundreds of helicopters. 'There will be countless thousands of men on the front line.'

They can hardly articulate their worst thoughts: that brothers and cousins will have been sucked up into the vast machine and will be waiting, ill-prepared and fearful, along the borders, ready for the order to attack.

'Make no mistake, Saddam will sacrifice whoever he must to win. You know that. And we are stuck here. We don't even know if they are at war yet,' Hameed says, banging a fist on the table.

'But what is he fighting for? To avenge the attempted murder of Tariq Aziz? The Khuzestan oilfields? Surely not.'

'This is not a war about oil. It is his vanity. It is always about his vanity. He wants immortality. He wants to be worshipped by his people in songs, poems, books and paintings that tell of his great deeds. Saddam, the fearless leader of men.'

'And don't forget how many Arab countries support him,' Nabeel says. 'The Ayatollah Khomeini and the Islamic state are next door.'

Hameed sighs. 'You are right, of course. But we feel so powerless. Even here in Germany.'

With news of Iraq virtually non-existent in the East German press, the *émigrés* feel their isolation keenly. Nabeel has numerous prearranged phone conversations with Jabbar, who shares the news from France. 'Brother, there are skirmishes up in the border towns.'

'Do you know anything of Tariq?'

'Nothing. You know they will try to conscript him, Nabeel.'

There is nothing to do but wait, like everyone else, for the most dramatic reports to filter through to the newspapers. It doesn't take long. On 22 September the Iraqi Army crosses the border into Iran, and strikes are launched against the cities of Khorramshahr and Abadan. The two countries are now officially at war.

This prompts Nabeel and Nada to revise their plans. Although neither has said so, they have been hoping that perhaps they will be out of Iraq only for a short time. This thought helped to sustain them through the months of turmoil. Now the possibility of an early return has gone, and Nabeel knows that he must find a country that will take them in permanently.

He and Hameed go out for a beer one night to talk over his plans for the future. 'Hameed, you have been more than kind to us, but we should leave you soon. We must find a home. When we escaped from that shark, His Excellency the President the Leader God Placed Him, I thought the world would open its arms to us. "Just call up the ICP in Prague, they'll get you a nice job at the university or somewhere." But no. And because of me we have been in France, Prague, Damascus and Beirut. I don't think Nada and Yamam can take much more of this. The Communists may not want to help me any more – they certainly don't care that I risked my life writing for their papers while others fled – but I have to keep trying.'

'Look, Nabeel.' Hameed sips his beer and considers the matter. 'Let Nada and Yamam stay here while you go back to

Prague. They're not half as much trouble as you anyway.' He smiles. 'Go and see the deputy secretary of the Party. I know him, and you should mention my name. We will apply to get Nada's visa extended. Perhaps you should think about living here. I could look into an academic scholarship at the university.'

Nabeel leans over his beer. 'You are kind, Comrade. I will go to Prague, but on one condition.'

Hameed eyes his friend with care.

'Though I'm not sure any good will come of trying in Prague you must promise to visit us when we are finally settled.'

'Of course, my friend.' Hameed raises his glass. 'To your home, wherever it might be.'

In Prague the deputy leader is sympathetic, but the doors remain closed. He respects all that Nabeel has done but there is no lectureship or any other position for him. Nabeel is not a member of the Party so the deputy leader's hands are tied. As he leaves the Communist headquarters, Nabeel realises that nothing has changed since he left Iraq. He is still ostracised, but this time by the Communist Party.

So, on a gusty October afternoon Nabeel finds himself contemplating a return to Beirut. Sitting alone in the Café Bratislava, a long-time haunt of Iraqis in Prague, he resigns himself to life in Lebanon. The biggest obstacle will be telling Nada. He resolves to use his last dollars to buy a ticket that afternoon. Then she will not be able to dissuade him.

He finishes his coffee, but as he turns to leave, he sees,

tucked away at a table by the door, a man he recognises from home. 'Falih?' he says, in disbelief.

The man is scribbling notes in a book. He looks up 'Nabeel!' He leaps to his feet, scattering papers. 'I don't believe what my eyes are telling me. You got out! This is incredible. I heard a rumour that you were in Beirut but no one was certain. Everyone is saying it's crazy there.'

'I was there in the summer. In fact, I'm on my way back now. I'm going to the travel agent this afternoon,' Nabeel says ruefully.

Falih presses his palms together in the sign of thankfulness. 'But this is indeed fortuitous! I am leaving for Beirut in my car. Why not come with me? We can talk and catch up.'

'Are you insane? It's fifteen hundred miles or more!'

'Pah, a few days, five at most. We share the driving, you pay half the fuel and save yourself the cost of a plane ticket. We discuss books and poems, politics and art. And I have many friends across Eastern Europe.'

'What about visas and permits?'

'Easy. We'll get transit visas at the border crossings. Even for Syria. Once we reach Damascus, we're as good as there.'

Ordinarily Nabeel wouldn't have given Falih's plan a second thought, but he knows it will save him a significant amount of money. In fact, it's a bargain. And in his current state, a week will make no difference at all.

'OK, when do we leave?'

'Tomorrow, if you like. Why not? We could go to your apartment, pick up your things and be out of the city before the traffic gets bad.'

Falih leads Nabeel across the road towards a small white car parked in a bay behind a tree. It is a Lada. He bangs his hand on the bonnet as they reach it. 'Don't worry about the rust.' He runs his hands round the rim of the door. 'The rain here has been eating the car alive but she is as sound as any in Iraq.'

◈

As they sit in the traffic on the way out of the city the following morning, Nabeel stares at the grey leatherette seats, the same colour as the cloth upholstery in his Lada had been. Despite the misted display panel, the broken fuel gauge and the roaring holes in the dashboard, where the air vents should have been, Falih's car is comfortable and reassuring. With its smell of cheap cigarettes and the creaking, it could almost have been his. He pushes a carton of Marlboro and an envelope of dollars into the glove compartment, and realises he is looking forward to the drive. It is a relief to be on the way somewhere else

'It is time we see for ourselves the Europe everyone keeps talking about,' says Falih, enthusiastically. Taking the E5 out of Prague, they inch south towards the Hungarian border.

The first five days, as they pass through the fields and pastures of southern Czechoslovakia and into picturesque northern Hungary, are blissful, with vistas, hills, fine weather and idyllic hamlets dotted here and there along the roads. In Bulgaria Nabeel takes over the driving while Falih sleeps. He keeps up an almost constant pace into the night, only stopping to eat, refuel or pee at the side of the road. As they rise into mountain passes towards the border, he sees the moon in a cloudless sky and wonders if his mother is watching it and whether she has forgiven him yet for leaving. He has been away longer than six months already. Will she hold him to his lie? Her prayers and blessing now seem so important. He is out in the world alone for the first time in his life.

The spell of these unhappy thoughts is broken suddenly by a low grinding from under the bonnet. They slow, the car stalls and the engine dies. Nabeel wakes Falih and they both stand in front of the car. He knows it is pointless to look under the bonnet since neither of them understands a thing about mechanics. But in the blackness he can see a cluster of lights peppering the land below them. 'Falih, those are lights from the last town we passed. Turn round and roll back down.'

'You're crazy! Those bends will see us off the road and over the side of the mountain. We have no lights and the brakes have never been good. Let us hope we live to tell our children about this foolish idea.' But the high moon casts just enough silvery light for them to see the road. With Nabeel guiding him, Falih manages a cautious rolling turn. Then, releasing the handbrake, they coast through the blackness to the village below.

The car stops on a flat patch of road on the outskirts of the village. No sooner have the two men begun to argue about whether they should wake anyone before dawn than they are interrupted by a middle-aged man in his dressing-gown and boots shining a torch at them. Winding down the window, Nabeel explains, in gestures, smiles and snatches of English. 'Broken, broken,' he repeats. The man and his son push the car along the road and into a concrete garage. A minute later the village mechanic appears, pulls on an oily overall and begins work on the car. As he examines the engine, his wife sits Nabeel and Falih on a bench at the side of the garage and goes to lay a fire.

Eventually the mechanic calls them over. Lifting the car's

dynamo from its cavity, he tries to explain that it has given out. Nabeel nods furiously, using a combination of English, German and Slavic words encouraging him to fit a replacement.

'Where are you from?' he asks, in his slowest Slav, hoping they will understand.

'Iraq,' Nabeel replies.

Falih reaches under his sweater for his shirt pocket. 'My passport,' he explains, but the man waves it away.

'Maybe they think we've come up from Kurdistan to escape the war,' Falih whispers in Arabic.

'Do you really think they care?'

The mechanic's wife brings them hot coffee, bread, goat's cheese, homemade damson jam and wedges of warm omelette.

'We have only one problem, Nabeel,' says Falih, through a mouthful of food. 'We have no Bulgarian Lev and we cannot speak Slav.'

'We will have to use dollars, then.' Nabeel shrugs his shoulders and takes a fifty-dollar bill from the envelope he had stashed inside the glove compartment. The mechanic takes it and goes to show his wife. Together they shake their heads and come to Nabeel, gesturing at the pocket of his trousers for the envelope.

'We have insulted them,' Falih says. 'I said this would happen. We're in trouble now. These are mountain people. They're all crazy. Who knows what they might do to us?'

Nabeel holds out the envelope with its few remaining bills. 'Take it.' He points to the bills.

The man laughs and looks through the cash, takes a twenty and slips the fifty back. He offers his hand. 'Thank you, friend,' he says, in English, pointing up the mountain road. 'You can go.'

The disarming kindness of the Bulgarian villagers stays with Nabeel as they funnel through the southernmost checkpoint in the country and into Turkey. But these feelings of warmth don't last. Turkey has endured a summer of unrest. Demirel's pro-Western elected government has caved in under pressure from extremist groups and there has been yet another military coup. To prevent a total slide into anarchy, martial law has been declared. The border guard tells them they are fools for even trying to cross the country but he cannot stop them and stamps their passports, gives them a forty-eight-hour transit visa, then waves them through the barrier. 'There are bandits and gangs of looters on the roads. Don't stop unless you have to.'

Even in normal circumstances they would have to race to reach the Syrian border in such a short time. With chaos around them, the Lada faces its greatest challenge yet. 'Just what we need,' whimpers Falih. 'There will be soldiers everywhere, and bandits. Nabeel, have you considered what will happen if we break down again? Turkish prisons are worse than Iraqi ones.'

Around Istanbul they see the return of the driving rain that had dogged them in southern Hungary. Lying in the back seat, trying to rest, Nabeel wonders why he agreed to the trip. In Prague it had seemed a sensible prospect, enjoyable even, yet now he finds himself again in a lawless country with dangerous terrain and a co-driver who is nervous of everything. Pockets of thick fog slow them and oncoming cars appear suddenly, their headlights obscured in the murk.

Without warning they bump up on to a bridge that crosses the mighty Bosphorus. Rattling over it, suspended in an opaque white cloak, they can see nothing in either direction. 'Ever since I can remember I have wanted to see the Bosphorus,' Nabeel says miserably. 'Stop the car – I must at least

246

get out and smell the air.' Falih pulls over and Nabeel gets out to peer over the railing for an impression of what swirls beneath. Another car looms out of the fog and he is drenched as it hits a puddle. His cigarette falls apart and his shoes fill with water.

They stop in Ankara to find food, then push on down the dusty road to the south. Sitting in the passenger seat, eating *pide*, Turkish flatbread baked with meat and tomato, and running his index finger along the map, Falih suggests that they should head for Antakia. 'It will save us half a day.'

This turns out to be yet another poor decision. At dusk, they come face to face with the lawlessness of which the border guard had warned them. Soldiers, rebels and mercenaries lurch out of the shadows into the road, jumping at the car as it passes. Small fires burn in camps from which men run to intercept them, waving guns and screaming for money. Nabeel swerves to avoid them. Falih quakes with fear. 'Remember, the guard said don't stop. Can't you go any faster?'

As Nabeel pushes the accelerator of the protesting Lada to the floor, a hail of rocks hits the roof and bonnet. 'If we skid off the road we're as good as dead.' Falih lights two calming cigarettes and hands one to his friend. Nabeel follows the road, outlined in the thin light of the headlamps, the white-tipped Marlboro drooping from his lips. As he swerves to avoid more rocks and debris strewn across the asphalt, ash falls gently to his lap. Something smashes one of the headlamps and he feels it is only by a miracle that the windscreen has remained intact.

Eventually the bandits disappear and the terrain erupts into the crags and slopes that lead to the border.

'Look!' Falih says, pointing ahead. 'We're almost back on Arab land.'

There, by a fork in the road, is the sign they have been

waiting for, illuminated by the car's lone headlamp. The road to Damascus.

They drive along poor, deserted roads and come, an hour later, through a high mountain pass to their destination. A dividing fence, a steel gate and a one-storey whitewashed hut guard the way ahead.

Nabeel and Falih park outside the hut and walk across to the door. After such an ordeal and nearly twenty hours of almost solid driving it feels good to stretch their legs in the fresh mountain air. Nabeel knocks several times on the door but there is no answer. Ordinarily he would have driven on but to be caught without the right papers and stamps in Syria would result in an immediate spell in jail or deportation to Iraq. He is about to turn round when a tiny hatch half-way up the door slides back and someone demands to know their business. Nabeel bends to look at the face: the man is middle-aged with a pale moustache and his eyes are puffy with sleep.

'We are Arabs returning home. We need to get our stamps and cross the border in our car.'

'Do not try anything. I have a gun.' He jabs the butt of a double-barrelled rifle out of the hatch. 'And, for your information, you are already on Syrian soil so be careful how you proceed.'

The two men look at each other, bemused. Nabeel is about to ask what the guard means when the gun barrel jabs him in the shoulder.

'Reverse the car.'

'What?'

'You heard. Take your car back. I want it fifty metres away

at least.' He gestures with the rifle back down the mountain road.

'Are you saying we can't come through?' Falih asks, indignant.

'That is exactly what I am saying. The gate opens at eight and not before.' The rifle is withdrawn and the hatch slams shut.

Nabeel shrugs and winds his scarf round his neck. 'Let us do as he says. Maybe we should have breakfast at one of those villages we passed a kilometre back. We can get some sleep, maybe.' Falih agrees when the hatch slides open again.

'And you may not drive away from here either. You have already crossed illegally on to Syrian soil. You will stay exactly fifty metres back until I open.'

Falih gets into the back seat, curls up and drifts off under his thick army coat. Nabeel wishes he was relaxed enough to do the same. Now, ten days into this disastrous road trip and they are only just at the Syrian border. He lights a cigarette. The poor-quality Turkish blend fills the car with smoke and he coughs violently. Winding the window down, he lets in a stream of thin mountain air to clear his lungs. Each inhalation brings calm. He gathers his coat into a makeshift pillow, lays his head against the window frame and drifts off.

He is woken by a warm, wet sensation. It seeps into his subconscious and filters into his dreams. Something is nuzzling his head, something alive, with breath and a tongue. He sits up with a start, and as his eyes adjust, he sees an animal making for the scrubland. He turns on the Lada's single headlamp. A grey wolf pauses by the edge of the road, unblinking, then turns and disappears into the trees.

And there, in the silent chill of the mountain pass, Nabeel has a revelation. He is lost. He is far in every way from where he should be. Adrift in the world, miles from anywhere, his family strewn here and there, unable to talk to each other. Now he is on his way back into a war zone. In the last forty-eight hours he has been attacked and stoned and he has spent more than six hundred dollars, on food – mostly for Jalleh's stomach, expensive fuel, further car repairs, maps and border charges. It is twice as much as it would have cost him to go by plane, and he still isn't in Beirut. Everything has to change.

The editor of the Communist magazine is pleased that Nabeel has returned and passes him several stories. To Nabeel, this is vindication of his choice to come back. During the last part of the drive through Syria, he had reflected on his moment of clarity in the mountains and made a plan: he will work as hard as he can for six months, then return to his family for good – after all, he had fled Iraq so that he, Nada and Yamam could live without fear of being separated. And in the spring when he returns to Germany with money, he will be bringing them choices too: his earnings will buy them time and freedom.

He produces the commissioned articles with characteristic honesty, not wanting his work to be seen as more of the self-indulgent propaganda that many, even in Beirut, get away with. But the pieces are not well received.

Since he cannot afford to speak to Nada on the phone he explains what has happened in a letter:

I have had to leave the magazine. They wanted only propaganda and you know I cannot write what they want to hear. But, please don't worry, I will write for others. My aim remains the same – to earn enough money to keep us all, then return to you both.

Nada is unhappy without him and wants him to come back: '*I told you not to go there,*' she writes. '*It is not safe, regardless of what job you are doing. And we left Iraq to live. We will manage somehow. Do you need to risk everything? Yamam still asks about you every day and I don't know what to tell him.*' But she has good news too:

> *Hameed sent off the papers to Berlin and we have a small extension on our visas. We can stay for another two months. Hameed thinks we should try again in January. Dudi, will we see you before then? Yamam is growing very fast and talking in German. We miss you.*

Now that he is without a job he moves into a smaller apartment, with his old friend Mudhir. He allows himself briefly to imagine settling in Germany, with a role for himself at a university – Middle Eastern studies, or as a professor of literature. He wonders if he will ever again be considered a poet. The crowds, the readings and plaudits are so remote now, as though they happened in another life.

Slowly, he builds his freelance contacts and a few commissions come in. One paper has asked him to write a piece about literature under dictatorship and with this and other pieces – reviews, a couple of poems – he finds the weeks pass quickly. But Nada's next letter brings bad news:

> *Hameed applied to Berlin for another extension to the visa. But we have been turned down. Dudi, at the end of January Yamam and I must leave. Where should we go? Back to Jabbar? Will you write to him for me? We will wait for you in France, Dudi.*

Nabeel reads her letter in the dim light of his apartment. He keeps it as dark as he can. In a block of flats down the street, neighbours have been shooting each other through the walls and windows, and although he is not persecuted as he was in Iraq he is mindful of the disorder, wanting to steer his way through it unobtrusively. He had been feeling optimistic and had written to Nada earlier about a poem to be published in *Al-Safeer*. It is called *The Statue and the Museum*. It is about his mother's grief at his departure. It is the most painful piece he has ever written; his emotions, kept in check, have finally forced their way out. As he rereads Nada's letter Nabeel feels wretched. He begins a letter to Jabbar. There has to be a solution, a way forward . . .

With the sound of gunfire and shelling in the distance, Nabeel recalls a conversation he once had with Abo Gate'a, a writer of folk stories and one of his more trustworthy Prague contacts. Abo had told him to consider Budapest. 'Life is much freer there. It would suit a man like you.' At the time he had thought little of the idea. He was focused on Czechoslovakia and finding a prestigious position among the Communist élite. It was, after all, what they had promised him.

Now, separated from his family in Iraq, his wife and son, he knows he must try something else. He will meet Nada and Yamam in Poitiers and from there they will go east together. Of course, he cannot know if Hungary will welcome them but it cannot be any worse than this.

Qadisiyat Saddam
April 1982

Tariq watches Sabria run a duster along the lacquered wooden frames of the family photographs. They hang on the wall under the window next to a portrait of Imam Ali: Jafar at school, Jabbar on his graduation day, Yasin with Amel and Aqbal to either side of him. Although some of them are still living at home they have all changed. Jafar is forty-two and married. Juma'a is almost forty. Aqbal works at the Iraqi National Bank, and little Amel is at medical school. Even Tariq is now twenty-two and training as a civil engineer. If the country hadn't been at war he would have described himself as a young man with good prospects.

There are pictures of Nabeel, too. In one he is with Nada and Yamam, but the other was taken when he first found fame as a poet – thick, wayward hair just above his collar and a rather earnest expression.

Since Nabeel left, Sabria has been quieter; the loss of her husband and part of her family has made her fearful and uncertain. With conscription looming, Tariq knows he is about to add to her worries. Unlike Jafar, who is too old to be called up, and Juma'a, whose position as a teacher will save him, Tariq is young, the ideal conscript.

Newly graduated from university, he no longer has even the excuse of his studies to put to the conscription board. Although he has ignored their letters, he knows evasion is impossible.

He watches his mother pay homage to the Imam. She thanks him, as she does every day, for sparing Nabeel, Nada, Yamam and Jabbar. In the weeks following Nabeel's departure she and Behija, Nada's mother, spent their time together wailing and hugging each other. Now, with war raging on the eastern front, she is glad, for the first time, that Nabeel and his family are no longer in Baghdad.

'It is the those of you here with me who I must pray for now,' she says to Tariq, as if she has read his mind. 'I want you to be spared from the vanity war of His Excellency the President the Leader God Placed Him.'

'You worry too much, Mama. I'm a survivor.'

'I know, my son,' Sabria says. 'But that man has no thought for anything but war and you should not be caught up in it.'

'It is not even our war,' Jafar says, from the window where he is watching for the secret police. He has been tipped off that they are coming that afternoon. In the last month he has helped his brother slip out of the back door twice when the police came calling.

'Yet he calls it Qadisiyat Saddam, as if it is a modern-day holy war. He truly believes he is the incarnation of Sa'ad Ibn Abi Waqqas, a great voice out there defending the cause of Arabs against the Persians.'

'All he really wants is to send the intellectuals and thinkers to the front to be blown up so they can't criticise him any more.'

Jafar steps away from the window and settles on the sofa.

'It's a mystery to me why anyone still believes in him. Anyway, it's time for the news. Let's see what version of the truth he's peddling today.'

The newsreader talks of substantial Iraqi victories. 'Two thousand Iranians are known to be dead or injured in the latest battles. Six Iraqi soldiers have been injured and one has been killed.'

Sabria shakes her fist at the screen. 'What a shameful lie.'

They know from the numbers of injured men returning to their own neighbourhood that the bulletins are nonsense.

When they had first come for Tariq, not knowing who he was or his family's reputation, the draft officers had expected him to sign up there and then like everyone else. He had taken the form and burned it in the bread oven. When they had returned, several weeks later, he told them he had sent it back. Within a week the army was on to him. 'Iraq's most valiant soldiers are being slowed around Khorramshahr and Abadan. The Iranian resistance goes on and you are trying to dodge your duty. You *will* help your Iraqi brothers. We will return tomorrow to collect these papers, and your medical certificate.'

He had gone into hiding for a few weeks, hoping they would move on to someone else. Now that he is back he is living on borrowed time. If they discover that he is related to Nabeel, there will be a beating too. After the Mukhabarat had discovered that Nabeel had fled the country, they had imprisoned Tariq. Sabria had come to the prison and, together, they had signed a document disowning his brother. They had known that anything done in the name of the regime had no legitimacy. And Nabeel had asked them to do it.

'I am praying every day to Allah for the end of the war,'

Sabria says now, to her youngest son. '*Inshallah*, you will never meet the draft officers again.'

◈

In early February the Fifth Directorate of Military Intelligence, a Gestapo-like organisation, begins an investigation into Tariq Yasin and soon discovers that he is the brother of the exiled poet Nabeel Yasin. This, with his previous arrest record, catapults Tariq to the top of the enforced-conscription list.

Two officers from the Directorate storm the Yasins' house in the middle of the night, wrestle Tariq from his bed and charge him with 'concealing information'.

'I told you, I am sick. I have back problems. I cannot fight, I will be a liability,' he screams.

'Our doctors will decide if you're fit to fight.'

They take him to a military detention centre where, predictably, he is denied food, drink and sleep. He is beaten and his family is threatened. With only Jafar and Juma'a left at home to look after his mother and sisters, he knows there is nothing for it but to sign the papers.

They send him to join the 120th Infantry Division 31, stationed to the south-west on the Iranian border near Basra. He is not allowed to say goodbye to his family before he is driven to barracks on the outskirts of the city, handed an ill-fitting uniform, stiff black boots and a canvas patrol bag, then marched aboard a vanload of other recruits.

'Does anyone have any idea where we're going?' he asks the eighteen-year-old next to him.

'The "oven of the war", somewhere down south, close to the Shatt al-Arab.'

On arrival at the camp, the recruits are marched through the site and into a huge canvas tent where they wait to receive their first orders. Tariq shifts from one foot to the other to ease the blisters on his heels. They have taken his gold chain and his silver *misbaha*, and cut off his hair. Now his cigarette lighter is his only link with home.

The stocky quartermaster marches in, shakes sand from his beret and stands in front of the recruits. 'You know why you are here.' He looks them up and down contemptuously. 'You are the scum, the liars and cowards who thought they could cheat their way out of this noble war. And because of this we will now test your courage to the fullest. You will join the Scout Advance Party, active immediately. You will train today and tomorrow, and then you will be dispatched. You will now show your allegiance to His Excellency the President the Leader God Placed Him by leading the way into battle.'

This speech has the desired effect: the group are petrified. Tariq had imagined weeks of marching, manoeuvres and training in survival techniques, undertaken a long way from the front. He raises his hand. 'Sir, I am not the only man here who has no military experience. Should we not have full training?'

'Silence. The job of the Scout Advance Party is to listen and do as you are told. But, since you ask, no training is needed for the task you will undertake.' He strides out of the tent into the beginnings of a sandstorm.

As they journey into the fields, each man stares out of the back of the jeep, lost in thought as to what horrors await them on the front. When Tariq had asked the commissioning officer how long he would be there he had been told he would serve a year. But from the snort of laughter that followed, he knows he is not expected to last that long.

257

The prospect of carrying weapons depresses him. He has never even touched a gun before. His family are dissenters, but not one has ever owned a weapon. 'Your tongue is the quickest way into and out of trouble,' Sabria had told them.

He bats mosquitoes away from his ears and surveys his new world: men with the vacant stare he had seen when his father was dying, the smell of bad meat stewing, the dust in his nostrils mixing with the stench of effluent and diesel. He would rather be at the mercy of the Mukhabarat than here. As he contemplates the jeeps, tents, sacks of provisions and weapons, he realises that if he is to come out alive he must become the sharpest soldier out there.

Lying on a tarpaulin groundsheet with a coarse blanket over him, Tariq cannot sleep. In less than six hours he and his squad will report for duty. Staring up at the stars, he wonders how Sabria is taking the disappearance of yet another son without explanation.

Long before daybreak he can hear of ammunition being loaded into tanks and ground-to-air missile launchers being assembled. Men shuffle about by torchlight. 'They call us the walking dead,' the boy next to him whispers.

'Who does?' Tariq asks.

'The tank drivers. I heard them.' The boy pulls a packet of cigarettes out of one of his boots.

'Why us? Isn't everyone in this war walking dead?'

'Some are more dead than others.'

'What are you talking about?'

'You don't know yet, do you?'

'Don't know what?'

'We're minesweepers. That's why we haven't been trained. They don't expect us to live long. Our job is to walk out in front of the tanks and look for mines.'

The boy goes on: 'I spoke to the colonel yesterday. "Of course, we have the most skilled bomb-disposal experts," he said, "but we want to save them. That's why we send you out first." He laughed at me.'

It was well known that as the Iranians retreat they set mines across the swamps, scrubland and salt plains.

'They don't even bring the injured back to camp. If a mine goes off and you're maimed, they leave you for dead.'

They lie in silence, then the boy offers Tariq a cigarette. 'I'm Mahmoud.'

'Tariq,' comes the stifled reply.

Dawn breaks over the camp and the red streaks in the sky yield to brilliant blue. Tariq can see that the ground beyond the camp fences is churned up and pitted by explosions. Trenches run like scars for miles, hurriedly filled in as the Iranians retreat. Bodies, guns, jerry-cans and cigarettes are buried along with the shrapnel mines.

'Mahmoud,' he says, thinking he should plan for the worst. 'If something should happen to me, would you get news to my family? I'll give you my address and a telephone number.' In the first year of the war those who had died in battle were hailed as martyrs, their families given ten thousand dinars and a Toyota Super. Now, with so many dead, he would be lucky if they decided to bury him, let alone inform his family.

'I have the same worry,' Mahmoud says. 'Let us make a pact. I will find your mother and tell her, and you will do the same for me.'

'You have my word.'

259

A grandiloquent brigadier strides out before them with a megaphone as they stand waiting for their orders.

'Today you will advance in a south-easterly direction from the lines drawn yesterday. You know your positions, and the job you must do. The victory of this army depends on your vigilance. And remember, you do it in the name of His Excellency the President the Leader God Placed Him. Do not fail him.'

He disappears into the mess tent and a sergeant takes command of the troop, leading them on the slow trudge through the razor wire and down the lines out to the trenches beyond the camp. All around them, craters and shrapnel mark the progress of the day before. Tariq wonders how many were killed to get the tanks where they are now. Without much talking, the more experienced men take up positions at the front, spreading out slowly and carefully at intervals of two metres or so. He waits for the sergeant to lead off, then follows in silence, adopting the low, slow sweep of the man in front: with his eyes on the ground he looks between the fragments of wheel, headlamps, mortar cases and bits of twisted metal for the telltale disturbance of a landmine. Tariq has no idea what he is supposed to be looking for. He realises that he and the men around him, the draft dodgers and middle-class undesirables, are being used to detonate the mines, rather than finding and destroying them.

Step by agonising step he walks on for twenty minutes. Then the firing begins: shellfire and mortar explosions fill the air, intermittent and deafening. The Iranians have started the day's barrage, and as they find their range, shells land all over the no-man's-land Tariq is walking through. Unlike him, the enemy are safe in embedded armoured vehicles, now established as ground-to-air missile and mortar launch stations.

The ten boys who joined with him two days earlier are dotted to his right and left. Mahmoud is on the far side. They stalk on, heads sweeping from side to side. At every large explosion he cowers. Some carry on walking through waves of acrid smoke as if they have not seen or heard anything.

Their orders are to reach the row of trenches two hundred metres ahead, the point of yesterday's retreat. Tariq could have run the distance in a minute or so. Now, as he looks ahead to where a red flag flutters in the breeze, it seems impossibly far. Even the pain of his new leather boots against his blisters has changed: it reminds him that he is still alive.

Every now and then someone stops or falters, shouting that he has a mine. Tariq checks that his comrades are all still standing. Then, slowly, as the minutes turn to hours and the world beyond the nightmare recedes, he finds that he has established a rhythm of his own. Each step is a meditation, a complete activity in itself, taking him through fear into release.

By the middle of the afternoon with the high heat of the sun bearing down, it feels like a game, a glimpse of hell. Then comes a flash of light and a huge pulse of energy. There is screaming, torn flesh in the air. But no one stops. Tariq turns his head and sees the dismembered torso of the man he had stood next to that morning in the line for breakfast.

Little by little necessity sharpens his intuition and he learns to spot the telltale signs in the dirt, the patterns that suggest a human hand has been at work. New recruits keep arriving to replace the many who die.

In the fifth week news comes in that all but three of the next regiment have been killed at the battle of Khor az Zubayr. Stunned, many men retreat into prayer, and from every tent Tariq can hear the sound of men whispering the *bismallah* passages from the Qur'an. Here, on the front, nothing can hide the truth. They all know that with this regiment gone, and thousands dead just a few miles away, they will soon move up to replace it.

Tariq and his squad remain at the bottom of the camp hierarchy, the last to receive food, provisions, leave and privileges. In the early days Tariq had complained: 'There is no stew. How can I search for mines if I am hungry all the time? The other soldiers get rice and meat and bread.' He had been shouted down by a group of sergeants. It seems that he, like all the other men in the human shield, can do nothing to raise his status.

It is in his sixth week that Tariq begins to plan his escape. Among the chaos he has noticed a more personal agenda developing: the business of the regiment seems not so much conflict as commerce. Senior officers treat the war as a vehicle for their own ambition. While the dead and wounded are counted and shipped to mass graves or, if they are lucky, home to their families, the officers negotiate deals to increase their wealth, power and privilege once the war has ended. Men with skills and business acumen are being taken from across the forces for non-military assignments. Tariq has heard that a carpenter from the mine squad has been seconded to Basra to fit an officer's house with cupboards and new teak furniture. 'Can you believe it?' he says to Mahmoud, one night.

'The brigadier has sent two teachers to Baghdad to tutor his children in maths and physics. They were on the tank-maintenance detail. Are you trained in anything?'

'Of course. I'm a civil engineer, but I don't know how they could use that.' Tariq sighs.

'This war is corrupt,' adds Hani, from the bunk opposite. 'If you have any sort of trade, there's a place for you away from it. You just have to find out who needs what doing for nothing. Abdullah Karim was on the mines a month ago. Now he's driving a truck shipping black-market dates and fruit from the military storehouses to the general's family. I tell you, these men are making fortunes.'

'We must make our own luck in this life.' Tariq is thinking hard.

'Down here? Is such a thing possible?'

It is after some casual eavesdropping that he discovers the regimental general has bought a large plot of land and is having a house built on it. 'The project has fallen so far behind. I've made the investment, and intend to live there, but at this rate it'll never be built.' The conversation between the general and one of his colonels makes Tariq's heart pound. Project managers are hard to find at the best of times, but during a war, well, they must be like gold dust.

'Tools, materials, money and staff have all gone missing.' Mahmoud relays more detail from the grapevine. 'He doesn't want to waste any more money but he can't find anyone who knows what they're doing. You should talk to him. There will be no better opportunity.'

'It has to be worth a try. Where's his land?' Tariq asks.

'In the south-west of Baghdad.'

It cannot be far from his mother's house. If they send him to do a recce he'll be able to visit her. Spitting on his boots and shaking out his beret, Tariq sets off immediately in search of the general.

◆

The general's tent is situated at the heart of the camp. He has a fridge, a coffee-table, a large bed and a personal secretary. Two aides stand guard at the entrance. As Tariq strolls towards it he takes out a full packet of cigarettes and offers it in a friendly, easy manner. The first guard observes him. Tariq thrusts the cigarettes towards the second. 'They're Baghdad,' he says, turning the packet so that the corporal can see the logo. 'At home,' Tariq gestures at his uniform, 'I'm a civil engineer. A good one. I hear the general's looking for someone to help with his house.' He catches the man's eye and holds his gaze. 'I could do the job he wants. I have very good qualifications from Baghdad University.'

The guard puts up his hand and, after a whispered discussion with his colleague, ducks through the loose canvas flap.

A minute later Tariq is presented to the general. Close up, he is not as old as Tariq had thought. His hair is greying at the temples but his face is round and well fed.

'Yes?'

'Private Yasin, sir.'

'They tell me you have something to offer me?'

'Yes, sir. I'm a civil engineer. The best. I hear you need one.'

'I need many things. But go on. Tell me your background. What is a civil engineer doing here on the bloodiest front?'

'I graduated from Baghdad University with a good degree in civil engineering and was working in the city when the call came.'

'The call?'

'To come to the front, sir. It was my wish to serve my country in the best way I can so I signed up.'

The general eyes him suspiciously. He knows that anyone on mine detail is usually a rebel or a criminal.

Tariq goes on, hoping he will not undermine his chances: 'My family live in south-west Baghdad. I know many builders and tradesmen there who can help—'

'Quiet! I don't care about your background. How can I be certain you will do a good job?'

'I am young, sir, with something to prove. I will work hard. Besides, you are my general and it is my job to follow your orders. If I do one job well, perhaps a second will follow.'

'Between me and you, the house has become a depressing issue for me.' The general peers across his desk at Tariq and pulls at his thick leather cummerbund. 'It's full of problems that I have no time to sort out. Perhaps you can help me. You will go . . . for two weeks and if I see progress you will return there for two weeks in every month until it is finished. Now, go and await my instruction.'

'But I am in the Scout Advance Party, sir. Perhaps I will not be alive to return.'

'Indeed. Perhaps, on reflection, three weeks at the house is more realistic.' He inclines his head and waves Tariq away.

When Tariq arrives at the general's plot a week later, his heart sinks. The villa is little more than a series of concrete posts and slabs arranged haphazardly in the ground. The plans, such as they are, bear little resemblance to what he sees. And although he is dressed in full uniform and armed with a curt official letter, none of the workmen seems troubled by his presence. The four builders, dozing under a makeshift canopy, barely move as he walks on to the site. Bags of cement and marble slabs are strewn across the vast courtyard.

'Who is the foreman?' Tariq adopts the irate tone of his patrol sergeant.

'There is no foreman,' a man answers, squinting at Tariq, who stands over him. 'Who wants him anyway?'

'The general! He is very unhappy with the progress you've made and I am going to sort it out before we all end up at the front.'

'Good luck.' The man laughs.

He can understand their lack of drive: the slower they are in finishing, the less likely they are to go to the front. And they are paid simply for being there. 'I know why you're not working and I would do the same, but I have to tell you that the general is on to your little scheme. He plans to send you somewhere very unpleasant if you don't help me get on with it. There will be no more pay either, unless I return with reports of how well we are doing here.' Tariq looks them straight in the eye. 'And, believe me, I will fire any of you who does not keep up. The general is coming in a week, and we must have the hall and courtyard complete.' It's a harsh way to start, he knows, but he has enough cigarettes to buy at least some co-operation from them. That, and some horror stories from the front, should do it.

When the general pays his first visit to the site, he is impressed and full of camaraderie. 'Carry on, carry on.'

Sensing that he is in a receptive mood, Tariq makes him a

second offer. 'Sir, if you want this finished faster even than I told you,' he says, 'allow me to bring in my own men who will work hard for you. I will make up the shortage with four from my detail, all skilled in their trade. What is more, you will not have to pay them since they are already employed.'

The general laughs and offers Tariq a cigarillo from his engraved silver cigarette case. 'They will work hard because they respect me or because you have got them away from the front?'

'Both, sir.' Tariq takes a cigarillo and lights it.

'You're a clever man, Tariq. I like it. So, with your own men, how long?'

'We shall have it complete in twelve weeks.'

'Excellent.'

Back at camp he puts in a few days' service at the front. As he emerges from his tent on the morning he is due to return to Baghdad with Mahmoud and the rest of his crew, he sees a jeep with an old friend in the back outside the communications tent.

'Sadik?' he shouts. Sadik had been friendly with Nabeel, one of the group who used to hang around Tawfiq's shop. Now he is obviously shattered and bewildered.

'It's good to see you.' They cling to each other – and to a glimpse of what life had been before all of this.

'You also, Tariq. I cannot believe it. To see you here, in this – this vile cesspool . . .' He trails off. 'But what of your family? How is Nabeel?' he asks.

'In Europe still, perhaps in France,' Tariq ventures. 'The others are at home, working. When you come back to

Baghdad you should visit.' He grins. 'You know you will always be welcome.'

His colleagues are pacing back and forth from the truck with tins of oil and food, and he realises that Sadik's crew are preparing to leave. 'What about you? Are you being re-stationed?' he asks.

'No, we have to return to the front. We have only stopped to collect two extra men and more trucks.'

'What are you doing out there?'

'I am in the Dirty Task Squad. When they came for me, they saw I could not fight. It is my eyes. I thought perhaps they would let me off or use my brain to some advantage. But they mocked me, and put me here instead,' he says. 'So now I collect the bodies of the dead. We leave the enemy where he has fallen and take our own. But there are never enough bags for them all or string to tie them. Our truck has the smell of an abattoir with the bodies crammed in like carcasses, sometimes fifty at a time.'

Tariq swallows.

'It is easier when they are bagged but we can only do that when a body is in pieces – to keep the parts together. The army does not care about the dead.'

'How long have you—'

'Who knows? It only gets worse. We are under orders to deliver bodies to any family we can.' He gathers himself. 'Mothers, fathers, brothers, sisters – all attack us as we deliver their dead. They want proof, wedding rings, scars and birth-marks, and sometimes there is nothing left to show them. What can they do with a hand? I try to help them, but they don't want to talk, only to wail.' He pauses. 'War is full of prophets and writers. I try to find papers if I can. Letters from all those that we leave in pits. That is the real proof.'

'You are not to blame.' Tariq wraps an arm round him. 'Go. Find peace when this is over.'

'Thank you, Tariq.' He climbs back into the jeep.

As he watches Sadik bounce away, Tariq wonders what the future holds for him. No one deserves to be in the Dirty Squad but, as he has come to appreciate, nothing in war is equitable.

For now Tariq knows he must cherish his own good fortune. He is in demand. He has some tins for his mother and a request for help from another officer – the general had recommended him to a colleague – once this job is done. And he is on his way out of the camp. With Mahmoud and three other friends from his detail, he is on his way back to Baghdad.

Allah Karim
February 1986

The apartment block in Budapest is modern and attractive. Nabeel, Nada and Yamam have rented a flat on the eighth floor. It is the most comfortable and affordable place they have found since they left Iraq. Set in the sprawling eleventh quarter of the city, it has long views up towards the river Danube, two bedrooms, a living room, a bathroom and a box kitchen with fitted cupboards, a gas oven and a fridge. From the table next to the kitchen window they can see the small church, factory buildings and a train station. Across the river is one of Nabeel's favourite sights, the Gellert Hotel and its thermal spa.

The rooms are cosy: there are thick iron radiators and carpets. Even in winter, when temperatures reach twenty degrees below zero and hard-packed snow cakes the city, it is warm in the flat – quiet too, with only the faint sound of traffic and the occasional voice in the street rising up to them. Relaxed now, they all sleep well. They make time to be with each other and to explore new things. Nabeel has re-acquainted himself with Kafka, T.S. Eliot and Thomas Mann, and he and Nada have even managed a few trips to the cinema, watching Hungarian and Hollywood films in their newly adopted language. On Fridays they sometimes walk together along the banks of the river that divides the city in two but most of the time they stay in their flat, their tiny haven.

There is rarely any noise from the corridors or through the walls. Sometimes they exchange greetings with their neighbours but people here, though friendly, keep to themselves.

During the year they have lived in the apartment Nabeel has come to know a few of his neighbours. He meets one of them a teacher, who keeps similar hours in the foyer several times each week. The man had initially been so shy that he would duck if Nabeel said hello. It was hard to imagine him in front of a classroom of schoolchildren. Even his clothes looked uncomfortable on him. But the face beneath the broad felt hat was amiable and open. After a few months of waiting together for the lift doors to open, they had progressed through a series of short exchanges to more personal and revealing lines of enquiry. 'I have noticed we both work the same hours. You must be another teacher,' the man had said one day, out of the blue, taking Nabeel by surprise.

'Almost,' Nabeel had said, smiling, in his heavily accented Hungarian. 'I am finishing my PhD at the Academy of Science.'

'Fascinating. In what, may I ask?'

'I am assessing the effect on ideology and culture of economic and social development in Arab countries.' He does not say that it had come after a two-year quest to find a job. Or that during this period he had never stayed anywhere for more than three months and that the relief of being offered respectable work had been almost too much for him.

'You have been in Budapest long?'

'About four years.'

'Where are you from?'

Nabeel had paused to consider the question. 'Well, once I was a poet and a writer . . .' He paused. 'In Iraq. Baghdad.'

'Such a place of myth,' his neighbour cried. 'The cradle of civilisation.' Now each time they meet he asks Nabeel about the war. 'Tell me, Nabeel, what is happening in your country now?'

At first Nabeel had taken a deep breath, then embarked on a considered answer – to him there was no more serious matter in the world than his country's fortunes. But he had seen that almost as soon as he had begun the lift doors would open at the second floor and the man would step out, saying, 'Goodnight, Nabeel. See you tomorrow, I hope.' Nabeel had found himself standing there, his words trailing off into the empty air, wishing he had never opened his mouth. It dawned on him that the man did not require an answer of any depth: the question itself signified the limit of his interest. 'A little good, a little bad,' or 'The Iranians are pushing us but this has happened before,' is all that is needed. In Europe the war with Iraq means little, if anything. And why should it? Nabeel thinks. It is a world away.

Today, on this freezing February afternoon, returning early from the library, Nabeel hopes he will not meet the teacher. The news from Baghdad is bad and he cannot bear the thought of making small-talk: the Al Faw peninsula has collapsed and many thousands of soldiers are reported dead, injured or missing.

He has no idea if Tariq is at the front but assumes he must be. The word from the network of *émigrés*, who pass information diligently among themselves, is that every man

272

alive is being drafted. Nabeel holds little hope of the local television service showing anything of it on the evening news. In Budapest foreign reports stop at the boundaries of the Iron Curtain. Television here devotes time to Gorbachev's official activities, covering every visit the Soviet premier makes to a barracks or hospital.

Nabeel is stepping into the lift and wondering if he should go out and call Jabbar when the teacher rushes into the foyer on a gust of icy air. 'I have chased after you from the bus stop,' he exclaims, breathless with excitement. 'What great news, no?'

'I'm sorry. What great news is this?' Nabeel tries to conceal his anxiety.

'Surely you have heard? The offensive at Al Faw. What a triumph for Iraq, eh?' The teacher is pleased to have something to discuss with his Arab neighbour. 'It will lead to a great victory, don't you think? I hoped I would run into you yesterday when I heard. My wife and I wondered if you and your wife would like to come to us for a drink. We have Tokai. I hope that this means an end to your troubles at home.'

Nabeel follows him into the lift. 'Thank you for your thoughts,' he responds, as delicately as he can, 'but this is an Iranian victory. We are Iraqi.'

The lift stops and the doors part, allowing the teacher to escape. 'Do not worry,' Nabeel calls after him. 'It was a kind thought. War is so confusing.'

The lift doors close and Nabeel lets out a groan that lasts almost until he is inside his flat.

Everything is arranged carefully to utilise the limited space. Coats and hats hang on a stand next to the door, steel pots and pans have been tidied on to a rack above the sink, and a few items of hand-washing, which cannot be done at the launderette, are drying on a rail in the bathroom. The furniture is not their own, or what they would have chosen, but it is comfortable enough. In their time in Hungary they have gathered a few personal items, four plates, a jug painted with blue flowers, a little statue, which make the place their own. There are books and tapes too, collected from markets and second-hand shops, all stacked neatly on the wooden shelves. They are signs, small ones, that Nabeel and Nada are trying to make a go of their new life. And they are aware that, while they still feel markedly foreign, Yamam has effortlessly absorbed Hungarian culture. Undistracted with memories of Iraq, he has amassed a crowd of Hungarian schoolfriends and endless invitations to birthday parties.

Nabeel and Nada have talked it over many times during the last year. Should they settle in Budapest?

'Dudi, it is good that we are here, of course, but we are always going to be outsiders,' Nada had said one evening, as they read Yamam's glowing school report. 'We have no right to be here, even though Yamam is more Hungarian than Iraqi now. What if things change? Your work permit is only issued for a year at a time. There is no security. And I am not going to risk using another forgery from the Embassy of Nabeel.'

He laughs at the memory.

It had been one of Nabeel's boldest schemes. They needed papers. Their passports had expired the end of 1984, and unable to go near the Iraqi consulate or commission the services of an expert Arab forger, Nabeel had sat Nada down, told her she was not to worry and said he would forge new ones himself. Nada had almost fallen off her chair in shock. 'Dudi, one thing you are not is a master forger.'

'I don't see you coming up with a better idea. How hard can it be?'

Considerably harder than it looked in films, was the answer. It took meticulous planning and attention to detail. He'd used tape, an inkpad, glue, a thick black ink pen and an old Iraqi coin from Yamam's toybox. The hardest part had been to forge the consulate's signature, and create a stamp across the updated photograph. It had taken two days of practice, lots of coffee, some razor blades to slice the old photograph off the page, a hammer to hit the coin in order to leave an impression in the paper and their new photographs – but in the end they had brand-new documents. When she saw them, Nada had wept. They were indistinguishable from the real thing.

Looking out of the window, he sees Nada bobbing home with Yamam. Cocooned in her winter coat, snowboots and scarf, she is like a ball of fluff being blown across the snow. Perhaps she might have heard news of Iraq. If not, he will call Jabbar. The French always have news. They sell enough weapons to Iraq to be interested in what goes on there. He will not tell her about the encounter with their neighbour, the teacher. It will upset her.

Baghdad is always on his mind, interrupting him as he works, clouding his thoughts, defining his choices. Some-times when he is in the library or at the faculty building he finds himself gazing at the window, expecting to see an orange or banana tree like the ones outside the living-room window at al-Mansour. When he leaves the library, he imagines he is leaving the Baghdad University campus, on his way to visit Tawfiq. He wants Baghdad to remain fresh in his memory.

There is information, of course, that keeps them in touch, but it is unreliable. He has the odd conversation with Jabbar and news, passed like Chinese whispers, from others who have got out of Iraq. But six years into exile Nabeel has no idea if his brothers are in the war and, if they are, whether they are alive, injured or worse.

Of all the news they receive, they cherish most the letters to Nada receives from her mother and sisters. Although they are heavily censored each one cheers Nada for weeks. 'They are full of Mama's wishes and love. What more could I want?' she snaps at Nabeel, when he complains that they say nothing.

'She is so repetitive, even the censor must know them by heart.'

Nada knows it is difficult for him. He receives no letters from his own family. Sabria cannot read or write, and he had told his brothers and sisters not to risk their lives by sending anything to him.

Over the years he has tried to make contact. He has parcelled up photographs, notes and letters to his family, but visiting Iraqis, fearing association with a prominent opponent of the government, are reluctant to act as messengers. In Prague he had given a letter to his friend Mustapha, a reluctant Party convert who had come out of Iraq on a visitor's visa. 'Please take these to my family,' he had implored, and showed the other man a picture of Yamam as they sat outside St Stephen's Basilica. He had nodded, then turned the letter in his hands rather than putting it into his coat pocket.

'Don't take it if you think you'll have to throw it away before you get to the border.'

'No, no, it's fine,' Mustapha insisted, but as Nabeel watched his fingers drumming on the table he knew this was a lie and had snatched the letter back.

The following year Nabeel had approached an Iraqi diplomat. 'Don't talk to me,' the man had hissed, refusing even to look at him.

'I have a letter for my mother, nothing more. You must have family – you must understand.'

'Leave now,' the man had said. 'The regime sees everything. You are still a wanted man. Don't imagine you are free.' He had run off towards the river, crossing the road without looking out for traffic.

After this Nabeel had begun to play with the idea of calling home. He would tell his mother they were doing fine and that she mustn't worry. In turn, she would tell him they were all alive and well, that his brothers had returned from the war and that Amel was the best young doctor in Iraq. They would have time to say goodbye and 'I love you' and that would be that. 'But the Mukhabarat listen to everything,' he sobbed to Nada one night. 'How can I call?'

Nada had tried to calm him. 'You will have to be discreet, that's all. Just as my mother scrambles their names when she writes, you should not say yours. Call yourself Hussein Yamam, as she does. Pretend to be a family friend. Then you will mean nothing to the censors. They can't know everything about everyone.'

In the end, his call is spontaneous. As he settles down to prepare for a tutorial in his thick polo-neck sweater and corduroy trousers, Nabeel is inspired by the spirit of a fresh year. His tutor, Eva Anchel, one of the academy's finest professors, had been a pupil of George Lukács, the Communist philosopher, and although he knows she thinks highly of him, he remains in awe of the connection. He could claw his way up, become an academic, a writer of note, perhaps even a political commentator. As dusk closes in, and people crunch through the snowy streets on their way home from work, he is seized inexplicably by a giddy sense of bravado. Later Andras Tokai, a Hungarian poet he met at the university, and his wife will join him and Nada for dinner. It will be fun. He takes a tablecloth out of the drawer in the kitchen, then puts a Symphonie, the cheapest brand of cigarette in Hungary, into his mouth, lights it and picks up the telephone. Several times the line goes dead, then there's a crackle and, after a short silence, the long, mid-tone purr he has not heard for many years.

Sabria picks up. 'Hello.' She sounds gruff and irritated, but it is unmistakably his mother.

'Mama,' he croaks, as tears prick his eyes. 'Mama!'

'My boy! Is that you?'

'I'm here.'

'Oh, my child, my son, you are alive, *al humdullillah*, thank God. Where are you?'

'*Allah karim*, God is gracious.' He remembers he must be circumspect. If they are listening he does not want them to know of his whereabouts or what he has been doing.

'Where are you?' she says again.

'Working, Mama, and we are well.'

'But you are living where? Tell me that.'

To this, he replies simply, 'In the world.' It seems so stupid that she has asked him three times a question that he cannot answer.

Sobbing, she calls to the family in the room, to Amel and Juma'a and Aqbal. 'He is on the phone.'

'Mama,' he continues, 'we want to know how you are, how the family is. Tell us, please. Are you all well, from the eldest to the little one?'

'We are bearing up. No one is sick. And no one is in hospital.' He knows by this that she means his brothers are not in prison. Most Iraqis use code to talk undetected in front of the censors. 'And my little grandson? How is he?'

'He is well, and growing fast. Quite a big boy now. Lively two. Almost nine. He misses you.'

Nabeel wants to say more but is not sure how he can describe his son adequately. Even the brief description he has given has set her off. He was her first grandchild, her special boy, yet now he is a stranger to her. 'He is funny and full of ideas, and very popular. You would see yourself and Baba in him.'

The pain of the last few years claims her: 'Oh, my son, why do you not write to me, or call? Why do you not come home? Do you not love your mother, or respect her in her old age?'

'Please, do not say these things.'

'So, my son, tell me, when are you coming home?'

He has dreaded this question. 'No regime in Iraq lasts long,' he had said to his brothers, on the last evening they had spent together at the house. He had been wrong. 'You know we want to come home. All of us *want* to come home.'

'So, when?'

'Every day I think of you, Mama.'

'But when will I see you, Nabeel? When will I see Nada and Yamam?' she sobs. 'Would you deny me that?'

They are coming unstuck. 'I will call again, Mama, I promise. We will call with something to say, some good news, soon.'

Sabria, late 1980s

He hears the front-door key turn in the lock. Nada and Yamam are home. He sees their feet as they step into the hall, then behind them two more pairs. Andras and his wife are with them. Unable to meet their gaze as they pass, he turns to face the wall. They have come early, and although Andras and his wife are true friends he wants to be alone.

As his mother goes on, he hears them tiptoe through the living room to the kitchen, following Nada. They will see Nada's Porkolt stew, thick, slow-cooked, the home-made noodles and stuffed cabbage, rich with paprika. He hears the packets of pretzels being shaken into bowls and Yamam talking about his day at school.

'Mama . . .' Nabeel murmurs, remembering, with a pang, the way she had always ushered them to the table. With his forehead against the wall and his eyes closed, he can almost smell her bread baking.

'But when will I see you?' she asks. 'It is a simple question.'

'*Ma'as salama*, Mama,' he whispers. 'Goodbye.' They are both crying as he puts the receiver back in its cradle. The clock on the wall tells him he was on the phone for less than seven minutes. They are all alive. After so many years there is nothing more to say.

Letters, 1989, 1990

In the spring of 1988 a trip to the doctor reveals that Nada is pregnant. She feels her distance from her mother and sisters more keenly now than she has at any time since they left. 'Dudi, I need them,' she had wailed, when she was doubled up over the basin with morning sickness. 'I cannot do this on my own.'

Nabeel knows that whatever he says will be the wrong thing. He has tried to phone Baghdad twice but eight years of war have made contact virtually impossible. He cannot make this better for her.

But when the baby boy is born in November at the Taitni hospital, they are overcome with joy.

'We are a family of four.' Nada gazes at the child in her arms. 'He is so beautiful. Come on, Yamam. Look at your brother.'

The thirteen-year-old leans across and kisses his brother's forehead. 'What are you going to call him, Mama?'

'We thought Hanin.'

'Hanin?'

Nada nods, and draws her elder son to her.

'Does it mean anything?'

Nabeel looks at his wife and son. 'Nostalgia,' he whispers, 'and longing.'

While Nada struggles to balance the day-to-day chaos of life with a new baby, Nabeel tries to get the news into Iraq to their families. He writes scores of unsigned letters and sends them to friends and family hoping that one, at least, will get through. But by Hanin's first birthday they have not heard back.

'Baba, is Hanin an Iraqi like me or Hungarian?' Yamam asks his father one morning.

'Hanin has Iraqi blood,' Nabeel had said solemnly, 'though he lives in Hungary.'

'We are an international family now,' Nada adds cheerily, not wanting to dwell on what cannot be changed. But both she and Nabeel wish their second son could know his parents' homeland.

It is hard to acknowledge this. Talking about home brings only pain and sadness, so they allow family life to absorb much of their attention. There is work, too. Nabeel has completed his PhD and been awarded a research post and grant. He is working on a renewable year-long contract, though he returns to poetry intermittently. Ideas form, but with no one to read his words he feels as if his thoughts are only half expressed. For him, so much of the meaning of his verse comes through in the performance. The words need to live, to reach other people in song.

Nada, too, has been busy. She also has done a PhD and now works at the Arabic school, teaching the language and literature of her mother tongue. But Yamam is the beacon of progress. Quietly, without his parents being aware of it, he has developed a considerable reputation as a talented footballer.

'He is brilliant,' Nabeel delights in reminding Nada, as they watch him at his weekend training sessions. 'He takes after Jabbar. He was always out with a ball. Mama could never get him inside.'

'The school coach told me Yamam could go all the way to the national trials.'

'Imagine!' Nabeel laughs. 'The first Iraqi in the Hungarian side!'

With the baby tucked into Nabeel's coat, they cheer Yamam's team on to victory.

One Saturday in February 1989 when Nabeel is alone at home Sa'ad, Selwa's husband, calls the flat. He is visiting Bucharest with a delegation of engineers and brims with news of their families, Selwa's children, Jafar's, and the president's latest projects too.

'To celebrate the victory against Iran, he has built an extravagant mosque. He is building palaces everywhere, and another bridge across the Tigris in Baghdad.'

Nabeel remembers the foreman he and Jafar had hired to oversee the construction of the family house in al-Sayydia. He had disappeared without warning and not come back for more than a fortnight. Not even his wife knew where he'd been taken. When he surfaced he told Nabeel that he had been accosted, blindfolded and taken to a site in the desert two hours outside Baghdad. There, in his capacity as a master tiler, he had been made to complete the halls and bathrooms for one of Saddam's luxury retreats. It had been the best quality marble and slate he had ever worked with.

Eventually Sa'ad can no longer disguise the real reason for his visit. He lowers his voice. 'Nabeel, I am sorry to do this to you after everything we have just enjoyed but . . .' Nabeel knows that terrible news is coming. 'I bring bad news. It is Hamed, Nada's father . . . Well . . .' Sa'ad is struggling to tell Nabeel what he already knows now. 'He became very sick and was no longer able to walk, or speak.'

'I understand,' Nabeel says.

'The moment of his passing was very sudden.'

'But why not send a letter or call us?'

'They knew Nada was pregnant and did not want to worry her. They were praying he would recover.'

Nabeel feels panic blossom inside him, overriding his own sadness at Hamed's death. It is only the hope of seeing her family again that keeps Nada going. She will surely sink into depression when she hears.

'How am I to tell her?' he mutters, as he turns to the window looking out over the city.

Sa'ad shakes his head emphatically. 'No, no, no. You are not to tell her yet. Behija gave me strict instructions, Nabeel. That is what the letter I have is about. You must respect her wishes. She wants you to tell Nada only that her father is ill. This will prepare her. Do you understand? You are to tell her that he is disabled, and unable to speak. Later they will write and tell her the rest.'

'I see.' How well Behija understands her daughter, but what a terrible thing she is asking him to do.

Sa'ad lays his hand on Nabeel's arm. 'This is what Behija wants, Nabeel.'

Later that night Nabeel tells Nada her father is ill. He cannot bring himself to ask her to hope for his recovery. That would be too cruel.

'I should go to him,' she wails. 'He will be asking for me, I know.'

'He is in good hands. Let's wait for more news. They will

find a way to reach us if there is a turn for the worse.' Holding him in the dark, she trusts him.

For two years the pretence goes on. Nabeel waits for the letter from Behija that will tell all. But while the usual censored letters continue to arrive, each compounds the lie. He watches Nada slice open each one and unfold it. He watches for any change in her expression, but it never comes. 'Baba is neither any worse nor any better but sends his love.' Nabeel feels he should tell her the truth, or at least introduce the idea that the illness is worsening, but she is bound to ask how he knows and then the deception will be exposed. She has a right to know, but there is never a good time to tell her.

When the US-led coalition forces launch the Desert Storm offensive in response to the Iraqi invasion of Kuwait, Nada still does not know her father is dead. On the night it begins, 17 January 1991, Nabeel spends the evening with his friend al-Jawarhiri. The great poet, now ninety-one, has come to Budapest to visit friends and give a talk. They had first met twenty years earlier when Nabeel had started going to the Iraqi Writers' Union. Al-Jawarhiri had been a mentor, guiding his talent, and had worked hard to have him reinstated as a poet. Although he is now long past his golden period, he is nevertheless a literary icon, whose celebrated work *Good Tigris* is universally loved across the Arab world.

They spend several hours together, in the small apartment where al-Jawarhiri is staying, discussing the looming war.

'The Americans are just waiting now, baiting Saddam.'

'They're going to come in hard. It'll be ugly.'

Al-Jawarhiri sits up and nods. 'They want Saddam but the whole country will suffer. It is already broken, Nabeel, damaged beyond repair. Eight years of war with Iran saw to that. But the Americans will not care. They will bring his capital city to its knees to ensure victory.'

'I can only think of my family.'

He shrugs. 'If it means things change and you can return a free man, it is not necessarily a bad thing. In my case, the Lord will be sending almonds to a man with no teeth.' He laughs wheezily.

Nabeel goes to empty their ashtrays, then lights him another cigarette. 'How is life in Damascus, these days?'

'Even in Damascus an old man like me isn't free of the Saddam,' al-Jawarhiri grumbles indignantly.

'But you have always been independent of him.'

He shrugs again. 'I could not be in his pocket. He asked me once to write a poem about him and his conquests. "Why do you not write about me, al-Jawarhiri? Am I not great enough for you to include in your poems?"' The old man tuts at the impertinence. 'I said to him, "Your Excellency the President the Leader God Placed Him, I have written about historical events since 1919. Although you have done many things, you are not history yet." Can you imagine it, Nabeel?'

Talking to al-Jawarhiri gives Nabeel hope that one day he might be accepted again in Iraq. In the end the rebels always become the establishment.

If there is to be any possibility of this though, he must publish again. He had written only two poems of any note in all these years, *Romance* and *The Death of Yasin*. They were well received, but such a meagre output suggests that the president is indeed the victor. He must galvanise himself.

Al-Jawarhiri is already ahead of him. 'So, Nabeel, what have you for me to read?'

'Nothing, I'm afraid. But in the last few weeks I have started writing again. I can feel it flowing. There is certainly enough to write about.'

He has been working with a solid idea. He had seen footage of the Iraqi Army occupying Kuwait the previous August and had jotted lines of verse on scraps of paper. It was as though he was back in his old bedroom or at a table in his old haunt, the Christian Club. The lines had come easily, and, to his surprise, with his old clarity. But now he doesn't speak with the idealism of the young man. Now his concerns are those of a man in the middle of his life, with years ahead and behind him. He is no longer writing songs of innocence but of experience. The exuberant confidence of youth has been replaced with a vivid realism. There are echoes of his 1974 epic *Brother Yasin*, but stylistically and in tone this new work is richer, more mature.

'It will be a poem of truth,' he says, as much to himself as to al-Jawarhiri. 'Seeing you has reminded me that I must get on with it.'

'You had better be quick. You never know what may be round the corner.'

It is almost two when he leaves the old man to go to bed. Outside, a cigarette between his freezing lips, he waits for a taxi. It is twenty degrees below zero and the air coming from Siberia stings his face as it whips between the buildings and through the trees. He flags down a taxi and jumps into the back. 'Eleventh quarter, please,' he says, and relaxes contentedly in the seat. In front, as they speed through the empty

Nabeel in Budapest

streets, the radio plays Hungarian rock music. As they pull up
outside Nabeel's apartment block the music is interrupted:
'The Allies are bombing Baghdad. They've just gone in. We've
got it live on TV.'

The taxi-office controller broadcasts a general announcement to all his drivers. Nabeel throws a mixture of notes and
coins to the front of the car. 'I'm Iraqi,' he says, when the man
looks round in bewilderment. 'Thank you but I have to run.'
Too impatient to wait for the lift, he runs up to the eighth
floor by the stairs. As he comes through the front door, the
phone is ringing.

'*Ahlan*, hello.' He answers instinctively in Arabic.

It is al-Jawarhiri. In the background Nabeel can hear the
BBC World Service. 'It has started,' the old man says
solemnly.

Nabeel keeps the television on all night as Baghdad is
bombed. Saddam has declared this to be the great show-

down, the mother of all battles, but his city is being deci-mated.

As he watches the air-strikes rain down on the city, Nabeel remembers the legend that every Baghdadi child is told of the seventh bridge. During the Abbasid Caliphate a seer had proclaimed that Baghdad should have no more than six bridges. At the construction of the seventh, so the fable went, the city would be razed to the ground with fire. Saddam Hussein had built the seventh bridge. And now the city is burning.

President Bush appears at a news conference, proclaiming there will be no mercy for Saddam. US Nighthawks and Apaches will continue to bomb strategic targets until Iraq surrenders. By 5 a.m., the television images have begun to repeat and Nabeel decides he should try to sleep. When Nada wakes at 6.30, she finds him fully clothed on the bed. 'Has the war begun?' she whispers.

Without opening his eyes, he reaches for her hand. 'Yes. They have been bombing the city through the night.'

'Baba!' She puts her head into her hands. 'Dudi, what about my father? He is an invalid. He cannot walk. Will there be time to move him to an air-raid shelter?'

Nabeel knows he should tell her but on top of everything else it would be too much for her. 'Your mother is a clever woman and your sisters are resourceful. They will have prepared for this. You know Umaima will have left nothing to chance. Please, be calm. We will try to call later.'

Distractedly Nada gets dressed and prepares her papers for the day's teaching. Nabeel leaves her tea on the table and goes out to fetch the newspapers. At the coffee shop news-stand, the front pages of *Magyar Hirlap*, *Nepszabadsag* and *Nepszava* are full of dramatic pictures of the bombardment. 'One of each,' he says to the rotund man on the stall.

'Are you Iraqi?' The man looks him up and down as Nabeel tucks the pile under his arm and hands over coins.

Nabeel nods.

'He's an Iraqi!' the vendor announces to others gathered at the stall. They swarm about him as if waiting for a revelation. The eight-year war with Iran had been of marginal interest to them, but this new war, with its live television images and the involvement of the Americans, is a sensation. He answers their questions as best he can, then breaks away and hurries back to the apartment.

'I was asked by fifteen people at the coffee shop what I thought was going on,' he says.

'I don't care about the stupid people at the coffee shop,' Nada snaps. 'What about Baba?'

She sweeps out of the flat, with the boys in tow, and he decides he must try to get through to Behija or Selwa. He spends half of the day in an international phone booth at the post office. Eventually an operator tells him that the Baghdadi telephone exchange has been destroyed and the city's lines are all down.

Nabeel and al-Jawarhiri follow the war's progress from coffee shops and at the homes of their Iraqi friends. Images of grey sand, smoky skies, missing buildings and blood blast across the television screens.

'The Tabbe, the Al Qushla and the Justice Buildings – we are lucky they are still standing,' Nabeel says. 'They have dropped so many bombs.'

When the ground offensive begins, leaving a trail of dead and injured in its wake, they know it will soon be over. The television shows long lines of ragged prisoners dragging their feet across the flat, sandy roads towards Iraq.

Jabbar calls in panic. 'Brother,' he gabbles down the line in Arabic. 'I have just seen Tariq on the news. He is in a line of prisoners walking from the front.'

'What?'

'They have our brother!'

'No, no. That cannot be.' Nabeel is unprepared for news of this kind. Every day of this war he has been focused on helping Nada, sensing that Tariq will be fine. There have been endless conversations, over almost a decade of war, about of his brother's welfare and Nabeel has kept faith. He recalls the collapse of al-Faw in 1982: they had been both terrified that Tariq was dead and certain that Iranian victory would signify Saddam's downfall. Standing in a phone box at the end of the street while Jabbar relayed the news, Nabeel had pushed an endless stream of five-forint coins into the slot as slush seeped into his threadbare shoes. They did not know for several years if Tariq was alive but Nabeel had never stopped believing he was. 'He is in my heart,' he had explained to Nada. 'I see him there, and he is alive.'

'Jabbar, please, you must tell me what you saw.'

'He is being taken back across the border. There are thousands of them, all together.'

'Don't tell me that you can see the face of one man amid thousands?'

'*Yes*! Thousands of them are walking from Kuwait City towards Safwan, but it was him, I know it. He looked at the camera.'

'Tariq is older now. You saw a younger man who looks like him. His hair, his face, they will have changed.' Nabeel turns to the main channel – an action film is showing so he turns to

292

another to find a chat show. His war has been ousted already from the schedules. He picks up the soft-top pack of Marlboro reds, bought for him by Nada, and fishes out the last one.

Jabbar is enraged. 'Do you think I would not recognise my own brother?'

'Jabbar! Come on!' Nabeel barks into the phone. 'It is eleven years since I saw him, nearly fifteen since you did. He is not the boy he was. He is a man now.'

'You just don't *want* to believe it.' Nabeel has never heard his brother like this. But, as he is discovering, in modern war, those who are absent can see everything but do nothing.

On the morning al-Jawarhiri leaves for Damascus, peace is officially agreed. Nabeel, who is taking al-Jawahari to the airport, arrives well before sunrise. Wading through knee-deep snow to the entrance of his friend's red-tiled apartment block, he puffs out white clouds, a mixture of smoke and condensation. Inside, he finds the old man sitting in a chair. 'Nabeel,' he looks up listlessly from the transistor radio, 'it is over. His Excellency the President the Leader God Placed Him has signed the end of the war – in a tent, on the border at Safwan.' Nabeel leans against the wall, stunned. 'They have let him go.'

When he returns to his own apartment later that morning, he is startled to find a fat airmail letter postmarked Jordan. It is in Selwa's hand and addressed to him. He takes the lift up to the apartment, and lays it on the table.

As soon as Nada sets eyes on it, she knows something is wrong, 'It is from Selwa. Why is it addressed to you? Is he dead? Nabeel, tell me.'

Nabeel sits her down at the little table.

'Nabeel!' she shouts. 'Is Baba dead?'

Nabeel nods slowly, and Nada howls.

'Read the letter. You must read it.' He is battling to make her hear through her tears. 'There are things you do not know. Things, I am ashamed to say, that we have kept from you.' He sits opposite her and takes her hands. 'Yes, he has died, after a long illness. But it was before Hanin was born. You were pregnant and your mother did not want you to know – she wanted you to stay strong for the baby.'

Nabeel gives her the letter. 'Read it.' He helps her to tear open the envelope and slide out the pages.

The letter tells of how her father had mourned Nada both when she left and after he became ill. When he lay dying he had wanted only to see her one last time. He asked for her and her name was the last word he uttered. 'Nada,' he whispered, and then was gone.

Happy Birthday, Mr President
April 1993

In 1993, with the people of Iraq weary, undernourished and in mourning for the 750,000 soldiers killed or injured in ten years of war, the president issues an edict that declares his official birthday, 28 April, is to be a national holiday and to celebrate there will be the most lavish party the country has ever seen. Every citizen is ordered to arrange their own festivities and the Ba'ath Party generously offers suggestions for honouring their great leader: songs, cards, banners, decorated portraits and birthday-cake recipes.

Sabria, Jafar and Amel, at home, are scornful.

'The man must walk with a mirror in front of him.' Jafar sniffs.

Sabria refuses to consider participating. 'I will not throw a party for the man who has forced so much pain on my family.'

'He is mad. Does he think we'll forget our worries for the day?' Amel, who works at the al-Amarah hospital, is home for the weekend. 'We hardly have enough flour to make bread in the morning, let alone birthday cakes and party food. He does not care that the country is starving. He is too busy with his plans for another Nebuchadnezzar's palace at Babylon to think of his people's welfare.'

'He is showing the world he doesn't care. In return for their sanctions, he will host a birthday party and show the world that his country adores him.' Jafar, says.

'Come on! How much longer can the world be fooled by him? We have been forced into these stupid parties for ten years now. Surely everyone must realise it's a pretence.'

As Sabria speaks she thinks of the pictures of Saddam as a Nordic hunter in the snow, a Kurd, a German in Lederhosen, a southern Iraqi peasant and an ancient king, displayed at his annual portrait exhibition. 'It isn't even his real birthday,' she adds.

And indeed this is true. Until the 1970s many Iraqis had used momentous events to mark the passage of their lives. Sabria, for example, always gave her birthdate as 'the year of the cholera'. Yasin had come of age at the time the British put an end to the Ottoman Empire, and Jafar had been six months old at the time of the coup. 'I remember the British bombing the military compounds on the outskirts of Kar-radat Mariam,' Sabria would say, in answer to a question about her eldest son's age. Later Jafar discovered this to be 1941.

President Kassim had brought the country more up to date with the introduction of identity cards and declared that all Iraqis who didn't know their exact birthday would share the same one, 1 July. This had caused some hilarity among Sabria and her friends. 'All Iraqis should get along fine, now,' went the joke, 'because they share the same birthday.'

Of course, some knew their real birthdates. Sabria knew Nabeel's because Uncle Rashid had marked it on his winning lotto ticket. 'A boy,' he had written, 'born today, to Sabria. Named Nabeel.' And Nabeel, in turn, had noted both Tariq and Amel's births in the navy blue Iraqi Petroleum Corporation pocket diaries given to him by his father, which he had carried with him all year.

But they were the exception rather than the rule. Birthdays were considered frivolous and selfish, even narcissistic in a country that preferred communal celebration.

'Ah yes, but it is a well-chosen date nevertheless, three weeks from the founding of the Ba'ath Party.'

'That self-proclaimed son of Muhammad will do anything in his own cause. And you can be sure that this year's celebrations will be bigger than all the rest combined. Still, Mama,' Amel sighs, picking up a copy of the Ba'athist *Athawra* newspaper, 'we will not be alone if we don't celebrate. Half the public workers in this country are not being paid any more. Most people are buying rice on the black-market, even when it is full of weevils. *Our friend* should get out his crates of French cheese and sausage, not to mention his warehouses of unused wheat, and share them out. If fear does not bring them out food will.'

Sabria looks at her youngest daughter, matter-of-fact to the last.

As the great day draws near Sabria, her sister Makkya and Tariq, in their daily walks through the diminished market-places of Al Sayydia, watch labourers string bunting, with red, white and green flags bearing portraits of the president, from block to block.

'At least it is a break from the usual,' Makkya says, as they hunt for a meat vendor with something to sell. '*Our friend* will have to show his face in public, no?'

'Him and a thousand tanks.'

'Ssh, sister. Ssh. And what about us? Will you go out into the streets with the parade?'

'Not a chance. It's the one time I'm glad women are no

longer allowed out on their own. It's the perfect excuse to stay away.'

'They're saying it will be the biggest march in Iraq's history. Are you sure you want to miss it? Perhaps you could go with Jafar or Tariq.' Makkya prods Sabria in jest, glancing back at Tariq, ambling behind them. 'Surely, anyway, you will bake a cake?'

'Certainly not!' Sabria whispers indignantly.

But the presidential bureau leaves nothing to chance. They want cakes baked across the land and the president's special forces are ordered to parcel up provisions and distribute them through out the city. In a news announcement, citizens are informed they will receive generous gifts that they can use to make their own party cakes: flour, sugar, oil, rosewater, nuts and butter. Two days later a young sergeant delivers a stamped crate of supplies to the Yasins.

'Your gift, *makrouma*,' he says, dropping the box into Sabria's arms as she opens the gate. 'Be thankful for the generosity of His Excellency the President the Leader God Placed Him.'

At one time, accepting such items would have weighed on Sabria's conscience. Now she will not look a gift horse in the mouth. Used sparingly, the ingredients in her parcel could last for weeks.

Turning back to the house, she nods at Juma'a. 'Look at this!' She holds the box aloft. 'The special forces delivered it.'

'And you took it?'

'Of course! I am thankful. I thought they were coming for you again.'

The militia have kept Juma'a under observation for ten years. It has been relentless. They come regularly to interview him, and he must report all his movements, no matter how small. Accusations of involvement in clandestine activities are made frequently, all of which Juma'a denies. If they decide he is lying, he is taken in and interrogated. He knows by name most of his interrogators and the secret policemen.

'I am fifty years old,' he tells them. 'I am married, with children. I look after my ageing mother, and if you hadn't sacked me, I would still be teaching your children. You can put me back in prison, you can take my job away but you will find nothing. You have never found anything in all the years you have been coming for me. Now even the Soviet Union has collapsed.'

Sabria scours the kitchen for her cigarettes and, failing to find them, begins to pull the items from the box. Such lovely things. Pine nuts! Fine caster sugar. Soft butter, requiring a fridge. So much has changed. In the days before the Ba'ath, she had enjoyed family parties and celebrations: dinners for forty people, with thirty dishes or more, salads, omelettes, meat stews, bean stews, baked fish, baked aubergines, piles of rice, spices and pickles, sweets and fruit. The colours of the Al Bayaa orchards light up her mind: trees thick with blossom and, later, with clementines, lemons, peaches, apricots, pomegranates, apples and plums, but that abundance belonged to another life. She looks at her Singer sewing-machine, barely used these days except for patching and mending. Even a solitary orange is considered a luxury now.

Come the great day, Sabria, Makkya, Amel, Aqbal, Tariq,- Juma'a and his wife gather to watch the birthday celebrations at home. Jafar too stays with his wife and daughter at home. Iraqi national television shows hundreds of thousands of

Ba'athist and secret police members parading the streets, spilling out round the city's main landmarks and on to al-Kindi Street, past the presidential palace and Saddam's official residence close to the Tigris, all praising the great leader. On the road from Tikrit to Baghdad, white marquees offer tea and shade to the loyalists walking from town to town in displays of unity. Trays of sweets are handed among the crowds, caramel-coloured, syrupy pastries to bribe those who accept them into self-conscious displays of gratitude for the cameras. A group of girls in scarlet spotted dresses wave Iraqi flags. Men carry giant paper hearts and flowers daubed with messages of love, honour and national pride. And everywhere, images of that face, proud and self-righteous, look out on his people.

'Saddam the powerful!'

'We love you, Saddam. Long live Saddam Hussein.'

'Yes, yes to the great leader, Saddam.'

'Our blood, our souls, we'll give for you.'

Others are more political. 'Down, down U-S-A, down, down Is-ra-el.'

'How much do they pay these people?' Amel blinks at the joy of the crowds. Young men and boys, all singing and dancing as they march through Haifa Street, fire their weapons into the air.

Sabria clucks loudly. 'See the tiny soldiers? These uniforms come from that Romanian, Ceaușescu. But they are so little – what do you think? Five or six at the most. Your brothers didn't even have a cap gun at that age! No wonder they don't need teachers like Juma'a any more. A boy has only to fire off a round of bullets now to find himself showered with sweets and posters of Saddam.'

Television cameras high on cranes and gantries swoop

across the city and remind viewers of their leader's great architectural contributions: palaces, four-lane highways and hotels, a new Babylon erected over the ancient ruins. Close-ups show that every brick glorifies the president. His buildings are emblazoned with vast, detailed murals, depicting great battles and victories in which Saddam has placed himself as the victor. The palace doorways are huge and carved, like the Gate of Ishtar, and from domed room to domed room only the finest materials, marble, black slate, gold, silver and onyx, have been used; every column is carved into a fitting homage. And all the while the presenter lists the great achievements of the leader. 'Are we really to endure an entire day of this?' Sabria grumbles, as she pours herself a glass of water from the jug by her chair.

But this is merely the warm-up. After a few minutes the presenter falls silent and the cameras cut away from the brightly coloured crowds and fade to a more secluded setting. His Excellency the President the Leader God Placed Him is making the long-anticipated television appearance that will bring him into every home in the country. Sabria is surprised that he has made a public appearance at all: she has heard from Amel the rumours that he no longer dares to appear in public for fear of assassination.

'He has someone testing his food, and his swimming-pools. And he stays only one or two nights at a time in his palaces. He even makes people strip off and wash before he receives them.'

Wondering if he could ever be quite as afraid as his people were, Sabria shouts to Aqbal, 'Come here. The coward is about to speak.'

'Mama, how can you watch it? Even Nabeel made better television than this.'

They all fall about laughing. When he was just sixteen Nabeel had been on a television quiz show and won a gold watch.

'My boy.' Sabria flushes with pride. 'He answered all his questions correctly, no?'

'Yes, but wasn't he funny in his shirt and tie?'

'Maybe, but not as funny as this.'

Hundreds of children are lined up along the sleek marble corridors of one of his newly built palaces. They are wearing frothy white dresses or little tailored suits, standing solemnly, holding hands. Returning to the room with tea on a silver tray, Aqbal sighs. 'What an idiot. Does he think anyone believes this? Those children look terrified. They have probably been told they will be beaten if they don't cheer. One false move, a twitch or a fidget, and they'll be whisked away. They've probably been there since before daybreak without a chance to sit down. You remember what happened to the general.'

The general, an acquaintance who had fought in the war, had been plucked from his house at two in the morning, blindfolded and driven to an unmarked building. After standing for three hours without coffee, water or any explanation, he and several hundred other men had been taken off and given a plain grey robe and clean socks. They were then led through several halls and made to wait again, in silence, for several more hours. Still no refreshment was offered. They weren't even permitted to use the lavatory. Later they were taken in blacked-out Peugeots to another location, ushered through more halls, and left waiting once more. They were unclear who was behind it, or what they were there for. It was after ten the following evening when, after a small period of activity at the main entrance, His Excellency the President the

Leader God Placed Him appeared. Everyone around him, including his guards, was terrified. The general assumed he was about to be shot. The smell of breaking wind pervaded the room.

The president paused in the doorway to observe the lines of weak-legged, dry-mouthed men, then slipped on a pair of felt gloves and moved slowly, expressionless, towards them. He issued each with a medal for devoted service during the war. Every man had been instructed to remain motionless. 'No matter how long His Excellency the President the Leader God Placed Him stands before you, do not exhale. Only when he has passed to the next man may you move your head and breathe. He does not want to feel your breath on his face.' The general's lungs were nearly bursting when he received his own medal.

Despite their revulsion, everyone in the house is mesmerised. Sitting forward, elbows on her knees, Sabria cannot take her eyes off the screen. 'There must be miles of fabric,' she mutters, knowing from her days as a seamstress what quantities have been used to dress the children. 'Some of us have no more than the clothes we stand up in, yet he finds French lace and organza. How can he use children like that when they know no better?'

'He has been using children for years,' says Makkya. 'Remember the edict. "We shall put an eye in every house, and this eye will be the child."'

As tinny music blares out through loudspeakers the children start to sing.

Saddam our glorious leader. Saddam, oh, Saddam, we love you so.

As the presidential train draws into view the Yasins clamour at the television, in a chorus of clucking and hissing.

Their president sits on a filigree golden carriage, which is drawn by a majestic white horse. The mare, her mane and tail strung with ribbons of white, silver and gold, her nostrils flared, clips slowly and tightly into the first of Saddam's opulent halls.

'He is taking the horse and carriage into the palace!'

'Do you think we're supposed to light the candles on our cake as we watch?' Sabria whispers. The family erupt into laughter. This is a more appalling display than even they had imagined.

The children wave and sing as the portly figure in white passes. The mystery of their billowing outfits is revealed: they are miniature versions of Saddam, children of the father, courtiers to the king, angels to his Godhead. The television presenter, whose voice is deep and regal, quivers with emotion as he proclaims the president the symbol of the homeland. 'The birth of the leader is the birth of hope. It is an opportunity for all of us who love him to demonstrate and renew our allegiance and faith to our great leader. He is the man who represents all that is great and true about Iraq.'

Sabria closes her eyes as a parade of ministers and officials proclaim, each more volubly than the last, that Iraq is a free and victorious country and that it is His Excellency the President the Leader God Placed Him who has made it possible. 'It is a sickness,' she croaks. 'There is no other way of looking at it.'

'Yes. And almost everyone is infected,' comes Amel's reply.

Eventually, the horse and carriage reach the inner atrium and the children lift their hands to the sky to praise him. At the finale, the camera cutting between them and the radiant Saddam, they break into a rendition of 'Happy Birthday'.

'I am shedding tears for them all,' Sabria howls, as the

president clambers down awkwardly from his carriage and positions himself next to a giant seven-foot cake, a cascade of bridal tiers topped with sugary icing. He takes a long sword from a waiting aide and slices through it. As the blade disappears, legions of attendant footmen bow and the children clap and cheer.

'Can this really be our Iraq?' Sabria says, to no one in particular. 'And what do you think Nabeel or Jabbar would say if they could see this? What would they think?'

'They would be open-mouthed, like us,' says Amel, 'and ashamed. After watching that, who could not be?'

A Hem, a Cuff,
a Poem, 1991, 1996

The turn of the decade brings change to Hungary. The Iron Curtain comes down, and the Soviet tanks and patrols that have been such a regular sight on the streets of the capital disappear for good as the Soviet machine rolls eastwards to Moscow. Hungary, free of its Communist master, is gripped by a new nationalism, and life becomes less certain for the Yasins. The tensions that arise persuade them that they should leave, and in August 1992 they fly to London and take refuge in a small rented house in Chadwell Heath, near Romford in Essex.

Here, the English family next door befriends Nada and the boys, and Nabeel resumes work on his poem. Entwining his own journey round Europe with the imagined struggles of a man returning home to a country cowed and broken, it will prove to be prophetic. He writes late into the night, sitting at the table in the living room with the curtains drawn behind him, smoking and scribbling until it is light, making notes, annotations and references and composing lines of verse. He has not written like this for more than a decade, and works through the night to complete the forty-eight-page poem.

The words are precise and alive, the rhythms, the metre, the sense and essence strong. It is a painful process but he is pleased with the result. It is as if everything that has gone before, from the fight against the injustices of the Ba'athist regime to the tanks and patrols rolling from Budapest back to Moscow, has been distilled into a single experience that he has committed to the page.

> Once again, on the journey home,
> On the journey home through this barbaric world,
> People, waiting in silence, to make the long, long journey home,
> Here I stand in life's desert,
> Composing a song to pass the evening,
> Holding my questions in my hands,
> So that when the journey has been long and the steps to my home few,
> I know the way . . .

It is the story of life contracting and unfolding, the slow dawning of its pointlessness and the redemption that comes only from love and family. Now he can see how his work had suffered for years before he was forced to leave his homeland.

He shows it to Nada, and then to friends within the Iraqi community. The response is sufficiently positive for him to raise enough money to have a thousand copies printed at a private press. The slender orange volume arrives at their flat in cardboard boxes and is taken immediately to the Arabic bookshops in London. It sells out within a few weeks. To see it stacked on the shelves of the Al Saqi bookstore reminds Nabeel of how he had felt when he was riding the wave of acclaim in Iraq. One afternoon he stands in the shop and watches a young man take a copy from the display, flick through it and put it with his other purchases. His heart feels as if it will burst.

True, the poem had come from him and his experience, but it no longer belongs to him. Now it is up to anyone who reads it to find their own relationship with the words. As a younger man Nabeel had been desperate for others to think as he thought. He wanted them to understand his work in precisely the way he intended it to be understood. Now it was almost the reverse: what mattered was that people responded to his writing by creating their own meanings, imagery and feelings.

He gives the remaining copies to friends and acquaintances, keeping just two for himself.

With this first frenetic burst of activity over, Nabeel and Nada turn their attention to making a new life in London. Nada finds work almost immediately as a proof-reader, and Nabeel begins slowly to establish himself as a journalist, writing opinion pieces for the Arabic newspapers *Al Hayat* and *Asharq Alwsat*. A year after their arrival they move to a new flat in the lively west of the city, at Hammersmith, and for the first time since they left Baghdad, they find themselves living almost entirely in the present. In London they have, at last, found a home, kind neighbours and friends, days off and walks on the common. The city has a large, active Iraqi community, too, with whom they share their history and experiences.

He is asked to perform *Brother Yasin Again* at an Anglo-Iraqi poetry evening. Iraqi writers working in London have put him in touch with the organisers, who are only too pleased for Nabeel to attend. Although it is intended to be an Anglo-Iraqi poetry evening, all the Anglo writers are Irish and the Iraqis – other than Nabeel, Lebanese. But Nabeel is delighted to have this opportunity: now that he is part of the community in London, he wants to take up his public life again, in whatever way he can.

At the dark-stained oak bar of the Victoria, a well-known Camden Town pub, he listens as his fellow poets read their work. Many are young and earnest, as he once was. To them, he is just a man in his mid-forties with greying hair. Beneath the horseshoes, mugs and football memorabilia hung on the walls of the room he watches and applauds each speaker. His friends have done him a good turn: he is back in front of an audience.

Nervously he steps on to the ramp that leads to the stage. Members of the audience raise their pint pots and whisky glasses, spurring him on. He gives a small bow and presses 'play' on his tape-recorder. The tape is one he had used in Iraq. He had found it at the bottom of a small cardboard box in the hall cupboard. Qatari seafarers' music begins to play and Nabeel is transported back to his youth. As the sound builds, he begins the poem. He is neither speaking nor singing. 'It's the Iraqi Bob Dylan,' hecklers call, to ripples of amiable laughter around the room.

Nabeel doesn't falter. They are free to shout, join in. It seems to him marvellous that, even in dissonance, they should all be together, beers in their hands, raising their voices to the roof. By the time he has finished, the room is mesmerised. Even though the words had been incomprehensible to almost everyone but himself, he had managed to convey something of the poem's intention. He bows to the cheers and walks off the stage, his heart full.

While Nabeel, Nada, Yamam and Hanin get on with their lives in London, the poem begins its secret journey to Iraq.

A female poet from Jordan packs the five copies she was given into her suitcase and flies back to Amman. She keeps one for herself and puts the rest for sale at the front of her gallery bookshop. They take pride of place on a small ebony table among a range of other poetic works.

Within a few weeks a man visiting Amman from his homeland, Kurdistan, sees the book. Intrigued by the vibrant orange cover, he looks more closely and discovers it is written by Nabeel Yasin, and the book's title is *Brother Yasin* and it contains both the title poem and a new sequel, *Brother Yasin Again*. 'I know of this man and his poems,' he says, 'but I have heard nothing of him for years.'

'He escaped Iraq and is in exile in London. This is his latest work. I got it two months ago.'

'I will take it,' he says. 'Two copies. I know someone who will be very happy to see this.'

With the books safely in his bag, the traveller returns overland through Syria to his home town of Arbil, once an important stop on the Silk Route, in the Kurdish north of Iraq. Here, he keeps the books until he can take them to his friend Hassan, a rebel and sometime smuggler of literature. Before Hassan even opens the book he gazes at it with incredulity. 'Where did you get this? My brother Tawfiq is a great friend of the poet. Please let me take it. I must go immediately to Baghdad to show him.'

Hassan rises at four and walks to the truck depot before it is light. The long-distance drivers, just waking from a night spent in their cabs, are preparing for the long drive south. Hassan, travelling on one of several false identities, negotiates himself a ride on a vegetable truck bound for Baghdad; he offers two packets of quality cigarettes and a few coins in exchange for a seat. In northern Kurdistan, a relative haven from Saddam's iron rule, he is safe enough, but as they journey south, the book he is carrying will become increasingly valuable contraband. He knows others who have been imprisoned and tortured, and is only too aware of the penalty if he is caught. But that will not stop him making this journey. An ardent believer in freedom, and a long-time opponent of the government and its policies, he has willingly appointed himself a courier of illegal material into Baghdad for his brother and other friends; over the years he has carried many banned books south.

Settling back against the crates of fruit, breathing in the scent of orange and mint, he checks his papers, plans his story and waits for the first roadside checkpoint. 'My aunty is old and unwell, and I, being unmarried, have been sent with messages for her recovery. And since I should take her some fruit,' he will tell them, 'I am lucky to have found myself in a greengrocer's van.' It is easy to make them think he is an ignorant peasant. Their belief in their superiority has always been their weakness.

He feels the slim volume against his chest, safe in his shirt pocket, as the truck bounces along the pitted roads from Arbil through Kirkuk, to Tuz Khurmatu and on, if he is lucky, to the capital.

Tawfiq's glass-fronted shop is still at the same address on Sa'adun Street as it always has been. It remains a place where, despite the surveillance, the little tailor encourages free expression. He is no longer the celebrated young designer of the

1970s, but the shop continues to do well because his customers are loyal. It remains the best source of good cloth in the city. What is more remarkable is that, over the years, the place has become a clandestine lending library, containing snippets from thousands of banned books, pamphlets and magazines, cunningly hidden in it.

The buzzer sounds as Hassan sweeps through the glass door. The men at the front nod to him in greeting. Through the pair of heavy curtains that conceal the back of the shop, he can see the outline of his brother. 'Tawfiq!' he calls. 'It is I, a surprise visitor from Arbil.'

Tawfiq raises his arms and comes through to greet him. 'What a happy surprise. What are you doing in Baghdad? Is everything OK?'

He glances about for a stool, then clicks his fingers impatiently. One of the men seated behind the curtain puts on his sandals and hoists himself on to a nearby bale of alpaca cloth.

'Sit with care,' Tawfiq jokes. 'That fabric is new in, and only for the finest rear ends. Come, come, you must be thirsty, brother. It's dry and dusty out there today.'

'Water will suffice, thank you.'

Tawfiq scowls at him. 'You must have tea. The man next door makes the best black tea in this whole cesspit of a city. I will not be long.' Then he is gone, slipping out of the door, leaving Hassan staring at the strangers, who smile at him. He cannot be sure they are trustworthy so leaves the book in his pocket.

When Tawfiq returns it is with a small tray of glasses and a silver teapot. 'So, how are little Nabeel and Nada?' Hassan asks, with a broad smile. Tawfiq had loved Nabeel and Nada so much that he had named his two children after them. 'Well, as a matter of fact . . .' and Tawfiq is off on a long-winded description of life at his house in the suburbs.

'And business?'

'It has been busy, and I'm in need of a rest but I cannot complain. One day honey, another day onions.'

When, finally, everyone says their farewells and leaves the shop, it is nearly closing time. A moment of calm descends. Hassan pulls out the book and hands it to his brother. Behind his glasses, Tawfiq's eyes prick and he looks up in consternation. *Brother Yasin?* The words, printed clearly in Arabic, are unmistakable. When he looks back at Hassan his eyes are filled with tears. 'A sequel! After all these years, Nabeel has written a new poem. Can it be true?'

'It seems so. It comes from Amman.'

Opening the book, Tawfiq starts to read.

Once again, on the journey home,
On the journey home through this barbaric world,
People, waiting in silence, to make the long, long journey
*   home,*
Here I stand in life's desert,
Composing a song to pass the evening,
Holding my questions in my hands,
So that when the journey has been long and the steps to my
*   home few,*
I know the way . . .

'I know his style anywhere. This is an occasion,' Tawfiq says, when he looks up at his brother. He fetches a stool, climbs on to it and drags down three heavy bales of cloth from a high shelf above his head. He plunges his hands into the first and pulls out a stack of coloured folders. 'Some Tolstoy,' he says, 'and . . . here we are! Nabeel's poems.' The folder is marked in small letters *The Picnic, Baghdad's Elegy, The Bloody Grassland* and *Brother Yasin.*

'Now, brother, I must know everything, especially how you came by this. Did your contact meet him?'

'No, but . . .' Hassan begins, but Tawfiq is already busying himself in the back room.

'I must make a copy for myself tonight and get the original to Juma'a. He must see it as soon as possible. By the way, did you know that Juma'a has become a cloth importer? Yes, it's true. When they sacked him from his teaching job he set up with some friends in the business but the sanctions have even stopped that from doing very well now. The secret police are all over him, questioning him, pushing into his business, but that's life.'

'Hold on, brother. Don't copy it now.' Hassan cannot believe Tawfiq intends to transcribe the entire poem. 'It's very long and it will take ages. I will get you another copy.'

'Don't worry. I'm in the modern world now. We have a photocopier. Can you believe it? The little machine is a great help. Only lack of paper and ink will stop me making enough copies to supply the whole of Baghdad.

'Look,' he gestures towards a shelf on the back wall, 'we have many, many books' worth of material here now. I will make copies and pass them to all of my contacts.' He pulls back the shelf to reveal a second, deeper ledge behind the cloth, a gap in the wood. And on this makeshift ledge, barely visible in the shadows behind the cloth, are numerous piles of papers. 'Who would have thought I'd become a publisher with a printing press?'

Hassan blanches at his brother's audacity. 'Tawfiq, I worry about you. Why don't you let someone else take over?'

314

Tawfiq shrugs. 'I cannot help myself. If I didn't do it, what would people have left to read? Military literature commissioned by His Excellency the President the Leader God Placed Him?' he says sarcastically. 'Everybody deserves better than that. Have you read any of it? Even he must know it's doggerel.'

'Look at the example he was set. Do you remember that terrible book his uncle wrote?' Published by the president's uncle, Wali Baghdad, *He Created Them by Mistake: the Persians, the Jews and the Flies* had been almost mandatory reading.

'All I'm asking is that you be discreet.' Hassan puts his arm round his brother's wiry frame. 'The scale of your operation is too big. You already know you are being watched. They will swoop on this place one day and I can tell you now they won't bother to put you back in prison.'

It was true. Tawfiq had been walking a fine line for many years. Poems, plays, novels, even articles and criticisms smuggled in from around the world, all are copied, printed and inserted into the bales of cloth stacked floor-to-ceiling all around him.

'I have all the classics now – Tolstoy, Gogol, Neruda, Dickens, George Eliot and Shakespeare. If there is a better-stocked library in the city I don't know where it is.' People from all across Baghdad and beyond bring him books daily. They may not be brave enough to pass them round themselves, but they know he is.

'I am a broker, that's all,' he says to Hassan. 'I trade in ideas and the human imagination. There should be no harm in that.'

He picks up a copy of one of Tolstoy's essays on art and hands it to Hassan. 'Read it. I have dug this out for a man who will come later. It will change the way you think about art.'

He closes a cupboard door, trots across to an alcove at the back of the shop, and moves several more bales of fabric to reveal a wooden trunk.

'Yes, you can see it is still being put to good use!' He gestures at the box, knowing his brother will recognise it as one of his old tailor's trunks. 'They make a good pair, the trunk and my new machine. A perfect fit.'

Inside is the portable photocopier. 'It came from the Ministry of Information and Culture. What an irony, eh? It broke and no one knew how to fix it so they threw it out with the rubbish. My radio producer friend rescued it. Now, of course, he is banned and works in a restaurant.' He chatters away as he pulls more bales to the floor. They thud as they land. He points to the third of the yellow folders, unmarked and thick. 'There's some blank paper in that one. Pass it to me, quickly.'

'Tawfiq, you have unbelievable nerve. I don't know who is more cavalier, me or you. But at least I live in the north of this country, and I intend to stay there.'

Tawfiq ignores his brother and puts the machine on the floor, squatting alongside it to fiddle with the flex. Although it is old, the copier has been fastidiously cleaned and maintained. His tailor's eye for detail has detected every last speck of dust and driven it out.

'Little by little, that is how the best things are done. A piece of paper here, a book there, Chekhov, Woolf, Ovid, Yasin, and soon the country will be filled with new ideas.'

The photocopier emits a high whine as it warms up. Hassan looks at his brother apprehensively.

'Don't worry. This is a noisy city.' Tawfiq reaches over and switches on his tape-recorder. 'And with a tape on who will know?' It bursts into life with some Iraqi folk music and he begins to copy the pages of the orange book. Half an hour later he has all forty-eight. With his tailor's tape still about his neck, he lays them out in order and fastens them together with string. He slips them into the Nabeel Yasin file and returns it to its hidden shelf. With the machine safely stowed in its trunk and the orange book in his hand, he settles in front of Hassan. 'Now, I must take this immediately to Juma'a. Please stay here and keep the shop open. When I return we shall go for supper at home.'

Tawfiq walks towards the bus station and searches for the bus to al-Sayydia. Twice in recent months the Mukhabarat have accosted him and turned out his bag of samples on the street, looking for contraband. They have been to the shop, too, but always, by some miracle, left empty-handed. Tawfiq offered tea as they pushed over his mannequins and took his friends aside for questioning. They are always watching him, but he knows that these thugs are illiterate, barely aware of what they do or why. If they had not threatened him so brutally, he would probably feel sorry for them.

Fortunately, his shop is a good cover. Everyone needs the services of a decent tailor and he is gifted. The moment he sets eyes on a person he knows what can be done: whatever the fabric, wool, silk, or cotton, he sees it draped round shoulders or falling from a waist. He loves to select material and realise a vision. Now there is less demand, less gaiety, fewer reasons to wear tailored clothing. This has become a land of military uniforms and informants; there is no call for tulle frocks and fine suits. There are no big occasions any more, unless you count the annual birthday celebrations for His Excellency. The men and women who had once flocked to his shop in search of Italian- and French-style couture suits are long gone.

Now, many wear *thawbs* and *abaya*s. With nothing to dress up for, why not pass unnoticed in a robe that allows you to hide extra rice on the way back from the market? This is the practical daywear of a dictatorship.

When he arrives at the Yasins' gate, he looks round to make sure he has not been followed. Then he presses the bell set into the wall. He can feel the book against his chest and his heart thumping. It is Juma'a's voice that he hears. 'Who is it?'

'Tawfiq.'

The gate swings open with a loud creak and Juma'a pulls his friend inside. '*Salaam aleikum.*' They embrace in the shadows and walk along the path to the house. Inside, Sabria and her grandchildren sit together in the cavernous reception room, glued to an Egyptian film on television. Tawfiq, a diminutive figure next to Juma'a, nods to each in turn. '*Salaam alaeikum.*' He retreats with Juma'a to a quiet area at the back of the room, refuses tea and murmurs, 'I have something for you. My brother brought it today from Arbil.'

He reaches into the breast pocket of his waistcoat and produces the book. Juma'a squints and leans forward. 'Is it real?'

'Yes. A friend of my brother Hassan got it in Amman – but look.' He takes the book back and opens it. 'It has the name of a printer in Wembley, London. I have not read it all yet but you can tell from the first words that it's his.'

Juma'a presses the tips of his fingers to his temples. 'Mama! Nabeel is publishing in London!'

'Can you believe it?' Tawfiq adds. 'We have a new poem.'

Sabria and the grandchildren gather round the table as Juma'a opens the book. Holding it carefully, so that he does not break the spine, he reads aloud the first page:

Oh, my family,
My angels did not return from their banquet.
I get ready to sleep for the last time on my damp sheets,
My bed of tears,
And just as the departed hum silent hymns,
I hum my hymns in silence,
So I may meet the morrow all alone.
My wisdom is my morning coffee
And my advanced years the light of my house . . .

I am the last wretched wise man in a time that detests wise
   men,
I am the last one clutching the dying embers as the fire
   burns out,
I am the last to burn . . .

Over the next two years, Tawfiq makes hundreds of copies of
Brother Yasin Again. While he was making the first batch he
remembered Nabeel once telling him about an antique book
he had bought at the old Abbasid market, a teal-blue and red
volume of the *Muqaddimah of Ibn Khaldun*, with yellowed
parchment pages. It had belonged to Nuri el-Said, the prime
minister during the monarchy. The prime minister's library
had been liberated by Kassim's regime, the contents spread
about the country like confetti. Nabeel felt blessed to find
such a thing at the market and had kept the book for six years
until the Ba'athists had snatched it from him as a punishment.
During his second year of studies, they had taken control of
the university: anyone who was not a Party member was

denied access. They set up a military-style checkpoint at the university entrance and regular patrols demanded papers and proof of identity. Nabeel had got up a written petition to demand free access. The Ba'athists had banned him from classes and chased him for his petition, anxious to know which treacherous students had signed it.

Denied entry by the normal route and with nowhere to keep his books, Nabeel had found a safe haven in a storeroom. From there he could slip unnoticed into classes, and he hid his books in a broom cupboard. It had worked well for almost a term until a fellow student informed on him. Then the guards had chased him through the corridors. They had lost him but found the broom cupboard and his books, including the *Muqaddimah*, which they had taken.

Tawfiq makes most of his copies of *Brother Yasin Again* with the machine, but when it runs out of toner or the president is punishing his people with another blackout, he copies it by hand in candlelight. Often he works well into the night, with half-finished shirts, suits and dresses on his bench. Then he passes on the finished work, delivering it with a pair of trousers or a new jacket. He often tacks a poem or a pamphlet into a lining, from which it can easily be removed.

'My work is still the best,' he tells his friends. 'His Excellency the President the Leader God Placed Him may prefer Gucci and Valentino but my customers' clothes are their equal in every stitch and much more besides.'

One night late in 1995 he arranges for a trusted contact to pick up a booklet. He has not asked for whom it is intended. He prefers not to. There have even been times recently when he has not passed something on – a sixth sense has prevented him. Perhaps they are closing in on him – or he is becoming paranoid in middle age. Increasingly, he has taken to keeping his papers in unlikely hiding places around the city. In Baghdad there is no shortage of bombed buildings, and sometimes friends will let him place a parcel behind a loose brick, or in a hole under a doormat. Much of his stock has gone this way as he tries to reduce the risk to himself.

Through the whir of the sewing-machine he hears someone enter the shop.

'Ah, Salman.' He whistles with relief. 'How good to see you.' His heart drops back to its regular rhythm and he returns to the false lining he is stitching into a beige jacket. 'Will you take tea?'

Outside it is dusk and shoppers flock the streets, with the arrival of cooler air. It is always the busiest time of day and Tawfiq finds himself casting metres of cloth on to the shop floor for several new customers. Khalid, a friend of his son's, wants a pair of smart trousers for a family wedding and two furniture importers wander in with a bag of fabric they would like made into English-style three-piece suits. As Tawfiq measures them, he calls the dimensions to Salman, who has decided to stay on.

Between customers, Tawfiq turns his attention back to the jacket. He had intended to finish it and drop it off with his contact that night, but by the time he closes he knows it is too late. The poem, hand-copied in tiny print, has been slipped into place and stitched in but he does not want to travel to the west of the city tonight.

'I will call in the morning. It is past eight now and I am tired,' he mutters to Salman, who has tidied away the teacups and tray and is hovering by the shop door ready to leave.

'My friend, you are doing too much,' Salman says.

'Maybe I am. It is all the worry of the shop and the children. I should take a holiday.'

'It is not the shop, but what you are doing outside it that is the problem. Everyone can see how hard it is on you.'

Catching sight of his haggard face in the glass of the window, Tawfiq fastens the door. 'Come, Salman. Let us leave. A tired man needs food and his bed.'

Salman embraces him by the door and waves.

As the key turns in the padlock of the steel grille, Tawfiq sees two secret policemen waiting in a doorway opposite. Normally this wouldn't worry him. But tonight, tired and feeling that his run of good fortune is at an end, he is more than a little shaky. He turns to walk in the opposite direction but they cut him off and push him back against the door. 'Open up,' they order.

He wipes his brow and prepares to deny everything. As usual he will protest only at their treatment of his shop. Experience has taught him that the worse his indignation as they bring his stock to the floor, the quicker they will leave. As they roll bales of fabric out on to the floor they fire off the usual questions: who are his customers, who does he visit, who does he supply, where does he get his banned material.

'There is nothing I can tell you. I am a tailor. I work all the hours to keep my family, making suits and robes. Nothing more. One day you will realise this and leave me alone.'

They empty drawers and turn over a table. He knows they will find nothing unless they dismantle his whole shop and they are too lazy to do that. They always reach for the nearest bale rather than climb a ladder. They will grow bored of bullying him soon. Then he has only to get home and this unrewarding day will be over. He will tidy the shop tomorrow.

Outside, as he draws the shutter again and snaps the lock, the streetlights begin to blur. People come at him from every angle, staring at him. From the corner of his eye he can see the two Mukhabarat men. As usual they appear to be following him home. But he is dizzy and unusually breathless, as if the last of his energy is draining from him. He stumbles on a dip in the paving-stones and loses his footing. He stops to steady himself and finds he cannot catch his breath. He turns into a street leading off the main drag and makes for a restaurant he knows. He can rest there until they decide to leave him be.

As he crosses the street he falls to his knees and collapses face down on the ground. The police, whose job has been done for them, melt away into the stream of shoppers, leaving him in the road to die.

All Things Must Pass,
October 1993 and February 1999

Padding down the hall of the small second-floor apartment she shares with two other female doctors, Amel dips into the tiny kitchen to make tea. She has not slept well again and her back is aching from the long journey south. The road from the capital to the Shia'a town of Al Amarah is rough and pitted and the buses are not built for comfort. It is always the same. Each weekend, unless she is on call, she leaves the hospital, makes the four-hundred-kilometre journey home to Baghdad, then does it again in the opposite direction a day later.

This relentless cycle would be bearable if she felt revived by the time she spends at al-Sayydia. It isn't her mother's fault, of course: she's getting old, and what with her brothers, sisters-in-law and babies all living at the house too, there is little chance of peace or the sleep Amel yearns for. There are occasional small mercies: she is not on the early shift this week.

Looking absently out of the window at the town, her eyes rest on a stream of raw sewage winding through the streets below. It oozes slowly along the drainage gullies to gather in pools round the playground. The children, playing amid rubble, seem not to notice.

She has long since stopped being surprised or saddened by anything she sees in al-Amarah. Most of the inhabitants are malnourished, in need of treatment for coughs and stomach ailments and unaware that life was once different. In all likelihood some have serious underlying conditions, cancers and blood disorders. The toxic waste that contaminates the water and the land in the aftermath of the war has devastated these people. The government won't admit there is a problem, let alone provide the resources for them to be treated.

Amel checks her watch: she has half an hour to get to work. There is no time for vanity in her morning routine. A quick wash and brush-up will do. Her clothes are simple, sombre and functional. A long dark skirt, white shirt and sturdy shoes. It hadn't always been so. As a student she had worn jeans almost every day, but things have changed since the war with Iran. She is often amazed at the clothes she wore back then. Now a new conservatism is settling on the country and many women are returning to thick clothes, the *hijab* and the *abaya*. 'Think as you like, but dress as others do,' is Sabria's advice.

She clips up her hair, takes her medical bag from the shelf behind the door and checks the contents: stethoscope, thermometer, a vial for boiled water, a box of scalpels, plasters, antiseptic cream, skin lotion, a roll of boiled bandage, safety-pins, sterilising tablets, her trusted medical manual. It has become a reflex action of late. Two years into this dreadful posting, she has almost no personal possessions apart from the bag. In not settling here, she is reminding herself that soon, with luck, she may move on.

The posting to al-Amarah had not come as a surprise. The Medical Bureau, which directs hospital placements throughout the country, knows exactly who Amel's brothers are and is not about to forget it. Since she had arrived for interview at the prestigious Baghdad Medical College in the autumn of 1978 armed with the best high-school results in Iraq, they had made sure she suffered for bearing the name Yasin.

During her first week, she had been banned from entering the campus. The dean had summoned her his office and had been forthright but unapologetic. 'Your brothers are known Communists, leftists and trouble-makers. One is an Enemy of the State.' Sitting behind his desk with a framed copy of the Hippocratic oath behind him, he had been unable to look at her directly. 'I see from this report that he is a writer of anti-Ba'athist propaganda. How unfortunate. Under the circumstances I cannot permit you to attend this school any longer.' He did, however, make her an offer as she walked in a state of shock towards the door. If she agreed to pledge allegiance to the Party and denounce all Enemies of the State, including members of her own family, she would be allowed to stay.

Amel had fled the campus and returned home to seek her father's advice. As he was head of the family, she needed him to agree to any course of action she might take. More than that, she knew he would be fair and pragmatic. 'Baba, they say I must become a Ba'athist.'

'And you are worried because you do not want to become one? Or because you do?' he had asked, without a hint of judgement either way.

'I am not Ba'athist, Baba. Nor should I become one. I may not be politically minded like the boys but I should not be made to sign. It is not right. I love medicine and I am good, Baba. This is my chance to do the thing I love. I have wanted to get to medical school for as long as I can remember. How dare they make me sacrifice my own freedom so that I can study?'

'Well, what can we do?' he had asked. 'Let us sleep and see how it looks in the morning.' He had pulled out his *mishaha* from the breast pocket of his slate grey shirt. Though he had often worried about how the boys' activities might affect his daughters' chances, he had not let it show. 'We will find a way round this. We will talk to Nabeel and see what can be done. There is always a solution if you are willing to compromise a little.'

A few days later Nabeel had petitioned some of the academics he knew with Amel's brilliant test results. Word got round to the president of the Ba'athist student union, who called Amel in to the university for a discussion about her situation. That she was a brilliant student was not in dispute: her background was the problem. He proposed a return to study at one of the other Baghdad colleges provided she renounced Communism. Once more she sought her father's approval. 'Baba, if I sign a contract saying I am not a Communist, they will let me into al-Mustansiriyah University instead.'

'Good. You're not a Communist anyway, are you?'

'No, Baba.'

'So, the next question must be, is it a good school?'

'Well, it does not have a great reputation but . . .'

'But it's a medical school where you can qualify to be a doctor?'

Amel nods.

'Then this is the school for you. You will become a doctor without needing to lie. Patience has rewarded you with sweet fruit.' Yasin had always marvelled at his youngest daughter's dedication. 'Sign it, *habibti*, with my blessing. Sign whatever they ask for. Why worry?'

'I do worry, Baba. I worry about what the boys will say.'

'Ah, your brothers.' Yasin had looked at her quizzically, then smiled wryly. 'Do not be concerned. They will support you.'

That autumn, only two months before her father died, Amel began at Al-Mustansiriyah University on the outskirts of Baghdad. She graduated seven years later with marks that showed her to be among the country's finest medics. Knowing how difficult it was for her in Iraq, her family had assumed she would go abroad as soon as she could.

'I suppose you'll be leaving us now, maybe for a research post in America or Canada?' Sabria had whispered in her daughter's ear, even before the graduation ceremony had ended.

'Who knows, Mama? I'm just thankful I've been able to graduate.'

In any other country achievements such as Amel's would have been accompanied by celebration and plans for a stellar career. But Amel, exhausted by life as a junior doctor, was unable to take much joy from her results. Her final year had included the stiffest apprenticeship: thrice-weekly shifts at the al-Yarmuk hospital, treating the war-injured from the front. She had felt too young for the carnage that faced her on the wards. Yet every day huge numbers of men were unloaded on to the beds, needing more complex treatment than she or any of the other doctors could offer. Men with burned faces and incomplete limbs, internal injuries and infectious diseases. After that, the graduation ceremony felt like a cruel joke.

She applied for every post she heard about, but over the following months she watched her contemporaries, most of whom were less well qualified than she, fall into the top hospital and university teaching jobs. Faced with weekly rejection it grew increasingly difficult to remain pragmatic.

At first she had believed it would be possible to study her way out of discrimination, to show herself so brilliant that they would have to accept her, regardless of anything her brothers might have done. The reality was different. Ba'athist policy meant that she had to suffer for the sins of her family. When she was finally offered a job it came as a shock.

The position was in Al Kut, low-grade, with no clinical expertise required. It was an insult to a woman of her qualifications. But she had accepted it. How naïve she had been! It was close to the front line and the town had been ravaged by war. Its hospital was flooded with wounded soldiers and civilians. And amid the casualties there was ordinary hospital life too. People got sick, people recovered; babies were born and the elderly died.

When she reaches the hospital complex, she can see patients already milling about waiting for the surgery to open. Many are poor, marsh Arabs, who have been driven out of the marshlands to the south-east by the president's drainage programme. The official reason for this is that it will yield fertile agricultural land, but everyone knows that it has been done in retribution. The marsh Arabs had sheltered deserters during Qadisiyat Saddam. Now, their homes and livelihoods gone, many families have been divided, some crossing the border into Iran, others forced into the city. Here they have nothing to do, no skills and no means of earning a living. Persecuted by the militia they exist in the most squalid conditions where illness and disease are rife. But of those who come into the hospital most are now turned away at the reception. Ever since the edict had been passed that doctors were to ignore non Ba'athists, it has become a punishable offence to treat such people. Most doctors are too scared to defy the ruling. Amel has no regard for it; neither does she worry that the Special Republican Guard is on hand, patrolling the corridors. What more damage could they do to her career prospects now? The hospital is large, with many rooms and corridors. There are plenty of places to treat all those in need away from prying eyes.

Sabria frets constantly about her daughter. 'I get Tariq back from the war and you put yourself in danger. Have you learned nothing from what has happened to your brothers? If you go looking for trouble, it will come. You are a clever girl. You should know that. Besides, who will look after *me* if they decide to punish you? You are the best doctor a mother could have. Why not get a job treating the needy here? You could even stay at home with me.'

And so it went on, every weekend: a relentless barrage of guilt that would end only when she had waved goodbye to her mother and boarded the bus south.

She had once attempted to reason with Sabria, but it had only compounded the problem: 'Mama, remember the Sulymany stone that saved Nabeel when he was bitten by the scorpion?'

'Ah, of course I do! Three times, if I remember. Those scorpions really liked the taste of him.'

The ancient brown stone had been named after King Solomon. It was reputed to give off heat that, when placed over a bite, would draw out the poison and stop it spreading.

'What if the wise man of Karradat Mariam had not come with his Sulymany? Nabeel would not be in Hungary now, would he? Nor would there be any Yamam. It is the same for me. I will heal any man or his child, regardless of whether he is a Kurd, a Christian, a Sunni or a Shia'a. There can be no argument, surely.'

These days, Amel is too weary to defend her choices,

preferring instead to let her mother have her say. It is pointless trying to win an argument with Sabria. Neither does she want to talk about things she has seen other doctors do in the name of the regime. With each cowardly action and brutal atrocity she witnesses, she understands a little better what her brothers have been fighting against all this time. If there are any compensations for an existence on the margins, this is it: people need her. It is that simple.

That day Amel sees more than a hundred and fifty people in the hospital clinic. The patients pass by in a long blur of sickness and misery. Some are much sicker than they know. Other than the Ba'athist policeman with a broken finger, most come in groups of two or three for support. The older women refuse to look at her; they are unsure how to talk about their symptoms so they speak through relatives. The few she is able to help are referred upstairs to X-ray or Oncology, or sent with prescriptions to the pharmacy in the hope that some medication will be available. For most, help will be too late.

She locks the surgery door after the last patient has gone, and slips a handful of sterilised needles into her bag. Then she goes up to the labour ward to wait for Zaynab, her flatmate. They are due to meet Mahmoud, another doctor, who has been providing them with black-market supplies. Today she is hoping for vaccine. She has earmarked a handful of families with young children to whom she will offer the jabs, hoping to prevent an outbreak of diphtheria.

Sitting in the doctors' green-painted common room at the end of the ward, she waits for Zaynab to finish her shift and for Mahmoud to arrive back from Baghdad. Briefly, she enjoys thinking of nothing.

When the door opens and the senior registrar comes in, she knows immediately that something is wrong. Usually affable, he seems ruffled and uneasy. 'Dr Amel, I must speak to you urgently.'

'Something serious?'

'I want to apologise straight away for what I am about to say.' His hands disappear into his pockets. 'There have been accusations from very high up.'

'Oh?'

'You have been treating people you should not be treating with drugs bought on the black-market. I myself would not comment, but this is what they are saying.'

Amel hopes Mahmoud and Zaynab do not sail through the door with their bags full just yet.

'Of course, I am sympathetic to what you are doing – we all are – but you cannot compromise the rest of us. We have our directives from the ministry and we *must* obey. Are you aware of the consequences if we don't?'

'I understand.' Amel does not blame him: he is a good doctor whose hands are tied. Every day they have to betray the Hippocratic oath, but that is the way of things now. The punishment for refusing is death.

In Al Kut, during the uprisings that followed the Kuwait defeat, she witnessed the regime at its worst. For their refusal to stop treating injured insurgents, several doctors had been murdered by the Special Republican Guard, who had rounded them up with some nurses and marched them to the flat roof of the hospital. There, they had forced the offenders at gunpoint over the edge. The bodies had been left below in a pile as a warning to all.

Hamza shifts about on his feet. 'Dr Amel, I'm so sorry, but I must ask you to leave. It will be better for you like this. If you are working with anyone else I suggest you tell them to stop. Now, you are a good doctor so I have found you another position. A friend has started work at al-Nahda hospital and needs more doctors.'

Amel thanks him and waits to break the news to her accomplices. Al-Nahda hospital, situated close to the dark slums of Saddam City to the north of Baghdad, has a well-deserved reputation as the worst hospital in Iraq.

At least her mother will be happy to have her home.

Amel is working on the emergency ward of the al-Nahda on the night of the great riots in early 1999. The Grand Ayatollah Sadiq al-Sadr has been assassinated with his two sons and crowds of protesters are spilling on to the streets to confront the police. An orderly caught on the fringes of a rampage comes running on to the ward with his own breathless commentary: 'It's madness out there, people running at the police with sticks and rocks. They're crying, "Death to Saddam" – can you believe it? The Guard are everywhere.'

Amel says nothing. She knows how it will end. The crowd will gather momentum and energy until they are chanting, 'God is Great, God is Great,' as one. Then *he* will give the order and the police will move in to kill them all.

'Check the radio,' she tells a nurse, as she heads for the ward. 'We should know if there is fighting anywhere else.' The old wireless set is there for the patients but sometimes it's possible to find an unblocked signal from a foreign station, Iranian or Kurdish. In some parts of Iraq you can even pick up the BBC World Service on short wave, if the weather is right and it hasn't been jammed or blocked. These stations offer the possibility of real news, not the lies that Iraqi Radio forces on its listeners. As she goes to change the drip on a young mother with a failing kidney, she prays that the protesters will go home. But al-Sadr was loved by millions of Shia'a. They will not stop until they have avenged his violent death.

The sound of gunfire is soon heard, sporadic and muffled, but unmistakable. Then a strange silence, followed by the almighty pounding of artillery fire. 'This is it,' one of the doctors says, as the blitz begins. 'Be ready, everyone.'

The police fire automatic machine-guns at the crowd. In a matter of minutes they have closed in. Trying not to flinch, Amel checks the IV needle in the young woman's hand. 'You are not to worry,' she says, squeezing her fingers. 'They will not come in here.'

As the words leave her mouth, a doctor skids in from the corridor. 'Downstairs, everyone. The wounded are coming in already.'

The doctors run down the corridors and into the wide marble foyer, where the air is full of men's screams. In the bare neon light bodies, twenty or more, lie on the floor. Blood seeps across the smooth tiles, great pools of it, thick and dark. Out of the darkness, beyond the glass doors, Amel can see crowds running in the distance. A man at her feet with a bullet-hole in his shoulder begs, 'Help me! They are shooting everyone. There are hundreds on the ground out there.' Amel dispatches the porters for stretchers, then bends down and starts to work.

Along the corridors men and women are searching for brothers, fathers and sons, calling their names. One man, unable to find his son, stops a passing nurse: 'Where are they taking the dead?' The nurse whispers that the morgue is fast filling and that they have opened one of the offices as a makeshift store until the panic is over. He should try there.

Amel sees a boy slumped against the wall, unconscious. He has been hit in the chest. 'Come, he is still alive.' She grabs a porter. 'If we get him to surgery he may have a chance.'

'I have no stretchers left, Dr Amel. We'll have to carry him ourselves.'

'OK.' They lift the boy off the floor and shuffle along the corridor to the theatre with him.

They lay the man down in the theatre and Amel runs back along the corridor to the storeroom for bandages and morphine. It is unlocked and probably empty, but it's worth a look. She runs her hands along the wall for the light switch. It isn't working so she feels along the shelves. Outside, footsteps pound along the corridor. Amel steps into the light from the open door and sees several officers run past the hospital. It has been seized by the Special Republican Guard.

Looking over at the small ward opposite she can see her colleagues through the glass doors, huddled together at the end of the room. Two guardsmen watch over them, guns poised.

The captain kicks open the ward doors and jerks his gun in her direction. 'We know the names of all the traitorous scum in this hospital. You will stop treating these men, do you understand?'

'We are doctors and we have work to do,' Amel says.

He jabs the gun at her again. 'The men you are treating are Shia'a rebels. They are animals. They are against everything that is righteous. They are enemies of His Excellency the President the Leader God Placed Him and those who aid them are traitors.'

'We are doctors, not traitors. There are many injured people here. It is our job to treat them, just as I would treat you if you were wounded.'

'This is a zoo, not a hospital. And I am ordering you to stop.'

A colleague calls to her. 'Amel! Please do as he says. Do not fight them.'

'See? Your sensible friend understands.' He grabs her arm. 'We could execute any doctor trying to treat these animals. We will take them outside and kill them. It does not matter to me. I will walk from here and still sleep soundly in my bed.' The doctors stand in silence.

Out in the corridor there is a screech of rubber-soled boots. Another guardsman crashes through the door waving his gun. 'Come on,' his face is sweaty with adrenalin, 'there are more fools waiting outside.'

Amel's guard pushes past her and runs off down the corridor.

When Amel hangs up her white coat and leaves the hospital, quietly, the next afternoon, she knows she will not go back. Sitting on the bus as it weaves through the aftermath of the rioting, past the broken windows and burnt-out cars, she decides that it is time for her to follow her brothers Nabeel and Jabbar and make a new life outside Iraq.

The previous night, after the Special Republican Guard had dumped the injured outside, the doctors had worked through the night to save those they could. Removing their hospital coats and identity tags, they had taken it in turns to sit by the door and keep watch, while the others dealt with the mass of injured and dying. It had been a defiant last stand but Amel knew she was beaten.

To her three remaining brothers and Aqbal, the news is no surprise. Jafar had been expecting it, amazed that she had waited so long. 'The issue now is how we get you out.'

'Let us hope no one wastes our time with the kind of schemes Nabeel was offered.'

'That was nearly twenty years ago.'

'And nothing has changed!' Juma'a interrupts. 'People still think they can smuggle a woman out in a sack of dates. It's laughable – like that idea for Nabeel to dress as a Kuwaiti peasant and travel in the back of a fruit truck with a great beard on his face! I would have liked to see the border guards' faces when he opened his mouth to speak. The most educated and eloquent peasant in all history.'

'But how can she hope to escape when women have to travel abroad with an escort?' Sabria shouts from the sofa. She is resigned to losing another child. Better that than Amel being arrested and taken to one of the notorious women's prisons. Unlike the boys, there would be no way back for her if that happened. She cannot bear to think of her youngest daughter suffering in the same way as Juma'a, or Sa'ad.

Sa'ad, Selwa's husband, had been in prison almost five years for buying the wrong car. He had gone to a state auction in the north of Baghdad and bid for a Mercedes against a man in a brown suit and sunglasses. The day after his triumph, he was arrested and his new car taken. It was Selwa who later discovered that the man he had bid against was a personal friend of Uday Hussein, *al-Layth*, the Lion. Sa'ad had languished without trial for years in Abu Ghraib. Lying blindfolded in his cell one night, he had heard a sudden burst of activity at the steel door. There had been a sharp, brisk swish,

337

and a choked gurgle. Then he had felt a warm shower over his face. It was the blood of his cellmate. In the morning, his blindfold had been removed and he had seen the body. They had slit the man's throat. When Sa'ad had a heart-attack a junior guard had released him to the hospital. It had been his second chance.

Sabria is relieved when Juma'a takes over the escape plan. He has an eye for detail. 'There is only one way to do this. We must get an official exit visa, a *kafala*,' he says.

'But it costs four thousand dinars, nearly a year's pay! And even then they won't allow me to have one unless I'm with someone,' Amel protests.

'I have contacts, and we will find the money by selling and borrowing. Since you cannot travel alone, Tariq will go with you. Once you get to Amman you can go on alone. He will come home.'

The hardest part for Amel is not the preparations but watching her mother take it in. She is worried that Sabria's health will suffer when she is gone. As well as reassurance and companionship, Amel has provided essential medical advice over the past few years. 'Mama, promise me you will at least try to live properly when I am gone. You must take care of yourself, as well as the others. I know you understand what I'm saying. Try to rest more. Promise me that at least.'

'How can I rest?' Sabria clasps her bony hands together. 'I am too old to rest. It is the years of worrying over you and your brothers that have left me like this. Rest will only give death an opportunity to take me. *Our friend* and this country have just about worn me out. And for nothing. I am an old woman without my family.'

'Mama, you know I have a return ticket.'

'Nabeel once said something similar to me. Don't try to

fool me. You *have* to have a return ticket. They only let you go if it looks like you're coming back.' She stares at her daughter. 'I know what's going on. You're leaving me. That I can forgive. But, daughter, please do not lie to lessen the blow.'

We Are Seven
March, April 2003

For three weeks between 20 March, when the Allied forces invade, and 9 April, when Baghdad falls, the Yasins wait, like countless other Iraqi families, with their hearts in their mouths. No one dares to imagine that the American-led offensive might truly mark the end of Saddam's thirty-five-year reign. In exile, Jabbar, Amel and Nabeel speak to each other on the phone as the television pictures play out on CNN and BBC World, fearful for the family trapped in Iraq. They worry not only for their immediate safety under fire but also for the time when the offensive is over. After Desert Storm and the uprisings that followed, life in Iraq had seemed to revert to a stiff status quo. After all the hope that the regime would fall, that had been the most cruel outcome.

In Baghdad, Juma'a, Tariq, their wives and children take refuge at the house in al-Sayydia and wait for the soldiers to come. With the sound of each new explosion they try to guess where in the city the bombs are falling and who may have been hit. The power lines are the first services to go down, leaving each house darkened and isolated. Gas and electricity substations are taken out strategically by the Allied bombers and the main telephone exchanges across the city are dismantled and abandoned, then left to the bombs. No one knows what is happening: there is no reliable television or radio. The claims on Radio Baghdad that the Americans' reports of progress northwards are an illusion amount to propaganda, a chance for Ba'athists to proclaim Iraq's victories against a weakened oppressor.

'They will say there are no Americans at all, even when we are under their bombs. And then, when the Americans are inside the city, they will tell us that victory is Iraq's,' Tariq declares.

'Why bother to deny events that we can see for ourselves?' Juma'a replies.

Rumour, speculation and stray facts are passed from person to person through the neighbourhood grapevine. Nobody has any idea whether it will be over in days or if it will turn into another agonising war of attrition.

In Rusafa, Jafar, Aqbal and their immediate families are in their respective apartments in the old part of town. Despite their proximity there is no way to make contact. They are unaware that tanks, advance scouts and reconnaissance teams have crossed the Tigris and the Euphrates and are advancing towards the outskirts of the city to the south. Bombs are falling, planes, spy drones and jets cross the sky. While some of their neighbours have fled, most have stayed, hiding in makeshift shelters built from furniture and praying they will not be hit. Dark columns of smoke rise into the air and the thunder of explosions rips through the deadened city.

Jafar hears a rumour from his neighbour that Baghdad is undefended and that the Party faithful and main military brigades have left. 'His Excellency the President the Leader God Placed Him has moved his military forces out of Baghdad to strategic points to the south and north, leaving the city open to the advancing troops.' He is sure they will cross the line of defence with no resistance.

Watching from their windows, Juma'a and Tariq wait, day after day, until finally on the morning of 5 April Tariq spots a long column of tanks rumbling along the expressway from the airport. 'Brother, they are coming! Look! Children, look! This is history in the making!' He ushers his two little girls to the window on the stairs and points. There, in the sandy haze beyond the open scrubland, is a long procession of tanks and infantry. 'That is the American Army. They have come half-way round the world for this.'

'What are they doing here, Baba?' the children ask, as they scramble for a better view.

'We can't be certain but we are praying that they have come for Saddam and his supporters. If we are lucky, they will leave the rest of us alone.' He hoists his elder daughter on to his shoulders for a better view and leans out of the window. 'We shall know soon enough what their intentions are.'

'You idiot! Get inside!' Juma'a shouts. 'Do you want to get their heads blown off?'

'Don't be such a killjoy! They'll tell their grandchildren about this!'

'Not if they're dead they won't. Have you forgotten how *our friend* hid his mortars and missile launchers between houses and primary schools last time? Do you think the Americans are going to be happy that foolish men with their daughters on their shoulders are waving at them? No! They will look at every house with suspicion. Don't expect them to know you're pleased they're here. They'll take one look at you and think you're a sniper or a decoy.'

The children laugh nervously, unsure whether to be excited or to hide.

'OK, perhaps you are right,' Tariq concedes. 'But remember what you've seen, children.'

An hour or so later they hear a banging at the gate and someone begging to be let in.

Juma'a and Tariq stare at each other.

'It doesn't sound like anyone we know,' whispers Juma'a. 'It can't be Aqbal or Jafar.'

'Keep everyone out of sight,' Tariq whispers. 'I'll go and see.'

He signals for everyone to take cover and walks warily across the yard towards the metal gate of the compound. 'Who is it?'

'I'm just trying to get home. I've come from the south. I need help to get to my parents' house.' The voice on the other side of the wall is young. Tariq opens the gate a little way and sees an exhausted soldier with his hands in the air. His weapon, an automatic rifle, is on the sand beside him. He looks barely eighteen.

'Are you injured? Is this some trick? I warn you, my brother is here and we're all armed.' Of course he is lying.

The soldier looks up at him, and Tariq realises he is near to collapse.

'Let me in. Please. If they see me the Americans will come for me. Let me inside – hide me.'

'Where is your unit? Are there any more of you?'

'I'm alone. Everyone has scattered. We're supposed to be fighting beyond the airport but our general released us when the tanks came. It's muddy and hilly, and we couldn't find anywhere to hide. There are thousands of them. And we had no food or water, only a few guns. I have been two days without any water. I didn't want to fight and now the Americans will find me and take me prisoner. I just want to get home.'

Shooing his children inside, Tariq drags the soldier into the compound. 'Where do you live?'

'Saddam City.'

'You'll never make it dressed like that. The city's filling up with Americans. Once they've seized the palaces and government buildings they'll spread through every street.'

'Can I stay here?'

'No. But I can get you some ordinary clothes. Wait here and don't move, not a twitch.' Tariq picks up the soldier's weapon and gestures for him to sit on the ground. Then, with Juma'a watching, he jogs inside, throws the gun on to the bed and picks out some clothes from his wardrobe, a pair of trousers, a beige shirt, vest and sandals. He fetches a jug of water and a bowl of rice from the kitchen as he tells the others what has happened. Ten minutes later, fed, clothed and watered, the soldier is almost on his way again. Tariq gives him back his gun. 'I'd get rid of that if I were you.'

'I will, as soon as I can.' He leaves the gate with a bow and heartfelt thanks. 'I will not forget your kindnesses.'

As darkness falls others come. Tariq wonders if word has been passed back down the line or whether the desperate soldiers are trying every house in the neighbourhood. Tariq offers each of them a set of his clothes, but he hasn't enough shoes to go round.

Juma'a watches his brother in disbelief. 'What are you going to do with all those?' He points to the growing pile of uniforms and boots behind the gate.

'Don't you think every man deserves to be reunited with his family? They're just like me. They don't want to fight. You heard what they said. The generals are disbanding their units and getting out while they can.'

'They're lying.'

'Come on! You saw them. They aren't the Republican Guard. They're ordinary men doing dirty work. They were probably all conscripts, like me. Where's your humanity?'

'Just be careful. It is not only the Americans we need to look out for. We're all dead. It's only your usual good luck that lets me go along with what you're doing. But go and lock the gate now. No more soldiers.'

It is from within the fortress of their home that they hear the news on 9 April. On their tiny portable radio, it is announced that the Allies, now in control of radio transmitters and the television station, have taken charge of the city 'Baghdad has fallen,' they declare.

Tariq turns into the room with his hands together. 'Let this be an end to it all.'

In London Nabeel has been perched on the edge of his sofa for days, spitting at old images of Saddam Hussein as they are shown on television. Now he is too stunned by what he is seeing to take it in. With the BBC repeating that Baghdad has fallen, he calls Nada at work. Neither knows what to say. 'Is it really true, Dudi?' Nada's voice shakes.

'I think so this time.'

'And Saddam?'

'No one is saying anything yet.'

In the background he can hear other Iraqis chattering excitedly.

'I can safely say there will be no work today in the proof-reading department,' she says.

'I wish you were here, Nada.'

'So do I, but I'll hurry home. You should go out. Go to the café and see what al-Jazeera has to say.'

'Yes. Yes, I will.'

Suddenly Nabeel feels the need to be with people, his own people. He grabs his coat, then jumps down the stairs two at a time and goes out into the bustle of west London. Everything looks as it always does, buses, cars, taxis and people, all moving fast. But when he passes the Arab travel agent and barber, he sees that they are both shut. He takes the bus to the Edgware Road and heads for the Iraqi-run *gahawa*, coffee shop, al-Jazeera Café – they usually have al-Jazeera television running on a huge screen in the corner. As he walks past supermarkets, restaurants and clothing shops, he is smiling.

At al-Jazeera, the TV is on at full volume and the atmosphere is alive with noisy debate. He orders coffee and settles himself close to the screen. A huge statue of Saddam Hussein is being pulled to the ground by a determined crowd of men. Nabeel cannot believe his eyes. He calls Nada again on his mobile phone. 'The regime is gone.'

She cries with relief when she hears him. Beyond their own survival, this has been their single dream. For years they have wished for their country to be delivered. They had almost stopped believing it could happen but now it has.

Unable to keep still, giddy with emotion, Nabeel walks out of the café and on to the road. He heads towards Marble Arch and into Oxford Street then to the number-ten bus stop. There, surrounded by commuters and the central London traffic, the lights of department stores and offices, he is transported back to the morning when he left Baghdad with

Nada and Yamam. He had been young then, only twenty-nine. Now he is fifty-three, Nada too. And the garrulous four-year-old who had come with them is a strong, successful man in his late twenties. It would all be different in Iraq – even the family he left behind will have changed more than he can imagine. In his mind he holds pictures of much younger people. He allows himself, perhaps for the first time, to imagine what they are like now. Jafar and Juma'a are in their sixties, both certainly retired. Were they white-haired, as Yasin had been? Did Jafar use a walking-stick? Even Aqbal and Tariq were middle-aged. Amel had told him recently that Aqbal had born three children, and even Tariq was a father.

As the bus draws up slowly, he thinks of his mother. Sabria. He had hoped that time would obliterate the image of her on the crisp winter morning of his departure, crouched on the ground crying.

His niece Sura, Jama'a's daughter, had told him of her death almost two years ago at the beginning of April 2001. She had called the flat when he had been writing at home. He had known it was something awful as soon as he heard her voice. In the first seconds he had imagined it was Jafar. Had his eldest brother been shot or imprisoned? It had not entered his head that she was calling about Sabria. Like most children, he had assumed that his mother would pay no heed to old age or the laws that govern life and death.

'Uncle. Your mama died.' Rana was calm and definite. 'She was ill and . . .'

He couldn't speak. The only thought in his head was that he had left her with a lie. He had said he would be away for six months and now, twenty-one years later, she was dead, and the only contact they had had in all that time was a few unsatisfactory phone calls.

347

'When?' he had finally asked.

'Yesterday,' Sura said. 'We have been trying to reach all of you since it happened.'

'Was she alone?'

'You knew from Amel she had not been well, no? So many problems, Uncle. And here in Baghdad there is no medication. Amel did so much for her, when she was here, getting medicine, advising her, but after she went it became worse. Doctors need more than their bare hands to treat patients. She held on,' Sura pauses, 'but she was in a lot of pain. She could not wait any more.'

Early that evening at the flat Nada darts from room to room. She has her arms round Nabeel when the phone rings. 'It will be Jabbar from France,' she says excitedly, as Nabeel picks up the receiver.

'Tariq!' Nabeel almost jumps out of his skin.

Tariq launches straight into it. 'Hoorah! Hoorah! They are here. It is over, Nabeel.' Then, 'Listen, I can't talk for long. I have a friend who is working as a translator for the US here in the city. I went to see him today and asked him to come to the house so we could call you. I am on his Thuraya satellite phone now. It's the most amazing thing. No wires. And I am calling you from the garden . . .'

'Are you OK?' Nabeel asks, reeling from the sound of his brother's voice after so long.

'Yes, of course. I'm with Juma'a.' Nabeel feels the flood of relief and, strangely, amusement. Only Tariq could manage to get a line out of a city where all the phones are dead.

'Are you at home?'

'Ah, yes,' he says.

'The others, how are they?'

'We are all well.'

'Who is with you?'

'Jafar, Juma'a, our wives. And all the family are inside.'

'It is amazing. What about Aqbal? Is she OK? Have you seen her?'

'She's fine. We found this out tonight. What can I say? We're at the house, relieved and happy, and we are all alive.'

'I'll call Jabbar and Amel. They'll be overjoyed. We've been thinking only of you all for weeks – for years.'

'Tell them I'll try to ring from the satellite phone tomorrow. I'll get my friend to come back.'

'Tariq,' Nabeel says, as a huge lump forms in his throat, 'Tariq, we have come through this. We are seven again.'

Making Contact
July 2003

Six months after liberation, Nabeel sends Jafar an Orange mobile phone with a friend who is returning to Iraq. Phones with pre-paid credit are flooding into Baghdad and the newly established network is flourishing. Jafar has never seen one before, but to make it simple Nabeel has preprogrammed the phone with all the essential numbers and included hand-written instructions on how to use it. Nevertheless it takes them several attempts to connect. The first time Jafar calls Nabeel's phone he is diverted to voicemail. Hearing his brother's voice – 'This is Nabeel' – he immediately assumes he is speaking to his brother and tries to say hello. When the tone passes and the line goes silent he starts shouting: 'Why do you not answer when I speak to you? You are rude, brother.' Eventually, he tires of shouting into the phone and puts it down – without ending the call. When Nabeel picks up his message later that day there is a half hour voicemail that includes Jafar's frustrated attempts to talk to him and a meeting he has with two friends at their shop.

These early hitches are ironed out and the brothers establish a regular dialogue that encompasses episodes from their own past. Among them is Nabeel's box of papers at al-

Mansour: 'Nabeel, I am sorry, I was unable to rescue it. But I will go back there now and look for it. *Inshallah*, it has not been discovered,' Jafar tells him.

Since that night in January 1980, when they had sat together at al-Sayydia, neither has thought of the box. Jafar had not managed to return to al-Mansour after Nabeel's departure to hide some more of his brother's things, and since then he had assumed that anything left there must have been looted or burned when the house was taken over by squatters from Uday Hussein's private army.

The next weekend Jafar makes his way across the city and out to al-Mansour. The house is as big as he remembers and looks as it did over a quarter of a century before when his brother and Nada had moved there. He pushes open the gate and walks through the unkempt gardens and up to the front door. The house feels unloved and neglected. Jafar goes in, then up two flights of stairs to the little room that sits on the flat roof. Beyond the sand and plant debris, there is a rusty old table and chairs and the weathered remains of the old fridge. It is clear that no one has been up here for many, many years.

For most of his life he and his siblings have been hiding things, books, papers, from someone or other. He pulls back the fridge to reveal some planks, which he begins to drag away from the wall. A hole has been cut into its lining. The room is dry and airless, and he can hear cockroaches skittering about behind the panelling. He suspects these hidden linings of the house must now be crawling with life. No one can have sprayed in years. The general from Uday Hussein's private army who appropriated the house has done nothing.

Since liberation Jafar has been hoping that something will explain the pain and sorrow of the past thirty years. But there is only turmoil and uncertainty. The Allies have not managed to find the president. Many are saying that things will get worse before they get better. Saddam may be in hiding but he will undoubtedly be scheming too. What that might mean for himself and his family, Jafar cannot imagine.

He pulls away the last plank and feels around inside the hole until he touches the corner of something solid. It is the box. The last person to touch it was Nabeel. He can barely bring himself to pull it out. Eventually he hauls it into the daylight.

The following morning he seals it and, since there is no postal service, sends it with a friend who is travelling out to Amman and who has promised to post it on. He writes Nabeel's address on in awkward letters. Jafar does not speak English, but he knows that once the box crosses the border Arabic will not do. His Arabic print is clean and poetic-looking, every little curve in the right place. By comparison the English address looks clumsy. It is misspelt too. But it reaches its destination. Nabeel is touched when he sees the label: *Nabeel Yasin, Hamermsith, Englend.* This is his brother's first correspondence to him in English. The pieces of masking tape, and the knots tied in loose twine look intact. It has not been intercepted or slit open by Customs. This is a cause for celebration.

Nabeel, Nada and Hanin, who is enjoying the long summer holiday from school, are all at home when the parcel arrives. They leave it sitting on the table and just look at it for some time.

Then Nabeel acts. The tape is split, the string cut and the box is open. A whole life rushes back at him and Nada. Papers, their marriage certificate, letters, poems and so many photos and slides. There are faces, hairstyles and people from another time. Some are dead, some are still missing and some

Nada (third from right) with college friends, 1971

Nabeel & Nada on campus

Wedding (Nabeel, Behija, Nada), 1974

Nabeel, Nada, Yamam, 1976

forgotten. He sees his own handwriting on tiny slips of paper. The thoughts of his friends and family: love notes, messages of sorrow and condolence, cards and invitations, reviews from his days as a performer. All of it looks as fresh as if it had been placed in there only the day before.

There are tears and much laughter, too, at the pictures of their younger selves, whom they had forgotten. Black and white pictures of Nabeel as a boy with wild hair and hand-me-down shirts, a teenage Nabeel with Jabbar, Nada with her classmates, Jafar wearing a gold medallion necklace and trying hard to look like a Lothario. Nabeel and Nada walking together, sitting and talking, holding hands or running away from the camera. They hold the old Kodachrome slides up to the window to look at them, the colour so vivid and evocative of their age. Everything seems bathed in the warm yellow light of home. Hanin gazes at the pictures in wonder. His father looks so strong, his eyes so clear.

Nada reaches in and pulls out a picture of their wedding. There had not been many but she remembers this one. She squeezes her husband's hand as she looks at him in profile. His hair is a dignified grey now, but he is still the same Nabeel. She wants to embrace him, knowing they are both feeling the same emotion, but Hanin is full of questions, wanting to know who all the people in the pictures are.

This box of memorabilia is the first he has ever seen of his parents' lives in Iraq, and of his family, the uncles, aunts, grandparents and cousins. The picture he has built up over the years is, he knows, a distorted image of life gleaned from their memories – the night they had danced together at the Lawyers' Association jazz concert, the poetry gigs they loved, his father walking home singing, his uncle being seized and arrested and his grandmother watching at the window for her boys to return home safely. These images seem so different from those he sees on television or in a newspaper. There people look tired and worn. These people had been happy.

There are receipts, tickets, brochures from friends' exhibitions. Nabeel turns over a ticket stub for the Roxy Cinema, then picks up a snapshot of a young man and woman standing side by side, leaning in towards one another, smiling. The man wears a wide tie and pale suit, cut to fit in the way suits did in the late 1960s and early 1970s. The girl wears a crisp little coatdress, with white-edged cuffs and tiny buttons. On her feet she wears delicate pumps. What strikes him is that her legs are bare, or possibly covered with fine, flesh-coloured stockings. And, of course, although Hanin can't quite believe it, he can see it is his mother. 'Mama,' he gasps. 'Your dress!'

She pulls at the photograph. 'Let me see that.'

'Ah.' Nabeel laughs, gazing at the photograph. 'We were at the university when that was taken. I was just about to go to a lecture.'

Nada smiles and sighs wistfully. 'We really were on top of the world, Dudi, weren't we?'

The White of Paradise
July 2004

Nabeel removes his reading glasses and rubs his eyes. The situation in Iraq is causing him a great deal of anxiety, and it appears to be worsening. Each morning the newspapers bring conflicting reports from inside the country, and things are more confused now than at any time since liberation. He must talk with Jafar as soon as he can. His plans for their return to Iraq are going awry. Faced with the reality of going back, he is experiencing new, complicated emotions that he has never considered while he has been gone. There are practical problems too. The country is not safe. He was foolish to imagine it would be. From all he hears and reads, Iraq is more lawless now than ever. There are insurgents, some loyal to the regime, who are happy to kill, bomb and kidnap their own people and he must not forget that, to many, he is the same Enemy of the State he was twenty-five years ago.

He and Nada have been planning their return as a family for some weeks. Flights, time off work and school have all been looked into, and put on hold until Iraq is safe. They have all been busy gathering mementos of their lives outside Iraq to take home and show the others. Jafar and Tariq have asked for photos for the family album. Notebooks full of dates and places, people and events are piling up on the kitchen table and Nabeel has taken to pacing round the flat, trying to remember every tiny triumph and trial that might help explain who they are and where they have been.

'How do you sum up a whole life?' He laughs, as he and Nada pore through a bag of photographs from their time in Hungary.

'You don't,' she replies, holding up a picture of Yamam in his football kit with his boot resting on the ball. 'All we can give them is snapshots. Look at Yamam. Now he is a man, with a hundred friends and big business ideas. How did he jump from there to here? No matter how much we wish it, they will never know the life that we have had, and we will never understand how it has been for them. We can only feel sorry for what we have missed.'

'We had no choice.'

'Exactly, Dudi. Just remember how things were then. I can still remember how it was at the end.'

A large bag is being filled with gifts for the trip. They cannot go home empty-handed. And although he has never met his nephews and nieces, Nabeel wants to get it right. He has already made one of them cry down the phone when he forgot her name. 'Uncle Nabeel, he does not know who I am. I know him but he does not know me,' she had wailed in the background, as he talked to Tariq one afternoon.

He picks up his mobile and calls Jafar. It diverts straight to voicemail. 'Jafar, this is Nabeel. We must talk about my trip. Call me, please.'

He decides he will conduct his own poll – speak with Jabbar and his friends. Some have been back already and will know what may lie in store for them.

With a new Iraqi government in the making, Nabeel

finds himself called upon almost daily, by al-Jazeera, MBC, al-Arabia and ANB, to comment on 'the situation' at home. In the rational setting of the studio he often hears himself repeating the same old lines: his country must be given the chance to govern itself, and to do so democratically. Anything less would be a failure of all that had been so hard won. And although it might be alien, he wants his people to embrace this new concept and to accept that it comes with responsibility. Without modern democratic principles, Iraq will be doomed to endless coups and dictatorships. To many, his democratic perspective is both disarming and infuriating. He moves to the bathroom and pulls at his greying beard, trimming away the odd stray hair. Aqbal had called him a few days before to tell him she had seen him on al-Jazeera and that, with his beard longer, he looked identical to Baba. Baba! Who would have thought it?

Later that day, once the interviews are done and he has visited the offices of *al-Hayat*, he will meet his friend Hani in Westbourne Grove. Hani, another artist in exile, has a new show, Beyond the Face, opening tonight at the Kufa Gallery. The critics have previewed it and the reaction has been universally positive. With successful shows in Japan and Europe, Hani is becoming part of a new international establishment.

He is just removing his house shoes and putting on a tie when the phone rings. It is Jafar, who has been with Rana, his eldest daughter, at her gallery space in downtown Karkh. They, too, are preparing for an exhibition, Rana's second. 'I should like to see it when I'm there,' Nabeel says. He has already missed the opening of the gallery, the first of its kind in the city since liberation. His niece is intent on making a bold artistic statement and is not shy of controversy. The gallery has attracted praise and cynicism in equal measure. 'She is like you, Nabeel. Another hot-head, doing only as she feels, thinking only of the consequences when they are upon her!' Jafar laughs again. Then there is silence.

Nabeel knows bad news is on the way. Why else would Jafar be so upbeat?

'Nabeel, we have talked among ourselves and we do not think you should come. Not yet, anyway. We all agree. You have seen the news, and the situation is worse, much worse, than CNN are showing now. For you, it is doubly unsafe. You have spoken to Aqbal too, no?'

Aqbal, too, had been unequivocal, living in constant fear that her sons would be kidnapped. 'It is the bank. People know I have access to foreign currency, dollars, francs and sterling. I am a target, too. No one knows who is kidnapping Iraqis, Nabeel, the country is wide open.' Now the only time she ever walks outside is to go to her car. And other than school the boys are kept inside the apartment, like two caged cubs, week in and week out. 'People are disappearing off the streets. Remember Jassim.'

The news of the kidnapping of their elderly cousin Jassim had played on Nabeel's mind for weeks. He had been walking to meet his son for lunch when he was picked up by an opportunistic gang greedy for cash. They had demanded a ransom of half a million dollars within hours. This impossible amount was renegotiated, in a series of fraught phone calls between both sides, to twenty thousand. After Jassim had been released they discovered the kidnappers had taken him by mistake. They had meant to kidnap Jassim's son, a young doctor working in Amman. They had been tipped off that he was back in the city visiting his elderly father. 'The problem is that people think all foreigners are wealthy beyond compare. Take your sister's advice and wait a little longer.'

Jafar is less direct in his appraisal of Nabeel's chances. 'Look, it is your decision in the end but it is not a good time for you. People know who you are and they know you are from the TV in London now as well. Though many are proud of you, not everyone likes you here.'

'What if we decide to come regardless?' Nabeel thinks of what his writer friend Ahmed Goda had told him when he returned from Iraq. Nabeel's name had meant a lot.

'If you come Tariq says you will need bodyguards. Is that what you want? To come home surrounded by men with guns? A bodyguard costs money.'

'If I go home to Iraq I should like to see the old place as a free man.'

'We still have your voice and your face on TV and that will be enough until the country is safe again for you. Nabeel, you must not be rash or foolish over this. We all want to see you here but you should not put us in the way of more danger.'

Suddenly Nabeel senses there is something Jafar is not telling him.

'Has something else happened? Has there been more trouble?'

'Nabeel, it is Cousin Ra'ad. He was working in al-Latifiyah. He left Baghdad to make an easier life with his family. Of course, they were there, but he didn't know the place was overrun with insurgents. They shot him in the head as he got into his car. They left him bleeding on the road. There was no ransom, no warning and no reason. He was thirty-two and he leaves his wife and four children. Do I really need to say any more?'

362

The exhibition at the Kufa Gallery in west London is well attended, and by the time people start to drift away, several paintings are marked with little red stickers. After the guests have gone, Nabeel's friend Mahdi drives Nabeel back to Hammersmith in his old grey car. Over the soft Egyptian instrumental from the tape player, a crestfallen Nabeel tells Hani about his conservation with Jafar. 'I spoke to my brother this afternoon and he says we must not go back. He says it is too dangerous for me. I don't know what to think any more. You have been there. Tell me, what do you think?'

Mahdi shrugs, and casts an eye across the expensive white stucco-fronted houses of Notting Hill Gate. 'Nabeel, I think you already know what I think. It is not the same city any more. It is not the same country any more. We were in love with a mirage, an old photograph of a past love.' He breathes slowly, as if the words rising into his throat hurt him. 'I waited twenty-four years. Every day I thought about going home. I planned it and dreamed about what it would be like to set foot there again.' He takes a hand off the steering-wheel to wave it in the air. 'And now I have been, and seen that there is nothing of the city we left. I could find no trace of it.'

He pulls up outside Nabeel's block, the two men kiss each other goodnight and Nabeel walks the eight flights of steps to his flat. Inside the long hallway he slips on his house shoes. From the light under the bedroom door he knows Hanin is in his room, studying. Yamam is out again, he thinks, having fun with his friends somewhere in the capital. From the lounge he hears the television. Nada is curled up on the sofa watching an episode of *Friends*.

'Hello,' she says, glancing up at him. In the golden lamp-light, legs tucked under her slender frame, she looks deceptively young, like she did in 1968 when he had first seen her face among the crowd in front of the university lecture theatres.

'Jafar says we shouldn't go. I am the problem, not you. You should go if you want to.'

'Dudi, come and sit with me.' She pats the sofa next to her. She does not blame him, and she never has, for anything that has happened to them in their life together. 'When we go, we will go together.'

'Mahdi drove me home. He says that when we go back we will be heartbroken.'

'Nabeel, Mahdi is not the only one. Jabbar says the same – Hameed too. We should be prepared to cry. Everything we knew was *then*. Perhaps we will find that our home exists only in our heads.'

As he watches his wife stare at the screen, an image from his earliest childhood returns to him, as clear and detailed as if it were in front of him. He is three, perhaps four. It is dark and he is sitting on the ground outside the house, on a wool rug. Through the doorway in front of him his mother is sewing, singing quietly to herself. In the halo of the paraffin lamp, hung from the tree, he finds he is not alone. An old man, a vision of light, is at his side, his legs drawn up under him. His beard is long and pure white. He wears a turban on his head. His robes and slippers are the white of Paradise.

He asks the man, this grandfather of grandfathers, a question that has been bothering him for some time. The man looks at him calmly and answers. He is old and has the answer to many things, Nabeel supposes. At any rate, his words are to be trusted. Relieved, he falls into the deep sleep of childhood.

The next day, he tells his mother how he had sat and talked with his grandfather during the night. 'I can't remember what

364

he told me but I know it was good,' he said. 'I want to know. Can I see him again tonight?'

She had faced him and taken his shoulders. 'Nabeel, you have no grandfather. Both have already passed.' And this, as he later discovered, was true. Sabria's father, the rice merchant, had died when she was two, and Yasin's many years before that. 'It was a dream, my baby. A beautiful dream.' But he knew this was not so. The old man had dipped in and out of shadow, and he had even bent down to smell the oil. This was not a dream. They had been there together. 'What did he look like, Nabeel?' She squatted before him and asked him to describe the man to her. As he told her the details of the encounter, Sabria had fallen to her knees. 'Praise be,' she said, raising her palms to the sky. 'In the name of God, the Merciful, the Compassionate, you have seen him, Nabeel, not your grandfather but the Imam Ali. He has come to you.'

'You know there is more than one world.' Nabeel perches next to Nada on the sofa. 'And wherever you are, you can hold another in your mind.'

She sighs. 'Oh, Dudi, please . . . We have had a lifetime of this already. Let me watch in peace.'

'OK.' He tries to make light of it. 'What if we try to imagine the home we might buy on the Tigris one day, where we can settle and grow fruit and . . .'

She goes over to the TV and turns it off. 'I imagine it always,' she says, looking at the string of *misbaha*, sent to her by her father, that is hanging on the wall. The bright yellow glass spheres are carved into a perfect wave of increasing sizes and headed by a spray of fine silk string.

One day, he knows, they will go back. The phone will ring and they will all agree that the time is right. In this he has faith, for they are his family. He stands up. 'Come on,' he says, holding out his hand to her. 'Tomorrow I will install the video software on the computer. Then you can *see* your sisters when you talk to them.'

She smiles and takes his hand. What a wonderful thought.

Epilogue

Four of the Yasin children still live close to one another in Baghdad, while three remain in exile:.

Tariq and his family continue to live in the house in al-Sayydia while Juma'a and his family occupy the annexe. Jafar, now a widower, lives alone in the house he built in 1968. Aqbal, her husband and their three children live in an apartment nearby.

Amel has now settled in Brittany in northern France where she works as a doctor. Jabbar, now a French citizen, lives with his wife Sylvienne in La Rochelle. Nabeel, Nada and their two sons, Yamam and Hanin, are settled in west London. Nada was reunited with her three sisters and their families in Amman, Jordan in autumn 2005, where her sister Selwa's husband Sa'ad underwent open-heart surgery. His heart condition remains from his time in Abu Ghraib.

Nada's mother, Behija died in October 2000 and she and Nada's father, Hamed, are buried at the Abu Ghraib cemetery.

Cousin Kamil, a widower with five children, now lives near the al-Khadimiya shrine in Baghdad.

Hussein, Nabeel's cousin who secured the plane tickets for him, Nada and Yamam to escape Iraq, married his sweetheart before being recruited into the army and dispatched to the Iranian front in 1980. He was blown up in his jeep six weeks later, travelling home for his first leave.

The engineer who had been a cellmate of Juma'a's at the stadium prison in 1963 honoured his promise and went to visit his colleague's wife. He is now married to her and they live in exile in London.

Dr Safaa al-Hafihd and Dr Saba al-Dorra, two eminent members of the Communist Party, took the two passports that had been offered by Abo Hameed to Nabeel. They were caught trying to escape by the secret police and are believed to have died under torture. Their bodies have never been found.

Tawfiq, after many years acting in opposition to the regime, died of a stress-induced embolism in Baghdad in 1996.

Sabria, who died on 31 March 2001 is buried close to her husband Yasin at Wadi-al-Salaam, the Valley of Peace. Her sisters Makkya and Noua are buried there also.

Acknowledgements

My first debt of thanks is to Nabeel and his family, near and far. The openness with which I have been told about their lives at every stage, both in and out of Iraq, has been extraordinary and I feel privileged to be able to share it. Special thanks go to Nada, Yamam and Hanin for their welcoming ways.

Thanks also to Fadel Abbas Hady for his dedicated work in translating The Poets Satirise the Kings, Brother Yasin Again and others, to Tina Phillips for her linguistic clarity and poetic eye and to Mahdi Assaid for his specific insights into Nabeel's life during his heyday in Baghdad.

I am enormously grateful to my agent, the amazing Kate Jones, whose instinct has been faultless from the outset, and to Nick Davies at Hodder, for his trust in this project and wonderfully skilful guidance. Huge thanks also to Hazel Orme.

Finally, my thanks to John and Sarah Tatchell for the peripatetic but enlightening upbringing that led me here. And to Clifford Jones for making this journey with me, for his patience, inspired counsel, love and faith.